DECODING MADNESS

A Forensic Psychologist Explores the Criminal Mind

Richard Lettieri, PhD

Prometheus Books
Guilford, Connecticut

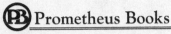
Prometheus Books

An imprint of The Rowman & Littlefield Publishing Group, Inc.
4501 Forbes Boulevard, Suite 200
Lanham, Maryland 20706
www.rowman.com

Distributed by NATIONAL BOOK NETWORK

British Library Cataloguing in Publication Information Available

Library of Congress Cataloging-in-Publication Data

Names: Lettieri, Richard, 1951– author.
Title: Decoding madness : a forensic psychologist explores the criminal mind / Richard Lettieri, PhD.
Description: Lanham, MD : Prometheus Books, [2021] | Includes bibliographical references and index. | Summary: "Dealing with some of the most heinous crimes imaginable, forensic neuro-psychologist and psychoanalyst Dr. Richard Lettieri gives a behind-the-scenes look at criminal psychology through case studies from his over 30 years of experience as a court-appointed and privately retained psychologist"— Provided by publisher.
Identifiers: LCCN 2020053577 (print) | LCCN 2020053578 (ebook) | ISBN 9781633886926 (paperback) | ISBN 9781633886933 (ebook)
Subjects: LCSH: Forensic psychology. | Criminal psychology. | Criminal psychology—Case studies.
Classification: LCC RA1148 .L48 2021 (print) | LCC RA1148 (ebook) | DDC 614/.15—dc23
LC record available at https://lccn.loc.gov/2020053577
LC ebook record available at https://lccn.loc.gov/2020053578

To my wife, Jeanne

A remedy for my pockets of madness

Faust: All right—who are you, then?
Mephistopheles: Part of the force which would do ever
evil, and does ever good.
—Goethe

CONTENTS

PROLOGUE

I was not always on track to become a forensic psychologist. Looking back, I'd say the spark that ignited the fire began when, as an undergraduate at the City College of New York, I was assigned to read sections of Sigmund Freud's *Civilization and Its Discontents*. Allow my indulgence to exhume a phrase from yesteryear and say the book "blew my mind." Freud bluntly claimed that an inevitable clash exists between impulse and restraint in everybody and that an unsettled compromise between the two is the price for civility.

Having been raised in a traditional Catholic family, I was keenly aware of the importance of self-control. But Freud's argument was different. He declared that the struggle to find accommodation between personal desires and community expectations was a basic condition for social comity, along with our willingness to live with the inevitable discontents resulting from such restrictions on self-indulgence.

On some level, I vaguely sensed all of this. But not like this, not so head-on. And then to realize that *I kinda* knew something, but didn't *really* know, was dizzying. For me, that was transformative. And so my journey began. A decade or so passed, and I was a graduate psychologist on my way to postdoctoral training in psychoanalysis, mental disability law, and neuropsychology.

Before embarking on this book, I had been practicing as a psychoanalyst in private practice and as a forensic psychologist and expert witness in criminal and civil trials. Over the years, I have completed more than a thousand criminal forensic examinations, and I have testified in many trials, ranging in cases involving multiple murders, assaults including sexual assaults, domestic violence, and more. Whether I was retained by attorneys or appointed by the court, I have offered opinions on many and varied legal questions, such as whether a defendant was insane at the time of a murder, if a defendant is at risk of becoming violent in the future, or whether an adolescent should be tried as an adult for a crime or remain in juvenile court.

You'll meet some of the defendants in this book. Like me, I suspect you'll sometimes be surprised by your reactions to them.

I have seen firsthand how mental disturbances can drive criminal acts. But my work in criminal psychology also has allowed me to vividly witness deep psychological truths, not only about the defendants who had lost the necessary control and comity required by society. The venue of the criminal justice system, with its daily exposure to primal emotions and the consequences wrought by their wanton expression, served as a petri dish to investigate the full spectrum of human nature. I employ the idea of *daimonic* as a driving force in us all that's the source of our constructive and destructive capacities. I do this by presenting detailed accounts of my examination of defendants, many of whom have perpetrated the most heinous offenses.

I also share what it was like for me to be exposed to the carnage human beings are so capable of exacting on each other.

In addition to being a forensic psychologist, I'm also psychoanalytically trained. It has served me well as a criminal forensic evaluator. And as a psychoanalyst, I'm accustomed to dwelling within the inner worlds of my patients and helping them to construct an understanding of the motivations and emotions behind behavior. This has been quite an asset, as the mental state of a defendant—what was on his mind at the time of the crime—is almost always crucial to the forensic issues. And, in addition to the usual tools available to the forensic psychologist like empirically validated tests, a psychoanalytic perspective has allowed me to develop a uniquely nuanced and deepened psychological understanding of defendants and their personal makeup.

In the process of exploring the many forensic cases and the issues involved, I also examine the ethical dilemmas faced by justice professionals and forensic experts who work within the system and how personal interests and inclinations, such as competition and cynicism, compete with the desire to be objective and just.

The book's central focus is a study in criminal psychology. But it's not solely about the criminal mind. It's a full-bore entrée into the imperfect human nature as revealed by all of those who operate within the system and the struggle to manage complex legal and moral decisions. I do so with the help of insights from psychoanalysis, psychology, and neuroscience.

Furthermore, I sometimes contrast the stories of my criminal evaluations with those of my private psychoanalytic patients, a juxtaposition that helps to drive home the point that emotional conflicts and raw emotions are inevitable but, when criminal proceedings are required, a heartbreaking tragedy has occurred.

In part I, I introduce the idea of the daimonic as an innate element of human nature, with its paradoxical potential for the savage and sublime. I also present a user-friendly explanation of psychological development that provides a context to understanding the forensic analysis of the cases that follow.

Part II accounts for the bulk of the book. Each chapter features an in-depth exploration of a case (or two) and describes the forensic procedures that lead to my expert opinion. For instance, I examine Randall, a charismatic man who turned out to be a stone-cold psychopath. I describe my emotional reactions as I became aware of the extent of his malevolent ruthlessness. Throughout, I explore the richness of our nature and its by-products—such as rage, deception, and also decency—through my experiences with both defendants and justice professionals. For instance, while I describe the conditions that led to violent offenses, I also examine the real-life consequences when prosecutors withhold exculpatory information. I also write about a jail mental health unit where the deputies are more compassionate toward very disturbed inmates than most private psychiatric hospitals.

Part III examines the implications of our daimonic nature, particularly its capacity to manifest as magnificence or malevolence. I contend that the legal system's view of human nature as governed by rationality sometimes leads to unjust outcomes. I integrate new insights from developmental and psychoanalytic psychology and neuroscience. The book ends on a positive note, as I argue that our criminal justice system is slowly bending toward the humane.

A few brief words about content and style. Case material was drawn from the scores of forensic evaluations I conducted during my decades of practice. I've combined cases and juxtaposed details so as to camouflage the identities and privacy of those involved as much as possible while maintaining fidelity to the psychological and forensic issues that I address.

In addition, I use male pronouns throughout the book, unless, of course, women are central to the discussion. I do so because the lion's share of defendants are men.

Part I

Human Nature and Its Discontents

I

THE DAIMONIC PARADOX

Nature, Mr. Alnutt, is what we were put in this world to rise above.—
Katharine Hepburn to Humphrey Bogart in *The African Queen* (1951)

Out of timber as crooked as that which man is made nothing entirely
straight can be built.—Emmanuel Kant

Driving down the freeway after spending the morning at the jail, I
looked forward to the afternoon in my cushy office and consulting room,
away from the steely setting of the county jail. I'm transitioning from my
morning job as a forensic psychologist to my afternoon gig as a practicing
psychoanalyst. What I'm not looking forward to is the conversation that's
about to happen with the defense attorney for Mr. Parcen, the inmate I
just interviewed. He is in his late sixties and has admitted to molesting his
nine-year-old granddaughter on at least two occasions. His lawyer, experienced in defending individuals for an assortment of crimes from public
drunkenness to felony murder, believes Mr. Parcen's behavior with the
child was likely an "aberration." After all, the inmate confessed when
confronted by the little girl's mother, his daughter, and he cooperated
with the police investigation. Because his history is free of bad acts and
he's a senior citizen, he deserves leniency. The attorney, Jon Cann, antici-
pates that a report from me will add some objectivity and psychological
weight to his client's case when he negotiates with the assistant district
attorney and the court. He hoped that I would flush out Mr. Parcen's
personal story, which is apparently fraught with neglect, to help construct

a somewhat sympathetic portrait of an individual who is a low risk to re-offend.

After I get to my office, I first return a few phone calls to patients and then prepare myself to speak with Mr. Cann. He's an attorney who is unfailingly committed to his clients. I admire his lack of cynicism or disdain for those he represents, regardless of the heinousness of their crimes. He's intrepid in his defense of the accused. His droll humor and natural sensitivity to the pathos of the criminal justice system are like shock absorbers when dealing with such primal dimensions of human experience. I'm about to give Mr. Cann news that will complicate his job, but I know he'll take it with his usual equanimity. As I usually do, I'll begin by describing interactions between me and the inmate and my observations that capture the essence of what shaped my opinion.

I watched as Mr. Parcen walked to the private booth at the jail where I was seated, waiting to interview him. He was escorted by two deputies, as is always the case when an inmate is charged with a sexual offense, lest he be attacked by another inmate if an opportunity to do so arises. According to jailhouse ethics, if a fellow inmate fails to exercise his duty to attack a child abuser, he may suffer the consequences from his jail mates.

Mr. Parcen had the bearing and gait of a self-possessed politician, not of a chastened sex offender. With his gray, balding hair, he looked his age. Yet his six-foot frame and thin body, together with his swift pace and his upright posture, gave him the appearance of a man with youthful energy. He greeted me warmly. Once we were alone in the locked booth, I explained to him the reason for our encounter. He knew I was coming and seemed eager to engage. In fact, he quickly took charge of the interview, not waiting for me to ask questions. He began by telling me about his life, some of which I already knew from conversations with and documents sent by his lawyer. Within a few minutes of observation and cursory exchange, I was impressed by his strangely bright demeanor and his blithe self-absorption.

A traditional man in many ways, Mr. Parcen made it a point to immediately highlight his conservative beliefs. He expressed pride in his status as a deacon at his house of worship. Indeed, he pressured all his grown children to send his grandchildren, for whom he expressed an abiding love, to a conservative Christian school. At a point when it seemed right, I expressed puzzlement over how his beliefs and affections clashed with his admitted sexual misconduct. After asking me if I understood Christian doctrine, which I do, he proceeded to explain that he needed only to ask for God's forgiveness. He placed the palm of his right hand above his left, and with a swipe of the adjoining palms, proclaimed that he would be forgiven by God, simply for asking. "I had time," he added. I asked, with some astonishment, if he meant that he had time to obtain forgiveness from God for his sins. He said, "Yes, that's correct." I followed up with a confrontational question, attempting to soften it by speaking with a balanced pitch, "Did you consider how destructive your behavior was to your granddaughter?" He momentarily paused before responding, "No, I never thought of that."

Though I had already begun to develop an awareness of his lack of consciousness, I was temporarily dazed. It reflected a stunning emotional shallowness and moral agnosia, with an inability to consider the emotional consequences to others of his actions. I found myself slipping out of my clinical skin for a moment and psychically migrating somewhere else. I thought of my daughter, Gina. I continued looking at Mr. Parcen, but with a wariness and distance, like I had to protect myself. Or was it moral indignation? What was happening is what psychoanalysts call countertransference, an emotionally meaningful reaction in the analyst evoked by the interaction with the patient. Of course, some kind of unsettling reaction to Mr. Parcen's disturbing sexual misconduct and cavalier rationale is reasonable and expectable. Nonetheless, my personal reactions said something about me, a truth I've learned from my training, including the years of having been myself prostrate as a patient on the couch. My reactions helped to inform me about Mr. Parcen's character beyond any explanation he could provide. My wariness was a familiar feeling, usually provoked when I encounter a person who, in spite of being extroverted, socially skilled, or even charming, is self-absorbed, self-serving, and emotionally unattuned. Though not necessarily predatory, such a narcissistic character style is usually accompanied by a vacuous inner life that allows one to seek gratification without awareness or concern for others and without expected restraint. Strangely, my emotional reactions are more simpatico with other personality types, even when the individuals have committed terrible crimes. I relate well to craziness and extreme emotions, so I think it's the lack of psychological activity in the narcissistic style that does it to me.

I psychologically shifted back into my clinical self, this time with an understanding of Mr. Parcen as someone capable of unreflective destruction, even to those he loves. We talked for a bit longer. I gathered more history and observations about Mr. Parcen's life that reinforced my developing picture of him. I terminated the interview early, feeling quite certain that Mr. Cann, the defense attorney, would not want a report from me. No sense wasting time and money.

When I phoned Mr. Cann about my impressions of his client, he seemed disappointed and a little surprised. I explained how the defendant's grandiosity and self-absorption had turned what should have been empathic and protective impulses toward his granddaughter into self-gratifying ones. He responded with a slight groan, followed by a moment of silence from both of us, a show of respect for the death of Mr. Cann's anticipated defense strategy for Mr. Parcen.

With that conversation over, I settled into the afternoon, awaiting my first patient.

***

Over the years, I've wondered why I practice forensic psychology and why I like it. I could remain safely within the confines of my consulting room, just me and my noncriminal patients. Certainly, doing long-term psychotherapy and psychoanalysis is gratifying. I get the privilege of entering into the lives of people in ways not usually accessible. The analytic relationship is peculiar in its circumscribed nature, a form of intimacy and deep emotional involvement that is conducted within the sanctuary of my office. Except for times of therapeutic impasse when I may consult with a colleague, I speak to no one, not even my wife, about these enduring and deeply private emotional encounters. I don't tell anyone about my affection for my shy, married woman patient who has been silently struggling with homoerotic fantasies since college that she can't understand or shake. Her fantasies remain sequestered within the confines of my consultation room. Then there's my engineer, who through years of treatment has been helped greatly with his panic and his relationships, but who nonetheless continues to live with a feeling that his head is stuffed with cotton, impeding full contact with the world. There's nothing medically wrong with him. I had hoped that as his anxiety waned, so would the cotton ball. That's how it is supposed to work, theoretically, but no such luck. I can sense his disappointment in me and our work together, despite his gratitude. I give voice to his dissatisfaction, letting him know it's okay to tell me. He demurs. He cherishes our bond and seemed afraid to rock it. I felt the same disappointment, along with guilt, for not being able to help him more.

My relationships with my patients are a lot like my other relationships, with some more intense than others. But our focus is predominantly on the interior of their experience, the nature of their interpersonal lives, and the complicated connections between the two. The shape of our bond is mostly in the background, but sometimes in the foreground, such as when something is said that provokes a troubling reaction from either one of us. An exploration of these incidents are difficult but could be very helpful to the patient. However the relationship unfolds, it's assiduously a private one, sequestered within the confines of my consulting room. As a psycho-analyst, I sometimes feel like I'm living an emotional double life of sorts. I'm ever aware of the responsibility that accompanies this kind of psychological work, with its attachments formed between me and my patients and my access to their inner worlds and to what the psychoana-lyst Christopher Bollas calls the "un-thought known."[1] To discover and touch that area of personal experience is deeply rewarding.

**

So why do I expose myself to the horror show that is so frequently the case when I step out of my consulting room and wade into the criminal justice system? Ironically, the seduction of criminal forensic psychology is for me in the baseness of it all. The opportunity to stare into the mind of the criminal is a rendezvous with something that is hidden in all of us—what Freud called the id and what I'll refer to as the *daimonic*—which is in balance in most of us, most of the time. It is usually regulated by social convention, fear, duty, compassion, courage, guilt, identifications with loved ones, or all of the above. All of that melds into something I'll call virtue while always teeter-tottering with its darker, shadowy side: those impulses to cheat, to wound somebody, to transgress the boundaries with-in which most of us remain silent and contained. "I wish he'd just die!" Such a thought is common in all of us but usually remains in the realm of thought or fantasy during moments of fleeting rage or irrationality. The impulse is controlled.

Not so with my forensic cases. The lid has popped off: a psychic hernia has occurred. A terrible act has exposed something about the hu-

man condition, a potential part of us all that cannot be denied, rationalized away, or controlled.

I've come to realize that my willingness to absorb the tragedy and
trauma inherent in maintaining a forensic psychological practice is a
compulsion to face a reality: the difference between the savage and the
civilized, the saint and the sinner, the ridiculous and the sublime is deep
yet dubious.

***

My private psychoanalytic patients are usually emotionally balanced professional types. Nonetheless, they—like all human beings—live with a
"monkey on their back" that won't let go, with desires, fears, and impulses they don't understand. Consider Dr. Vincent, a middle-aged physician with an illogical, destructive hostility toward his successful son that
unexpectedly surfaces at the most awkward of times. For instance, after
offering a toast at his son's engagement dinner, he made a tasteless sexual
wisecrack about his son's incipient baldness that embarrassed his son and
fiancée and infuriated his wife, almost ruining the event for his family.
Dr. Vincent knew his son always has been sensitive about his looks. He
loves his offspring, but he chronically undercuts his son and doesn't
understand why.

Dr. Vincent loves but becomes destructive to those most dear. Yet he
has never attempted to assault anyone or kill his son. We all have destructive, hateful urges. Consider anyone you know fairly well, including
yourself. What is the difference between someone who hates and someone who acts on hatred? What makes the difference between the husband
who says to himself, "I could murder him for saying that to my wife!"
and the criminal defendant who "crosses the Rubicon" and goes for the
kill? Is it in the defendant's nature, a predisposition to violence, a "bad
seed" within? Or is it a lack of nurture—early abuse or malignant neglect—that creates and fuels homicidal impulsiveness? Would such an
individual be different, a good citizen, if not raised by a crackhead mother
who allowed her child to be abused by her lover? Does nurture and early
experience really make a difference or are parents exchangeable, fun-
gible? There are so many individuals who were raised in the most challenging circumstances yet turned out to be quite resilient, whereas other
individuals raised in good family circumstances turn out to be fraught

with emotional fragility and unpredictability. Are our individual selves determined at birth—is biology destiny? What is the force that we call human nature that shapes us and is it malleable?

***

I use the word *daimonic* as opposed to "demonic" when describing the force in human nature that's played out and exposed so tragically in the criminal justice system. There is a big difference in the meaning of these terms, so let me explain.

Traditionally the use of the terms *demonic* and *evil* are used synonymously to convey the presence of something unnaturally or even supernaturally wicked on earth—an explanation for something that seems uncanny and unimaginable. Picture yourself having that first cup of morning coffee as you peruse the newspaper or the headlines on your smartphone. You fixate on a photograph of a mass murderer sitting in a courtroom next to his attorney, awaiting sentencing. The thought that comes to mind: "He's twisted." How else could someone perpetrate an act so aberrant?

The word *daimonic* has not always been associated with evil. The term derives from the Greek word *daimon*, which, curiously, means "divinity" or "deity." The Greeks believed in a host of gods, from the Olympian ones to lesser ones, all influencing us humans below. The gods visited daimones on humans to make sure mere mortals had a taste of good fortune and calamity. The Greeks used the term *daimonic* to convey a force that can take over us, a force that can be a blessing or a curse. "Eros is daimonic," said Plato in his *Symposium*. What did he mean? Erotic passion is clearly not evil, not in the "demonic" sense, but it is beyond logic and reason. It is an elemental force, like a Category 4 hurricane. Erotic passion is daimonic because it's awesome and instinctual, transcending rational thought. It's beautiful, impetuous, and intemperate, knocking over everything in the path of its desired object. It's a force that can go in different directions, for good or naught, moral or wanton.

The daimonic is human nature in its most natural and raw form. We feel its presence in the strength of a newborn's powerful grasp of our pinkie with her tiny hand and in her mighty bite and wail when she's hungry. It takes form in the soldier's act of heroism and the terrorist's slaughter of the innocent.

The daimonic exposes a basic human potential that is wide and deep. It includes the potential for magnificent love and generativity as well as uncorked hatred. It's the paradox and mystery of our being. Why does the daimonic surface for some in the creation of an inspiring song, whereas for others as an abhorrent sexual act? How does the dark and light sides of the daimonic duality influence each other? And what elements in an individual's history and endowment create the conditions for the dark, wicked side to unravel with such force that violates all notions of natural law and moral convention and destroys body and soul?

As a forensic psychologist, how am I to emotionally react when sitting across from a man who, hours before, killed his wife and two-month-old infant? Training and experience help, but they aren't enough. It requires something more, a personal something that came before my professional development. And that same "something" will shape how *you* react to my tales of human pathos. That "something" is the degree to which you and I are personally acquainted with the daimonic dimension of human nature. Such familiarity allows one to intuitively know that all of us are capable of good and evil and that human nature provides the building blocks that allows some of us to be capable of painting the Sistine Chapel and others to imagine and construct Auschwitz. The divide between the two extremes is gaping but fragile.

Emmanuel Kant is considered by many to be the greatest philosopher who ever lived. His powerful observation about human nature—revealed in the epigraph at the beginning of this chapter—and its inevitable crookedness has itself an ironic twist: to be psychologically acquainted with the full range of human experience is the antidote.

***

Questions about the extremes of human nature have been addressed by philosophers like Kant and by social scientists, neuroscientists, and psychologists, but perhaps most evocatively by Sigmund Freud.[2] He clearly saw the polarity in daimonic human nature and developed a psychotherapeutic approach to contend with it. One of his deepest insights into the daimonic was that our disowned, repressed emotions and impulses never die; they get buried alive and resurface in unpredictable, sometimes dreadful ways. When emotional pain and conflict remain unconscious and psychologically "unmetabolized," one is invariably confronted, sooner or later, with a "return of the repressed." The dark side may surface in various forms: persistent self-defeating decisions; projections of what is disowned in oneself onto others; irrational outbursts; or worse. In Jungian[3] terms, the shadow side, if not consciously accepted as part of the self, is ever present in its potential, ready to herniate out. Once in the light of awareness, it can be psychologically "metabolized" and owned, rather than one being owned by it and perhaps driven to demonic ends.

For instance, Simon, an easygoing husband who, after years of verbal abuse by his caustic, alcoholic wife, lost his composure and strangled her to death.[4] He described the killing to me. It was as though he was watching himself in a movie, depersonalized from the experience—it felt like it was both him and not him. His passion for his wife inverted from years of loyal commitment to murderous rage, seemingly out of nowhere, like a descending shadow.

It's not just defendants who expose the full range of our nature. Thomas, a terrified inmate, pleaded with me for help. He revealed to a deputy sheriff at the jail that a murder was about to happen in his cellblock. Now a "snitch" and a target himself, he asked to be placed in protective custody. The deputy refused and angrily told Thomas that he should have minded his own business.[5] Or consider a fellow forensic psychologist who told me he does not find the work stressful, adding with some braggadocio, "Because I don't care."

The deputy and psychologist learned to numb themselves to it all.

So many forms of destructiveness derive from attempts to cope with unrecognized helplessness, despair, and confusion. When such emotional states gain ascendance, a sense of anomie and drift follow in their wake. It's a pull on us all. When passions become aroused but are deemed unbearable and hence banned from awareness, the small and large evils of which we are capable become more likely.

***

In the ensuing chapters, I present a nuts-and-bolts look into what it takes to complete psychological examinations of defendants accused of committing heinous crimes. But I'm not solely writing about the madness of the criminal mind; I hope to shed some light on the nature of human nature. The examination of criminal conduct has revealed not only how mental disturbances drive crime, but it has exposed deep psychological truths about us all, especially our capacities to wreak destruction and to behave at elevated heights and on high moral ground. As such, as I reach my forensic conclusions in any given case, I stay cognizant of the line between mental disorder and destructive behavior resulting from those all-too-natural urges of inhumanity that we all experience at one time or another. This issue warranted particular concern in the chapters on psychopathy and the brain, or when mental illness is clearly present but not clearly driving the criminal behavior. Surprisingly, it's not always easy to discern the difference between the illness and the person acting badly.

Professionals and forensic experts who work within the justice system face daily exposure to human tragedy and the darkest of emotional experience. It is a psychological challenge to face the ethical dilemmas and moral hazards that arise from such conditions and to avoid the hard tilt toward cynicism, implacability, or even unfiltered competition, all of which clash with the noble desires to ensure justice and fairness. In the ensuing chapters, I tried not to shy away from times when professional judgment and the more noble angels of our nature seemed to have taken a back seat and succumbed to the darker end of the daimonic spectrum.

***

Psychological maturity, I argue, entails ample awareness of one's emotional experience, with a clear access to one's desires, goals, and ideals, along with an ability to manage potentially destructive urges. Long ago and most evocatively, Rollo May depicted the paradox of our daimonic, as both a troubling "gadfly"[6] and an inspiring muse, always provoking creative or unsavory potentials. The psychoanalyst Erich Fromm observed that destructiveness is the result of an unlived life and truncated psychological life,[7] a life denied its generative potential to strive and grow.

***

To be psychologically present requires a willingness to embracing the full ball of wax of who we are. It may seem counterintuitive, but accepting the more unsavory parts of ourselves and living in peace with the daimonic spectrum enhances our capacity for love and generativity.

This book is about understanding extreme human conduct. To a large extent, it is about the madness that drives much of criminal behavior. But my goal is to get a handle on much more—to demonstrate how crime and the methods and machinations of our attempts to control it reveal fundamental truths about all of us.

In the ensuing chapters I introduce you to an array of defendants and many others involved in the criminal justice system. You'll meet defendants, victims and their families, and justice professionals. Each chapter focuses on a different type of offense, which calls for specific questions to be addressed. Was this homicide a first-degree murder, second degree, or manslaughter? Was the defendant insane at the time of the offense? What caused a mother to kill her baby? What was her mind-set at the time? You're about to meet a few stone-cold psychopaths.

These are just some examples of the cases I share with you. In addition, I explore how our darker side sometimes seeps into the justice system and threatens its mandate to adjudicate fairly. I also highlight episodes when professionals working within the system behaved in ways that represent the apotheosis of our better side.

I end by making the case that, in spite of the cruelty and evils that are part of everyday life[8]—especially illuminated by much of the conduct displayed in the pages ahead—the justice system, like all our civic institutions,[9] is serving its basic function to elevate our better angels.

***

In the next chapter, I set the psychological stage, if you will, from which so much aberrant behavior and destruction flows. What are the forces of individual history and development that construct a mind capable of accessing the dark side of our human potential?

2

THE PAST IMPERFECT

The past is never dead. It's not even past.—William Faulkner

The end is always in the beginning.—Bruno Bettleheim

I've been living in southern California most of my life, since arriving from New York in my early twenties to begin graduate school. Here in the Golden State, I married and raised two children who are Californians. Yet I think of myself as a Brooklyn boy, a New Yorker, and I always will, even though I matured in California. This is why the early years are described as the formative ones; they have an abiding effect on our psyche and on who we are, for better or worse. To grow up in Brooklyn— circa late 1960s, early 1970s—was to live with physical density and human proximity. The people hurrying about, the jackhammer pounding roadside construction sites, city buses choking and huffing brown fumes, the smells and the police sirens screeching—it was like existing within a musty and churning machine. Contrast that with California's brightness, its spaciousness and easygoing, hang-loose style. Still, it's not me. It's hard to put down in words how that feels. But when I get back to New York, I think, "Yeah, I'm home."

Those early formative years determine who we are at our core: the die is cast and identity is shaped in some fundamental, abiding way. Think of the Russian nesting doll set, with the smaller dolls contained in larger, more "mature" ones. They're akin to different layers of a developing self, with the first-formed baby selves layered within, the ones that are tiny and fragile yet central to the fully formed edifice.

   Over time, our emotions and thinking become increasingly complex and mature, and early dispositions become tempered. The infantile expectation of immediate gratification gradually wanes, along with fear of the dark and the need for a soothing "blankie." As time passes—if we're lucky—we learn and internalize habits and ideals from loving adults that serve us well for a lifetime. Who we are—our identity—becomes more complex, sturdy, and mature as these layers of growth and experience become internalized. But all this is built around an inner core invisible to the outside observer and usually only dimly sensed by oneself, except when it unexpectedly rears its head. Those innermost "dolls" nesting deep inside are not obvious, but they are delicate and permanent.

                                             ***

Psychological time is different. Our early years carry a different weight that doesn't "slide" by in the same linear way that the later years do. Those early experiences, although intangible and murky in memory, have an impact that's psychically vivid, more set in stone.

   Freud famously asserted that time and the influence of our early experience on our mental life is ageless.[1] That's why our internal reality—the way we experienced ourselves during those early years—could be so varied from those who were there with us, partaking in the same external events; we all have our own psychic reality, with its sticky fixedness, particularly during childhood. Take the experience of loss, for instance. Deborah, a patient in my private non-forensic practice, lost her mother to a heart attack when she was nine years old. Without warning, Deborah's mother dropped dead in front of her in the family room. No one else was home. Although her memory is sketchy, she knows at some point she went to a neighbor for help. Deborah, her father, and her two older brothers were devastated.

   The family members supported each other through the tragedy and life went on, sort of. Her father eventually remarried a woman who was kind to my patient, but something was askew in Deborah that she couldn't quite pin down. Yes, she went on to be very successful, objectively. She studied hard, completed graduate school, and now works as a scientist in the pharmaceutical industry. But psychologically, she stalled. She can't tolerate loss. She broke up with her lover, a man that she knows wasn't right for her and whom she didn't love. Even though she couldn't wait for the relationship to end, she experienced a sense of catastrophic loss when it finally did. Deborah realizes that her reaction *must* be *somehow* related to the loss of her mother and not to this relationship, but she finds herself terrified and depressed nonetheless. She can't get herself moving. She knows her reaction is "irrational," but she can't help herself and she wonders why.

The experience of loss evoked an enduring reaction for Deborah, not simply a reaction to her current situation. It's not that she "unconsciously" really loves this man or is dependent on him. The end of their relationship elicited a black hole that feels as psychically permanent to her as the DNA that shaped the color of her eyes.

Traumatized by loss at the age of nine, Deborah now lives in a time warp that is unconscious most of the time. It rears its head whenever she experiences loss, although her conscious self realizes that it's an irrational reaction. It causes much emotional pain, but she can grapple and reflect until a measure of perspective takes hold, at least until the next loss presents itself.

Deborah's vulnerability to loss continues to stalk her. It's part of what formed her, a trauma that happened during those years that shape us, for good and bad. She was old enough to have a sense of herself that had already taken form; some Russian dolls were already nesting. Crucially, she also was old enough to use language as a tool to reflect on herself and her emotional life. She knew the difference between her thoughts and what was happening "out there" in the world. And she had a supportive family that made her feel secure and helped her manage emotional pain.

***

But what happens when an individual is a victim of trauma at a very early age? I'm talking now about those pre-language years when an infant or toddler doesn't know the thoughts are his or her own or that thoughts are different from the reality "out there." When I say trauma, I don't necessarily mean trauma with a capital T, like the trauma faced by a child whose father killed her mother in front of her. I'm including those everyday or common types of traumas, such as having had the misfortune of being born to self-absorbed or neglectful parents. Or even to parents who are good people but may have been too young to be good parents. Imagine parents, both twenty years old, who have an unwanted child. They take care of the infant's physical needs but are unempathic, regularly indifferent, and emotionally unattached during those pre-language, *really* formative years.

Those early years before language develops are especially timeless and consequential. There's no awareness of the psychological self yet, no firm "I." Experience just happens. Consider a baby discovering her own hand as it moves about, not even knowing that she is the mover, the agent, of its action. Emotions are basically biological happenings that stir up the infant or young toddler. The caretaker—mother, father, grandma—work to figure out what she is agitated about. It could be confusing, but with an adult who is basically committed and empathic, the task is do-able. Is she crying because she's hungry or her diaper's wet? After some trial and error, the baby is soothed. It's so natural in one sense, but it's a subtle, ancient psychological dance nonetheless. The caregiver must perceive *for the infant* her emotional state and respond accordingly to create a secure physical and emotional state in the child. As the infant matures and develops language, and with the help of empathic caregivers, a capacity begins to emerge *within the child* to do the same for herself, to be mindful of and know her own emotional experience. Now her emotions are not simply biological experiences but mental ones that she can recognize; she's beginning to *mentalize*, to *self-recognize* her inner states of emotions, wishes, desires, intentions, and so forth. A psychologically mindful self is emerging, one with self-consciousness and an ability to act with purpose.

What happens when things don't go so swimmingly for the caretakers and the infant? When one experiences the everyday trauma of a neglectful caretaker or the more serious capital *T* trauma of physical or sexual abuse? Without the empathy and emotional attunement that provides soothing relief, as well as a model of sorts for how to comfort oneself and others, the mindful psychological self becomes distorted. One develops an estrangement from one's emotional self, with devastating consequences. Emotions are misunderstood and unmoored.

Understandably, without a capacity for self-recognition of one's own inner states, empathy for and an understanding of the other's emotions and intentions is limited, and the emotional meanings behind behavior are prone to misunderstandings. Projection, or misattributing one's own impulses and thoughts to others, is commonplace.

Take Rodrick. He's an angry and disturbed teenager who was arrested for punching another teen in the face at a shopping mall for no apparent reason. He assaulted the other teen because "He looked at me." Upon further examination, it became clear that Rodrick felt this teen was looking *down* at him. Rodrick was on a senior outing from a private school for disturbed inner-city students. The group was at a mall in a suburban middle-class neighborhood when the offense occurred. Aggression and misunderstanding of others were not unfamiliar issues for Rodrick, as his school psychologist told me. Rodrick was raised in a chaotic home environment, rife with drug abuse and domestic violence. He had been shuffled around and lived with different family members and eventually in a variety of foster homes. He was not blessed with caregivers who were soothing and responsive during his early years. He never developed a mindfulness that allows him to reflect on his emotional reactions, to realize that his feelings are *his*, and that others may feel differently, with a variety of intentions and motives. Such a mindfulness and reflective ability about one's emotions and impulses allow for self-control, even under the harshest of conditions. This is not one of Rodrick's resources. His lack of perspective doesn't allow him to separate his inner experience from that of others. So instead of understanding others, he projects his inner anxieties onto them. He's easily disturbed and easily misunderstands. Rodrick's inner world is stark and foreboding, so he imagines the world as dangerous and offensive.

Both Rodrick and Deborah live in very different psychic worlds. Yes, Debora also lives with darkness and the fear of loss, but she knows it's *her* emotion, her darkness and fear. She's familiar with the contours of her psychological experience and can distinguish it from the world beyond. When she ended the relationship with her lover and felt catastrophic loss, she knew she was being irrational, even though she couldn't help it. She's reacting to what psychoanalysts refer to as unconscious fantasy, an enduring unconscious, emotionally tinged image or belief that shapes, and sometimes haunts, our conscious experience. For Deborah, it's something like, "Get ready to be shattered by love's loss." For Rodrick, it's malevolent, more like, "Don't trust anybody—fuck them!" Another difference is that Deborah knows her sense of danger is largely not rational. She tolerates being torn between what she feels inside and what she knows to be true: that her disturbed reaction is self-induced and actually uncalled for given her *current* circumstance. She doesn't blame her ex-lover for her misery. There's a dividing line between her psychic world and reality. Rodrick's experience is concrete in nature, with no dividing line between inner and outer reality.

Deborah is neurotic in her emotional life: she's internally conflicted but with a capacity to *mentalize*, a simple yet enormously important psychological function. It's what we mean when we think of someone who is psychologically minded, aware of having a psychological self, with others having their own separate psychological selves.

No such sophisticated awareness exists with Rodrick, whose psychological life is more primitive in nature, leaving him much less capable of understanding and tolerating conflicts within himself or with others.

I'm reminded of a psychotherapy supervisor who once wisecracked to me that to be neurotic is a psychological achievement.

***

By and large, my forensic inmates are not privileged to be neurotic like Deborah. Most have various types of derailments in their psychological development that make them susceptible to acting in ways that end up criminal. For instance, I evaluated Joan, a thirty-six-year-old woman who was accused of killing her estranged husband by shooting him in the back as he walked out of their house. They had been separated for a while, but he continued to visit their house, where she still lived, to spruce it up before selling it. Joan was accused of premeditated first-degree murder. Evidence of her purposefulness was that, about a month or so prior to the shooting, she screamed at him as he was leaving, "I love you to death." The shooting happened shortly after another of their toxic arguments.

Joan's defense was that she was acutely distressed, heard noises in the house and thought it was an intruder. She "lost it," got a gun, and blasted away, even though the victim—whether she knew it was her husband or thought it was an intruder—was leaving and had his back to Joan. She said she was "not myself . . . not thinking."

***

The psychological assessment was initially clinical, not a forensic one. I completed it about two weeks *before* the killing at the request of her psychotherapist, who was concerned about Joan's "love you to death" shriek. Although Joan denied any aggressive or suicidal intent, her psychotherapist began to question the degree of her patient's mental stability and wanted a second opinion.

I first met with Joan on a typical radiant California Saturday morning. I arrived at my office about twenty minutes before our scheduled appointment time. Since it was the weekend, there weren't many people at my office complex and the parking lot was spotted with only a few cars. As I pulled into a space and shut off my engine, I noticed a woman walking around the building. She looked like she was taking a morning stroll. She was in her mid- to late-thirties, casually dressed in a flowery dress and a light jacket, with short brown hair and a slight build. What struck me most about her was her gait: it had a light bounce to it. The shoulder strap of her cute little purse matched her dress and was wrapped slantwise, as it swayed slightly in time with her buoyant body. She seemed as though she hadn't a care in the world weighing her down. I wondered if this was the woman I was about to interview, the one who two weeks earlier had squealed "I love you to death" to her estranged husband. And indeed, it was.

After our mutual introductions and pleasantries, Joan completed some initial paperwork. Then I explained what we would be doing together for the next four to six hours. Joan told me how she felt about our consultation. Gently and with a slight, wry smile, she made it clear that she thought the evaluation was a waste. Her therapist had overreacted. She had no intention of hurting herself or her husband or anybody else. She expressed the opinion that her husband was going through some kind of midlife crisis and that they would eventually reunite. Nonetheless, Joan said she would cooperate.

Joan not only denied self-destructive or impulsive symptoms, but all signs of distress, unhappiness, or apprehension. Although she was surprised, even shocked, by her husband's wish to divorce, she was "going on with her life." Before he told her of his unhappiness with the marriage, she felt their marriage was idyllic.

As the session progressed, Joan's blasé acceptance was increasingly belied by her demeanor and interview behavior and the psychological testing results.

Joan had little to say about her early family life. Her memory was spotty at best. She was an only child. Besides being a "heavy drinker," her father was apparently diagnosed with a bipolar illness. "I'm not sure," she said. Their relationship, she nonetheless said with a lazy smile, was "normal." She couldn't describe for me in any concrete way the kind of man he was or the kind of activities they did together as a family. Joan's relationship with her mother was even harder for Joan to articulate. I couldn't get a mental picture of what their relationship was like or the ways of affection and strife that were part of the relationship. Joan's more meaningful comment was, "There wasn't much hugging." She couldn't articulate what kind of people her parents or other family members were.

Joan couldn't communicate to me much of what her parents or anyone in her early life were like as emotional people and what sorts of impact they had on her. For instance, I asked if her father's drinking caused any issues for the family. "Not really," she said, with a wan guise that suggested otherwise. She didn't have a well-formed psychological picture in her mind of him that she could communicate to me. As an example: "Yeah, he'd get mean when he drank, but not all the time. . . . He was really kind too. You know, he had a rough life too. . . . I used to resent him . . . not so much anymore." This difficulty with making a three-dimensional description of another's emotional state ("mean" sometimes, "kind" other times) is not uncommon among individuals with tenuous or insecure attachment histories. As I listened to Joan, I began to surmise that her early life lacked an adequate dosage of nurturance and mirroring of her emotions and inner states, such that Joan's awareness of her own emotional life was constricted. This left her with an inability to get a read on what others were feeling and for their psychological experiences to be opaque to her.

During her twenties, Joan was psychiatrically hospitalized several times for depression and attempts at suicide, all of which she dismissed as due to "boyfriend problems" at the time. She experimented with drugs. She had no criminal record. She had never been violent, but she was prone to emotional outbursts. Her adult life was marked by a search for stability, via relationships that usually ended poorly, multiple career changes, and numerous commitments to various religious groups. At the time of our interview, she was preparing to become a minister for the Salvation Army.

Psychological understanding of another is frequently revealed by exploring the seemingly mundane details of the person's life story. Frequently, it's not the specific details that are telling as much as what goes *unsaid*, what is opaque. That's how life stories sometimes expose meaning beyond what a person may know or be able to articulate. This was the case with Joan. She told me, in a matter-of-fact fashion, about how one day during her adolescence she returned home from school to find that movers had packed up her house. Her parents informed her *that day* that the family was moving. She had no idea that this move to another state was planned. During the course of the interview, she also told me that her current marriage was her third. Her first marriage ended when her husband, like her third, surprised her by abruptly telling her that he wanted a divorce after less than a year of marriage. Again, for Joan, this came "out of the blue," a total bombshell. Her second husband killed himself. His self-destructive tendencies were a complete shock to Joan; she was unaware that he was even depressed. I expressed puzzlement over this pattern she described of being repeatedly surprised by changes in the status of her relationships with intimate others in her life—her family's move and her obliviousness to the deterioration of her marriages. When I asked what she made of these repeated jolts and disruptions to her life, her reaction was strange: she seemed to unplug from our dialogue, as though she drifted very briefly into a mild trance before returning eye contact and saying she didn't know. She then asked, "What's next?"

I began to suspect that Joan's responses during the course of the interview thus far reflected a lack of psychological cohesion born of an incapacity or intolerance to recognizing her inner experience or that of others. She was unable to reflect on herself in relation to others, particularly if it threatened her desires and preferred perceptions of events, lest it provoke intense, confusing, and painful emotions too disruptive for a fragile psychological self. I saw this process in vivo when I invited her to consider the meaning of the abrupt derailments in her life. She disconnected from me and lapsed into a momentary protective reverie before requesting a change of subject ("What's next?"). She maintained her psychic stability at the expense of lucidity; for Joan, torn feelings, inner disturbances, and unwanted realities threaten to tear her apart. I suspected that she lacked the capacity for psychological mindfulness and organization that is present in Deborah, who is able to absorb her pain and emotions without using psychologically immature, reality-distorting defenses and strategies, such as the complete denial of what's in front of you. Deborah can feel torn without the fear of being torn apart. Joan had no mindful capacity. When she was faced with the reality of her marital dissolution, her intense and painful emotions completely overwhelmed her and she psychologically exploded.

Subsequent to my evaluation of Joan and prior to my eventual testimony at the appellate hearing that contested her first-degree murder conviction, Joan's aunt told me that she had seen Joan during times of stress—like after the breakup of her first marriage—go into a rampage, leave the room, and upon return a few minutes later, appear cheerful, as if nothing happened. Her aunt described such scenes as "bizarre."

Psychodiagnostic testing confirmed Joan to be an individual who was morbidly depressed, with indicators that she was chronically in psychological disarray with a fragile sense of self which was, at that moment, crumbling. I diagnosed her with major depression as well as borderline personality disorder. I noted that she might become emotionally unstable and self-destructive and that she employed immature psychological defenses like denial of reality to avoid pain. Her interpersonal relationship history was fraught with chaos, all of which reflected a precarious sense of self—hallmarks of a personality disorder. In my report, I also said she might well react to the emotional impact of loss in destructive ways.

I recommended a psychiatric evaluation for medication and close monitoring of her mood. Her behavior was unpredictable, and I suggested that she and her husband stay away from each other due to possible further decompensation. I emphasized her depression, her psychological fragility, and her lack of self-awareness. These issues, coupled with an impending loss, made her vulnerable to periods of poor reality testing and to destructive, possibly violent, behavioral reactions.

A developing self is ungirded by disruptions in the bond with caregivers. Difficulties can be augmented by an inborn temperament that doesn't match well with the lack of psychological supplies offered by caregivers. Gertrude Stein famously proclaimed, "A rose is a rose is a rose." Not so with people: under the best of circumstances, some people still have trouble, and under the worst, some still do well. But most of us do not thrive without early, imperfect, yet good-enough caretaking. Like Rodrick, Joan's insecure bonding to others led to unstable behavior, distorted perceptions, and impulsiveness.

Joan couldn't manage the intense rage she felt toward her husband. She didn't see the breakup of the marriage coming nor could she see her husband's growing dissatisfaction. She was limited in her ability to empathize and understand him, to grasp his mind-set that was in conflict with hers. She could not give what she didn't get. It was beyond her to distinguish her desire from his or her degree of love and happiness from what he was experiencing until reality was staring her in the face. And then it was literally too much for a fragile self to bear. It's not that she didn't know it's wrong to shoot somebody, even an intruder, in the back. But the intensity of her emotions ripped apart, at least momentarily, her power of will.

At her trial for first-degree murder, Joan was convicted by a jury of her peers. She was found to have committed a homicide knowingly and with conscious deliberation and premeditation. She was sentenced to life in prison.

***

Joan got a second bite of the apple. After the guilty verdict, her family hired an appeals attorney to review the evidence and the trial transcript. He found my report and argued that the original defense team was incompetent and deprived Joan of effective counsel for never offering evidence of a psychiatric condition that affected her mental state at the time of the homicide.

I had been surprised by the defense strategy at her first trial and at least had expected to be consulted by her defense team.

During the appellate court's hearing, I presented psychological evidence regarding Joan's mental state just prior to the killing and said her psychological fragility and limited ability to manage her emotions made her susceptible to impulsive rage reactions. I described borderline personality as a significant psychopathology that makes one susceptible to unpredictable emotional reactions to such an extent that reality testing may become impaired.

The three appellant judges unanimously concluded that not only had Joan's defense team deprived her of effective legal counsel by simply arguing that she was emotionally distraught and in a state of confusion at the time of the shooting, but that her conviction of first-degree, premeditated murder and her life sentence were to be vacated. The court noted that it is not uncommon for individuals with borderline personality disorder to sometimes commit destructive acts, including homicide, during periods of instability. They are likely to strike out in "infantile rage" and "destroy the thing they feel they are losing." Had psychological evidence been presented at Joan's trial, the judges wrote, it may not have excused Joan's behavior but may have helped to explain it. The psychological evidence of her mental disorder may have had bearing on her actual ability to formulate a specific intent to premeditate the murder. They concluded that because my psychological report was written just before the murder, it provided a clinical picture of Joan's mental state that was "the antithesis of evidence of premeditation and deliberation." They opined that it was reasonably probable that had the jury heard evidence of Joan's personality disorder and mental state prior to the crime, they may have found that she did not premeditate and deliberate the killing.

During a plea bargain process subsequent to the appellant decision, Joan pleaded to voluntary manslaughter. The appellate court described Joan as likely to have been in an "infantile rage" at the time of the homicide, with the mental state, the mens rea, of a child—a state that interfered with her ability to deliberate and premeditate. But her actus reas, her bodily movements, were certainly adultlike. She got a gun and shot her estranged husband. Joan's mind didn't develop naturally, commensurate with the maturity of her body. What makes our mental life vulnerable to being stuck in time and arrested in some fundamental way? As time progresses, the body matures biologically, but the mind within that body may become distorted, twisted, and weakened.

***

Besides corrupted experience and inadequate attachment patterns during those early years, there are a variety of other reasons why adults become mentally disordered. About 1 percent of the population develops schizophrenia (in all cultures and during different historical periods), a horrific disease causing hallucinations and delusions.[2] Contrary to popular belief, though, most people with major mental illnesses do not commit crimes. You're just as likely—actually more so—to be attacked by your normally friendly alcoholic neighbor than a schizophrenic. So why are many of us vulnerable—with or without a formal psychiatric diagnosis—to episodes of infantile rage and destructive behavior? Think of the nightly news reports on one of those gruesome and tragic outbursts of unexpected violence: a distraught father killing his wife and children before ending his own life. The neighbors are shocked; the family seemed so normal, the murderer a family man. What happened? What makes the majority of us who are not struggling with a chronic mental illness nonetheless vulnerable to mental states that compromise self-control and distort reality?

Let me return to my patients introduced earlier in this chapter—Deborah, Rodrick, and Joan. Deborah had the good fortune of being raised by loving caretakers who helped her survive the devastating death of her mother and to be gifted with a sense of self-recognition, an awareness of her "I-ness." She has self-reflecting ability, is able to mentalize, to stand back and observe her thoughts, wishes, feelings, intentions, and so on without impulsive action. She knows that, unlike concrete objects, the contents of her mind are imaginative and potentially changeable based on her ongoing experience in life. She understands that others in her life have their own mental lives, imagination, and life experience, which make them unique and different from her imagination and experience.

This ability to mentalize,[3] to realize that others have their own distinct experiences, sounds so simple yet is so profound. It is the foundation of an independent and stable identity, that sense of "I-ness" of oneself and of the other. Think about Rodrick, who lacked that simple mental ability and its consequences on his life—his vulnerability to action without thought and to profound misunderstandings of others.

Despite the loss of her mother at an early age, Deborah's temperament and strong, secure bonding with others in her early life allowed her to develop a sense of herself with an empathic understanding of others. Even when in emotional pain, she is able to tolerate that pain without her mind being torn apart to the point of distorting reality. The capacity for self-recognition allows one to gradually become conversant with one's personal desires and intentions and to know that others have their own desires and intentions. This enhances emotional control and the meaning emotions have to psychological experience. With such a level of psychological understanding, one is better able to tolerate our emotional intensity, even the most malignant impulses, without resorting to reality distortions and destructive behavior.

I think of mentalizing ability as providing a kind of psychic infrastructure wherein emotions and impulses are given space to be "digested" and tempered before they may be expressed in a destructively daimonic form. It provided Deborah with an inner strength to contain her pain and the courage to face herself without projecting or lashing out.

A radical limitation in self-recognition provides the psychological milieu in which daimonic malevolence is seeded. The word *radical* comes from the Greek word *radius*, meaning root. Limited mentalization is a deficit deeply imbedded within an individual's psychological makeup. This kind of personal limitation is not easily observable but profoundly consequential. Lacking it, Rodrick unconsciously projected his bad feelings about himself onto others. Joan was psychologically so unmoored that that she erupted in an impulsively homicidal rage.

Some, like Deborah, lucked out. But nobody's perfect and we're all subject to limited self-recognition and psychological anomia to one degree or another at one time or another. And that makes even the "lucky" ones capable of cruelty and brutality to one degree or another.[4] It's all in there, part of our daimonic nature.

As is obvious in the chapters that follow, many of those caught in the justice system have not been gifted with such a level of psychological achievement as Deborah. The imperfect past is timeless and haunting. It corrupts imagination and with it, reality and emotional understanding, bringing the full spectrum of the daimonic.

Part II

The Vagaries of Justice

3

TIES THAT BLIND

Whom the gods destroy they first make mad.—Euripides

Nobody realizes that some people expend tremendous energy merely to be normal.—Albert Camus

The walk from the witness chair to the double door leading out of the tenth-floor courtroom took forever. I hadn't realized its cavernous size when I entered to begin my testimony in Michael's insanity trial. That morning, I had felt less than my best. Saddled with nasty throat and sinus infections, my voice was hoarse and wispy. After the court clerk swore me in, the bailiff adjusted the microphone and sound system so that all in the gallery could hear me. As is usual when I'm about to testify, I struggled with an aching case of the nerves. It started the week before when I began to prepare for the big event. It peaked as I walked from the courtroom gallery to the witness stand, aware of the jurors staring at me, already taking my measure. The attorney who retained me began, "Tell the court about your training and experience, Dr. Lettieri," hoping to convince the jury that my opinions were worthy of consideration. Years of psychic hard work have tamed my proclivity to worry, but my neurotic self continues to look for opportunities to express itself, and this is one of them. The bailiff's mic change amplified not only my voice but my angst, a moment of panic but, as usual, it didn't last. I settled in for the ride.

After hours of testimony and tension, separated by a lunch break, the attorneys completed their questioning and the judge excused me. It seemed to have gone well. Walking toward the courtroom's exit, I realized that not only had I been unaware of the large size of the courtroom, but I hadn't noticed that the trial drew local media. Since murder cases are unfortunately not that unusual, I suspected it attracted the public's attention not because a killing had occurred but due to the tragic nature of the crime: a dedicated, loving mother who cared for her ill son had been slain by him. Michael stabbed her in the back, adding a layer of betrayal and symbolism.

I exited the courtroom and entered the hallway. Andrew, Michael's older brother, waited for me. The relief faded and my heart pounded. When he testified during the first phase of the trial, Andrew as well as his sister Michelle focused on Michael's psychiatric symptoms, his attachment to their mother, and his nonviolent history. I had interviewed Andrew several times. We had a good rapport, but my testimony exposed gaping miscalculations and misjudgments by the family about Michael's potential for violence. Andrew had told me of the agony and deep guilt he lives with for underestimating the depth of Michael's illness and its risks for their mother. I had just created a public record of the family's private emotional hell and deadly miscalculations.

A burly man in his late forties with a light goatee and thick torso, Andrew walked toward me. I stood there, wondering if his shame might have flipped to rage. It soon became clear that my insecurity was rearing its head. I fixed on his sad eyes and slight smile. He hugged and thanked me for helping people to realize that Michael is "so sick. . . . He's not a criminal. He loved my mother." Andrew's wife, Josey, who had been sitting on a bench in the courtroom's hall, walked over. She had been crying. Her eyes looked worn and reddened, and she carried a pack of tissues. Josey thanked me and took her husband's arm as they walked toward the elevators. Not wanting to ride in the elevator with them, I headed for the bathroom. I wanted an escape from the suffering.

***

Michael had a long history of mental illness, but nobody had fathomed such violence. Although a shy youngster before he developed his psychiatric symptoms, Michael had made a few friends in the neighborhood. He played sports and loved baseball. At age ten, his parents divorced. His mother continued her work as an occupational therapist. His father, a physician, moved out of state but kept in touch with the children.

Michael told me his family was supportive, his mother in particular. There were no early signs of emotional disturbance during his early years, no bullying of other kids, no fighting, and no signs of childhood depression. Michael wasn't oppositional at school or mean to other kids. Though he got along with other children and had some friends, he had no close buddies. He spent a lot of time by himself. He took part in social projects at school and through his church, like fundraising for the poor during holidays. In high school, he got involved in the Bible ministry program and even took a trip with a group of students to South America during his junior year.

Still, Michael struggled emotionally as he moved through his teen years. By his senior year in high school, his shyness had transformed into troubling social anxiety. Formal activities like sports or church events helped for a while to control his growing unease, but he got worse with time and spent less time socializing. His self-consciousness around others became increasingly painful. He stopped going out to eat with his church group. "Everybody looked at me."

After graduating from high school, Michael continued to live at home and attended a local junior college. He dropped out the first year. His anxiety and self-consciousness began to morph into paranoia. In class, he wondered if some of his professors could read his mind. The academic demands and contact with so many new faces took their toll. Michael had a part-time job at Target for a few months until he abruptly quit. A sense of peril weighed on him.

Before he quit the job at Target, something else happened that stoked Michael's insecurity and distrust. One evening, to fight off boredom, he went for a drive and ended up having a car accident. He hit a twenty-one-year-old pedestrian dressed in dark clothing who had attempted to cross the street against a red light. Michael saw him but couldn't stop in time. The police and paramedics arrived and took the fellow to the hospital. He was released several hours later with a mild concussion. The police found Michael's behavior suspicious. He hadn't been drinking, so they didn't smell alcohol. They misread his odd behavior—poor eye contact, mumbling speech, and guarded demeanor—and suspected he had something to hide. He refused to take an in-field sobriety test. They arrested him on suspicion of drug use, took him to the police station in handcuffs, and tested him. He was drug free. After speaking with his mother and a few witnesses at the accident scene, the police released Michael, but not before some psychic damage was done. During their questioning of Michael, the police threatened to charge him with a DUI with aggravating circumstances. They terrified him further by raising the specter of a civil lawsuit. The incident fueled his developing paranoia.

By now, the family realized something was wrong. His sister Michelle told me that by the time Michael reached his early twenties, she thought her brother might have a mental illness. He spent days holed up in his room. He stayed up all night. She had moved out of the house at the end of Michael's senior year in high school but visited regularly.

I queried Michelle about Michael's relationship with his mother. Matricide (murder of one's mother) and a destructive relationship between mother and son tend to go hand in hand. An insidious type of dependency and simmering rage sometimes defines the bond that's prequel to the killing.[1] Yes, Michael depended on their mother, but it was because he was so limited and couldn't function on his own. Michelle emphasized that their mother was not the controlling type. She tried to get Michael involved in church activities or to consider taking part in a day treatment program at a mental health clinic to no avail. The burdens imposed by having an ill son were heavy, but she persevered without obvious resentment. During a conversation not long before the murder, she told Michelle that, as much as possible, she treated Michael like he was normal.

During her visits home, Michelle thought Michael might have been lonely, though he hadn't complained about it. During those early years before it first sank in that her brother suffered with an illness, she'd make simple, encouraging suggestions to him. She made an offhand comment about calling friends from high school or junior college. His response took her aback. He felt "betrayed by everybody. Not everybody, but almost everybody. A lot." He complained about how the managers at Target had "run me down." It stunned Michelle. She spoke with her mother, her brother Andrew, and her sister Nicole about her concerns, but they did nothing. They hoped Michael would "pull himself together." It didn't happen.

***

Michael's mental condition continued to worsen. The family had to hospitalize him when he became so withdrawn that he stopped talking and eating. He lost almost forty pounds. After a brief, four-day psychiatric hospitalization, the doctors discharged him. At home, his isolation and paranoia gradually worsened, leading to more brief hospitalizations. His paranoid ruminations included the sense of being betrayed or followed. He'd take a bus and worry about passengers who got off at his stop. Were they shadowing him? Could they hear his private thoughts? Michael was diagnosed with paranoid schizophrenia.

Even when free of paranoid delusions, Michael continued to suffer from what's called "negative" symptoms. His facial expression was invariably flat, incongruously so. When everybody laughed over a situation, he wouldn't even chuckle. He was usually distracted and preoccupied. Any sense of social awareness eluded him: during family conversations, he'd get up and walk out of a room without comment. Ironically, the medications that helped with core symptoms like delusions worsened others, making him more withdrawn and lackluster.

Michael's chronic symptoms were made up of a mixture of paranoid ruminations, vague fearfulness, social isolation, and a poverty of expressiveness. His withdrawal into himself would get so bad that during one of his hospitalizations, a psychiatrist described him as catatonic.

Through it all, he never showed signs of aggression. He was never violent. In fact, during several of his hospitalizations, the staff placed him in assertion groups to encourage greater self-expression and less passivity.

Michael continued to live with his mother. For brief periods of time, he left the house and spent weeks living on the streets. He'd invariably get picked up by the police and taken to a hospital. After a brief stay, he'd return to live with his mother. The extent of his psychiatric treatment consisted of fifteen-minute check-ins with a psychiatrist at the county clinic every six weeks for his antipsychotic medications. A case manager was available once or maybe twice a month to speak with, if necessary. Eventually, Michael would stop going to his appointments, run out of his medications, become bizarre (e.g., pacing and talking to himself; refusing to eat), and end up rehospitalized, only to start the cycle again.

***

On the morning of the killing, the police received a telephone call from Michelle, Michael's sister. Michael had called her to say he had "done something. . . . I hurt mom. I thought she was sending me to hell."

Michelle asked the police to do a welfare check on her mother. They found her dead, stabbed in the back and covered with a blanket. After being told of Michael's whereabouts by Michelle, the police picked him up and arrested him. They charged him with first-degree, premeditated murder.

***

I began my interviews with Michael about one year after the homicide. Such a time lapse is not uncommon, but it causes problems. The defendant has time to think about what happened, work it over in his mind, and rationalize his behavior. Memory gets spotty and recollections of the actual events may be distorted. I design my evaluation procedures to compensate for these problems and, as best I can, to arrive at a clear depiction of the defendant's mental state at the time of the crime. In this case, I conducted multiple interviews with Michael, reliving the killing with him, comparing his recollections with the official record, and exploring discrepancies. I interviewed family members and reviewed the records of their interviews with police. I discussed and, when necessary, confronted contradictions in the emerging picture of what transpired. I also conducted psychological testing.

As usual, our first interview was a review of Michael's development and personal history, his criminal background, psychiatric and medical histories, family and interpersonal histories, and his educational and employment histories. Although I usually have read multiple psychiatric-medical documents that outlined a defendant's personal background before the interviews, hearing it from the defendant is extremely important: it provides the psychological meat that gives facts their unique flavor and intimate meaning.

The most critical part of the interview was a detailed examination of the Michael's thoughts, his feelings and intentions before, during, and after the killing, his mental state or mens rea that prompted the killing. What were Michael's thoughts before and while he stabbed his mother? How long had he had these thoughts? What motivated him to behave as he did after the killing? During multiple long (three to five hour) interviews, I drill down on the details of a defendant's thoughts and behavior until I develop a picture of his/her mental state at the time of the killing.

To prepare for my examination of Michael, I reviewed a voluminous police record on the killing, along with audio and video interviews of witnesses and of Michael that the police conducted. I reviewed an extensive record of his psychiatric and medical treatment, which confirmed his chronic mental illness. Crazy behavior doesn't suddenly "pop up" just before and after a defendant commits a crime. Psychopathology in adults usually leaves a paper trail. It's at least documented via observations by family or other intimates. In standard clinical practice, I don't interview family members before I treat patients for, say, anger or impulse control. For complex forensic cases, I consult with those in the defendant's life to get an objective perspective on the defendant's illness and behavior. It's an essential part of the evaluation process, adding to a three-dimensional view of the defendant and his illness, which may deepen my understanding of what led to the offense. My consultations with Michael's family, especially with Michelle and Andrew, helped enormously.

I also completed comprehensive psychological testing with Michael. Tests such as the Minnesota Multiphasic Personality Inventory (MMPI-2-RF)[2] help to reveal the extent and quality of an individual's symptoms (depression, anxiety, delusions). Because of the extensive research done on these tests, I was able to compare Michael's scores with those of other defendants and nondefendants (norms) who had taken the test, thus providing an unbiased measure of his psychiatric condition. These tests, with literally thousands of studies confirming their accuracy, have validity scales that appraise whether the defendant is answering questions honestly. Sophisticated statistical measures are used to ensure the results reveal a true picture of the defendant's symptoms. Optimally, the test results should converge with my developing clinical understanding of the defendant.

During the first interview with Michael, I explained that I'd be conducting a psychological evaluation in order to write a report and render an opinion on his insanity. I would give an opinion on whether he suffered from mentally disordered symptoms at the time of the crime. Also, I would evaluate if he understood that killing his mother was wrong when he did it. Since the court appointed me (unlike when I'm privately retained by an attorney), I told him that the results are not confidential or covered under doctor-patient privilege. He understood.

Michael was twenty-eight years old when we first met. He was thin and stood six feet tall. But with his drooped posture and slumped shoulders, he appeared smaller. He wore a clean white t-shirt beneath an orange jumpsuit that was two sizes too big. Together with his crooked posture, he looked like a man trying to hide from the world. His long black hair clearly hadn't been washed for some time. A striking feature of his demeanor was his poor eye contact. To avoid the discomfort of sitting with a stranger in a booth the size of most apartment bathrooms, Michael found comfort in fixing his gaze downward on the desk between us. His discomfort was palpable and infectious; I too felt the awkwardness. His speech was soft, with minimal verbal output, as if every word had a cost. His dejected manner was reminiscent of many schizophrenic individuals I've encountered through the years who were recovering from the active stage of their illnesses. They're free of severe symptoms like delusions, but they look as though they're withering away, like dried-up plants.

I began probing the homicide with Michael during our first visit after we had gotten reasonably comfortable with each other. We established a rapport by talking about his personal life, his friendships, his family relationships, sports, and his emotional struggle with social anxiety. About two hours into the interview, I felt we had developed enough comfort with each other to begin talking about his psychiatric condition, a segue into the more combustible topic of his mother's murder.

Michael had been treated with Haldol, an antipsychotic, for years, but it had been causing bad side effects for months before the killing. He had itching and burning sensations in his thighs, arms, and stomach. As is usual with individuals prone to psychosis, the symptoms had an irrational meaning for him: "I thought I was going to hell." The burning sensations convinced him "the sun was coming" and would take him away.

Because of the burning sensations, Michael's psychiatrist changed his medications, but the delusions about the sun had solidified in Michael's mind. He recalled a conversation he had with his brother when they were kids. Andrew said that if a UFO took them to the sun, it would take two weeks. The memory added to his panic. As time passed, Michael decided he had to act and save himself from such a terrifying fate.

Michael first believed that his psychiatrist had damned him to be burned by the sun by prescribing medication that inflamed his body. He rambled about the Bible and how hell is at the center of the Earth. Before the killing, he believed "The sun is hell."

Michael purchased a knife at Big Five and planned to kill his county clinic psychiatrist. Then, "everything would be normal." As fate had it, about one month before the killing, Michael received a call saying the psychiatrist had been transferred and that he had been assigned a new doctor. He decided not to follow up with a psychiatrist. For a brief period, he considered himself saved.

Two weeks before the killing, Michael and his mother took a ride to a casino in the Nevada desert. As they drove, "The sun got bright and light. Everything faded into a bright light." Before they reached the California state line, he made his mother turn around and go home. Now, he thought, "she's responsible for the sun getting close," not the psychiatrist.

Unsure what to do, Michael worried about running out of time. If he didn't do something soon, the sun would "gobble me up." He made multiple calls to Andrew, complaining about the sun getting closer. He told Andrew that their mother had special powers. "She's evil." Andrew told him that their mother was "good as gold" and had saved him from living on the streets. A day before the killing, Michael called Andrew, expressing fear of their mother. Andrew called her, concerned. She calmed Andrew down, saying Michael had never been violent or aggressive toward her. She added, "He doesn't have the nerve."

On the day prior to the killing, Michael had panic attacks "like I had never had. I couldn't control anything. I had too much excitement running through my thoughts at once." His thoughts about his mother were bizarre: "She turned people into locusts and grasshoppers." He thought to himself, "Who's going to send me to hell?" He said he then heard his mother say, "I am, if that's okay with you." At that point, he made the decision, "I'm going to do this. I have to do it or she'll send me to hell." He considered killing himself, but then he would end up in hell anyway. He decided that his only choice was to kill his mother so that the descending sun would stop. "Then everything would be back to normal."

The same thoughts kept running around in Michael's head. "If I didn't stop her, I'll burn in the sun." At the same time, he described himself as "sitting, staring at the wall." The evening before the killing, he visited a gentleman's club and had a beer. In the past, being at the club helped distract him from his ruminations. It didn't work this time.

The killing occurred on a Thursday morning, about 9:00. Michael had not slept much the night before. The bright southern California sun signaled to Michael that he had to act—immediately. He had taken the hunting knife he purchased weeks earlier from a drawer in his bedroom. He sat on the living room couch with the knife beneath his shirt, ruminating. His legs burned and itched. When his mother entered the living room from her bedroom, she began talking but he wasn't listening. She mentioned something about getting vitamins to help him with his burning and itching sensations. She headed to the kitchen, maybe planning to enjoy her first cup of morning coffee. If so, she never made it. Michael thought, "I've got to do this." He stood up from the couch and caught up with her before she got there. As she walked, he plunged the hunting knife deep into his mother's back, telling her, "You're bad." Before falling, she turned, looked at him in wide-eyed shock, and uttered, "You . . ."

Almost immediately after the killing, Michael's panic again kicked in, but now for a different reason. "I knew she didn't cause the problem. The sun was still there, close. . . . I killed my best friend." He ran to his car, sat, and considered what to do. "The sun didn't return to normal." He went back into the house and covered his mother with a blanket. He couldn't absorb the fact that he killed "my closest friend. It's like a dream." He called his sister Michelle, the only person he trusted. I asked why he did not call the police. "I don't trust them."

Michael had told Michelle he was calling her from a nearby pizzeria. She told Michael to stay put. She hung up and called the police, informing them of his location. They arrested him outside the pizzeria without incident. He told the arresting officers, "I just did the worse thing in my life. . . . I stabbed her."

I reviewed with Michael sections of his videotaped interview with the police detectives. Michael told the detectives, "I thought she had some control over me or something. She was playing a game in my mind." The detective asked if killing his mother was wrong. (If he knew it was wrong, he is legally sane, even with psychotic thinking.) Michael responded, "I don't know. She scared me so much I felt a little sick." At another point during the interview, the detective, with some exasperation, confronted Michael with the statement, "You knew it was wrong when you did it. Come on, be honest with yourself. You knew your mother was gonna die, didn't you?" Michael replied, "I guess." The detective then said, "Okay, now it's time. We need to go forward and find out what you really did. None of this sun stuff." Michael replied, "I thought the sun would stop, it would go away or go back to a place where it's supposed to be." One detective continued to press Michael: "But it was wrong to do it, right?" Michael, sounding befuddled, said, "It was real to me. I didn't know." The detective replied, "Yes, you did. Cause a knife in your mom is gonna kill her. You understood that, right?" Michael again responded, "I thought the sun would stop. It would go away. It would go back to a place where it's supposed to be."

I stopped the video recording and looked at him, waiting for his response. Michael just looked down at the desk between us. I pointed out the obvious—that the detectives believed he realized stabbing his mother was a crime and wrong. "Yeah," he responded. Then, for a moment, Michael's bland expression turned plaintive as he said, "I thought she was sending me to hell." He sat there, flaccid and lost. He killed the one who had been there guiding him through his troubled life.

Michael's odd demeanor and statements during his police interview were consistent with the clinical picture I had been developing from my interviews with him and consultations with his family. Michelle told me that their mother had said Michael had complained about burning in his legs for some time. Andrew told me that Michael believed his mother had special powers over him and was "evil." The family took for granted that Michael would never get violent, certainly not to the point of killing their mother. Michael's other brother, Benjamin, who lived out of state, said their mother mostly fretted about who would take care of him after she died.

The psychological testing was consistent with my clinical observations and Michael's psychiatric history. He suffered chronically from paranoid delusions. The validity scales of the MMPI-2-RF showed that he responded honestly, without exaggerating his symptoms or attempting to present a false picture of his behavior. His most elevated clinical scales were those that identify individuals prone to delusions or hallucinations. There was no evidence of antisocial tendencies or violent-prone behavior that was distinct of his irrational, psychotic thinking, which could have fueled his murderous conduct. In addition, his psychiatric records from his many psychiatric hospitalizations and his jail psychiatric reports carried the diagnosis of paranoid schizophrenia.

The clinical picture of Michael emerged of an individual with a serious mental illness. The only questions were whether his illness was active at the time of the killing and whether it had interfered with his ability to distinguish between right and wrong.

I concluded that Michael was mentally ill at the time of the killing. He suffered from the delusional belief that he had to kill his mother to prevent the sun from "gobbling me up." In my report to the court, I emphasized the extent and chronicity of Michael's mental illness and his delu-sional beliefs about his mother. Michael's irrationality drove his convic-tion that he had no choice but to kill her, lest he be cast into the firestorm of hell. In his psychotic mind, he was as righteous as someone who shot and killed a homicidal attacker. I offered the opinion that Michael was insane when he killed his mother.

**

During the insanity phase of Michael's trial, my testimony began with direct examination questions (as opposed to cross-examination by the opposing attorney) by Mr. Swanson, Michael's public defender. This part of my testimony was straightforward and gave me an opportunity to describe how I went about examining Michael and why I concluded he was insane. Questions like, "How much time did you spend in your evaluation of the defendant?" Or "Tell the court, Dr. Lettieri, what the evaluation entailed." "What tests did you administer, and how did they help you to come to your conclusion?" "What are your conclusions?" Finally, "Dr. Lettieri, were you paid to reach those conclusions or were you paid for the time to reach your conclusions?"

The sparks flew during cross-examination by the opposing counsel, in this case the prosecuting attorney, Mr. McDaniel. He cut an imposing figure in the courtroom. As an experienced district attorney—those who try murder cases are always the most seasoned—he knew how to get to the meat of the issue the jury needed to consider. As I said, during the insanity phase of Michael's trial, the essential question was whether he understood, at the moment he killed his mother, that it was wrong to do so. It didn't matter if he was scared, angry, or believed he was in danger because of his mental illness. It didn't matter that Michael was mentally ill at the time. Did his illness block him from realizing that his murderous behavior was morally or legally wrong? That was the question the prose-cutor wasted no time in addressing.

Mr. McDaniel was not only experienced but self-confident. He had won multiple jury trials over the years. With a voice booming and re-sounding through the courtroom, he began his cross-examination. He stood behind a lectern with notes he hardly glanced at, signaling to the jury his expert knowledge of the case and his certainty about what he needed to address in order to prove his point. At times, he separated from the anchor of the lectern and strutted about the courtroom as he asked his questions, again without notes. The focus of Mr. McDaniel's cross-examination centered on Michael's behavior *after* the killing. He highlighted Michael's alleged awareness of his wrongdoing by asking me to respond to a series of yes-or-no questions. This was also his way of exerting control of our exchange and my responses. "Did Michael cover up his mother's body after the killing?" Yes. His voice, a little louder, asked, "Did the defendant call his sister and tell her he did something bad?" Yes. A little louder, "Did he say he had made a mistake?" Yes. He showed segments of Michael's videotaped interview with the police. Michael told the police he did something terribly wrong. He looked distraught. He didn't look crazy.

As Mr. McDaniel posed those questions, he regularly glanced toward the jurors, calculating his impact. His demeanor was assured as he led me and them down a path that allegedly exposed Michael's culpability. He spent more time away from the safety of the lectern and casually strolled about the courtroom, like he owned it.

Mr. McDaniel shut off the video. He asked me if the evidence showed that Michael realized after the killing that he had made a horrific mistake. I answered yes. He glanced at the jury and sardonically asked, "Doesn't it imply he knew it was wrong to kill her?" This was a shrewd question. If Michael's behavior *implied* that he comprehended he was doing wrong when he killed his mother, it could possibly raise reasonable doubt in the jury's mind regarding Michael's irrationality at the time of the killing. I responded that no, it did not. With an overdramatic sigh, Mr. McDaniel asked me why not. This gave me an opening to explain Michael's conduct after the killing. I first made the point that at the time of the killing, Michael was in the throes of a fixed delusional belief that the sun was descending upon him and that he was about to be gobbled up because of his mother's evilness. After the killing, when there was no change in the sun's brightness, he realized that the killing did not change reality. At this moment, his capacity to perceive reality clarified, but that was *after* the killing.

I've witnessed a similar phenomenon with psychotic individuals in forensic and private hospital settings as well. I gave the example of a hospitalized psychotic patient who believed another patient was staring at him and thus causing the patient's derogatory auditory hallucinations. The psychotic patient smashed a chair over the other patient's head, believing the derogatory voices would cease. After the assault, the patient had an immediate moment of clarity and became suicidal, as the voices continued. Mr. McDaniel ended his cross-examination of me by repeating his questions and having me affirm that Michael was aware of and remorseful for what he did to his mother soon after the killing. I suppose he was hoping to convince the jurors that Michael was rational *enough* at the moment of the stabbing.

During the redirect examination—when Mr. Swanson, Michael's attorney, asked additional questions after the cross-examination—I clarified the severity of Michael's mental illness and how it warped his ability to understand what was real and true. I pointed out that years before the killing, records documented his paranoia and poor reality testing. Michael had expressed fears of the sun and of Satan. Mr. Swanson asked me to clarify some aspects of the psychological testing, which demonstrated that Michael suffered from a psychotic disorder. He wanted to eliminate any doubt in the jurors' minds that Michael's distortion of reality was severe and real.

After closing arguments, the jury deliberated for a day and half before reaching the conclusion that Michael was not guilty by reason of insanity.

The defense counsel spoke with jurors after they completed deliberations, a common occurrence. All realized that Michael suffered from a mental illness. The question of Michael's knowing at the moment of the killing that he was doing something wrong was the tough issue for them. The prosecuting attorney had been correct to focus on Michael's behavior after the killing. They considered several possibilities other than craziness, including an out-of-control temper outburst or old-fashioned family dysfunction. They were persuaded of Michael's insanity by the power of his siblings' testimony and their impassioned belief that he never would have killed his mother if he were in his right mind. My testimony on Michael's behavior after the killing—that this unaltered perception of the position of the sun and thus his catastrophic error—made sense to them.

During their testimony, Michael's sisters and brother described him as a loving son and never violent, not even during his delusional periods. Before the murder, all the family, including his mother, were confident that Michael would never hurt his mother. His paranoid beliefs about her evilness didn't sway that conviction. After all, he relied on her so much. And when he was relatively free from the pull of his mental disturbance, Michael enjoyed being with her, shopping or spending afternoons at a casino. Her devotion to him forged a bond much stronger than the force of his psychosis. So they thought.

Serious mental illness distorts reality and the perceptions of others' behavior and intentions. Those with whom the patient is most involved naturally fall prey to the psychotic distortions. Michael's mother was involved in his everyday life. In his mind, she was the "logical" one behind the malevolent force causing his impending doom. It's difficult for family members to fathom a son committing a heinous violent act toward a loved and devoted mother. That's because it's so difficult to appreciate the extent and *realness* of a psychotic reality to someone as ill as Michael.

Mental illness as a criminal defense is difficult for juries to accept. The mind is a mysterious organ, even more so when its penchant for irrationality is mixed in. It's particularly hard to swallow the notion that a diseased mind should excuse a horrific act like murder. A son killing his mother is even harder to justify under any conditions. Frequently, some form of a relationship has existed between murderers and their victims. But matricide is rare. It accounts for 1 percent or less of all U.S. cases, including homicides.[3] The defense of insanity is also rare, used in less than 1 percent of all criminal trials.[4] It's rejected as a defense by juries 75 percent of the time.[5] Again, jurors don't like giving anyone a pass for committing violent crimes. And there's always the possibility of fakery. Retribution seems moral and justified.

In Michael's case, the jury concluded that his delusional thinking transformed him into an irrational killer. It's ironic that the family members who underestimated his potential to act in a daimonic fashion were the ones who convinced the jury that his malevolence resulted from a diseased mind rather than pure evil.

4

LADY KILLER

Stronger than lover's love is lover's hate. Incurable, in each, the wounds they make.—Euripides, *Medea*

This case drained me, I told my wife. It wasn't just the horrifying circumstances—the mutilated body of ten-year-old Lisa and the almost-mortal injuries inflicted to the neck, back, and chest of her father, Bentley. What added to the emotional weight were my nagging doubts about Tina, the defendant, and my shaky understanding of her rage-filled emotions that motivated such brutality. What fueled such a seismic eruption of murderous rage?

During the past months, I completed an extensive forensic evaluation of Tina. Before our meetings, I reviewed thousands of pages of police reports, crime scene photos, autopsy reports and photos, previous psychiatric evaluations, and psychiatric hospital records. I spent hours listening to audio and video recordings of interviews with family members and friends of the victims and defendant. Because the carnage occurred at Bentley's house, police interviewed and recorded Bentley's neighbors as they "canvassed" the area. One recording was of the 911 call from the neighbor who was awakened by a half-conscious Bentley, screaming something about his daughter before collapsing from the lost blood squirting out of his neck. I listened to police communications as they responded to the crime scene.

It took days to review all relevant documents and listen to these audio and video interviews with friends, family, and possible witnesses and to police communications before and after the crimes.

Bentley and his family members refused to speak with me. Understandable. I watched—endured—the police interviews of Bentley, a devastated man. He looked like an empty vessel, still breathing but deadened. In his late forties, he's below average height and stocky, with small hands and thick fingers. This surprised me; I expected him to be tall, like Tina. To my eyes, they made an awkward pair. Although thin, she was wiry, so I saw how she might have overpowered him. He fidgeted in his chair throughout the long interviews, an inner agitation that belied his blunted exterior. He looked hollowed out, expressionless, his face caved, his eyes empty. His voice was soft, slow, and monotone when it wasn't quivering. His grief was thick and dominated the room.

The crime occurred in the early hours of an approaching Sunday. Bentley, Lisa, and Tina, Bentley's girlfriend, had spent the day together at Disneyland. Tina stayed the night at Bentley's house. Bentley and Lisa's mother divorced years ago; Lisa was spending the weekend with her dad.

Sometime in the middle of the night, Bentley awakened to use the bathroom, located inside the master bedroom on the second floor. As he was urinating, he felt a sharp pain in the back of his neck. He turned and saw Tina. She asked, "What's wrong?" as though confused. She had a knife in her hand. She then lunged forward, stabbing his neck and chest as she screamed something like, "You ruined my life. . . . I'm gonna ruin yours. . . . I've got nothing to lose. You took it all." They stumbled out of the bathroom into the hallway. During the struggle, he grabbed the knife from her hand just before he fell down the stairs. He managed to run out the front door and collapsed in front of his neighbor's house, who then called 911.

Later, Bentley recalled banging on the door and frantically telling the neighbor his girlfriend was going to kill Lisa.

When the police arrived, they found Bentley near death. The paramedics took him to a critical care unit at the nearest trauma hospital. Police entered the house with guns drawn. Tina was gone. They found Lisa on her bed, in a pool of blood, stabbed to death.

The police photographs documented the carnage. Lisa was stabbed multiple times in the face and arms. One arm was almost severed. Part of her right index finger was lying on the floor near her bedroom door. This was no cold-blooded killing; in a wildly crazed frenzy, Lisa was mutilated to death.

The crime scene and autopsy photographs left me in a strange dream-like state. It was too much to absorb. A weird disconnectedness followed me for the rest of the day. I've developed compassion for first responders like the police who walk into scenes like this one. It makes perfect sense that officers are frequently authoritative and detached, necessary postures for emotional survival after exposure to such unspeakable human tragedy.

About six hours after the stabbings, Tina was spotted walking south along a freeway, wearing a bloody nightgown, with no belongings. She was initially unresponsive to the officers' queries.

The police took her to a local hospital and had her medically cleared before they brought her to jail. A doctor's clinical note at the hospital described her as being in a dissociative state that was "probably psychogenic" in nature; there was no medical reason for her nonconsciousness. At one point, she said to the doctor, "We were struggling. . . . It was a mess." She asked a nurse, "Did he survive?"

***

I conducted multiple interviews with Tina that involved reviewing her family life, love relationships, friendships, work history, and medical and mental health history. Most important, we explored in detail the circumstances that led to the murder and attempted murder and her recollections of her thoughts and feelings at the time of the assaults. As usual, I administered psychological tests, including personality testing and sophisticated psychological instruments designed to help me decide whether she was being forthright.

Coming to conclusions about the forensic questions posed by lawyers or the court is difficult, but I'm usually able to do it with reasonable certainty. In this case the defense team wanted me to render a confidential opinion as to Tina's mental state when she stabbed Lisa to death and seriously wounded Lisa's father. Did she act with conscious intention to kill? Was she dissociated? Was she insane at the time of the crimes?

Although Tina seemed in at least a partially dissociated state at the time of the stabbings, I ultimately was unable to conclude that she was without conscious awareness of her homicidal rage. Nor could I conclude that she lacked an intention to kill or that she was insane. Here's why.

***

My interviews with Tina began about eighteen months after the homicide and assault. She was under medical care for a while and her legal team needed time to consider defense strategies. Since she seemed so disconnected from herself when arrested, she was first evaluated by court-appointed experts for her competency to stand trial. Did she understand the charges against her? Did she understand the nature of the legal procedures she was about to encounter, such as the legal system's adversarial nature? Was she rational and coherent enough to consult with her lawyers to help in her defense?

After two evaluations by the experts, the judge ruled that Tina was competent to stand trial for first-degree murder and attempted murder. It was at this point that Tina's legal team asked me to assess her. They wanted a diagnosis. And they wanted me to determine the degree of her dissociation at the time of the crimes. Did she have a willful intent to kill? If dissociated, did it compromise her ability to form an intention to act as malevolently as she did? Or did her actions lack willfulness, akin to someone who was having an epileptic seizure? Did she know what she was doing was wrong during the deadly assaults? In other words, was she legally insane?

During our many hours together, we spoke at length about her relationship with Bentley. They had known each other for several years before the assaults. She complained that Bentley put his work and family before her. However, she cared for him. She was trapped. They had ended the relationship several times but somehow always reunited. They had a very good sex life, which helped keep them together. Sometimes that made her feel desired, at other times used.

During our second interview, Tina said that she felt suspicious of Bentley before the attacks. Vague about her reasons, she mentioned something about money. He was wealthy and didn't like her involved in his finances. On the day before the crimes, Bentley made "secretive" phone calls, which gave her a "weird" feeling. She wondered if he had another girlfriend or if he were "plotting something." I asked if she currently believed that to be true. She didn't know.

***

Tina repeatedly denied having *any* memory of the stabbings. I reviewed many of the statements she made at the hospital only hours after the offense, some of which suggested that, at that point, she had at least a vague recollection of what she had done. She told me she had no recall of such statements to the doctor, which had been made soon after her arrest. She had no recall of asking a nurse, "Did he survive?" I tried to provoke her memory by having her listen to a recording of her statements made by a police officer who had been standing guard in the hospital room with his recorder on. No luck.

I questioned her many times about her thoughts, her feelings and impulses, and her reminiscence—no matter how fuzzy—before, during, and after the crimes. Tina repeatedly said she had no recall of any desire to harm Lisa or Bentley and no memory of the motivations that drove her to such deadly actions. She remembered the activities the day of the crimes: going to Disneyland with Bentley and Lisa, their dinner that evening, dosing off with the TV on. During dinner and while watching TV, both she and Bentley had several glasses of wine. Tina recalled feeling irritated that Lisa was around, since she was looking forward to an intimate weekend with Bentley. She had become angry earlier in the day when Bentley took calls for an hour on that Saturday. She denied having any paranoid or violent thoughts that day.

I asked Tina to tell me about a "DUI situation" that Bentley had mentioned to the police during his interview with them, saying she blamed him for her arrest. Her bitterness lingered, he said. About nine months before her arrest, she and Bentley had a "huge argument" at his house. She got up to leave but he insisted that she stay, as they both had been drinking heavily. She cursed him out and left. Tina admitted that she sped away from his driveway, which prompted Bentley to call the police, leading to her third DUI. This occurred during the time she had been back in family court over a child custody battle with her ex-husband. Tina admitted to me that she had been enraged at Bentley, feeling that he caused the arrest. But she also said, "I loved him. I'm kind of the forgiving-type person."

I noted that Bentley told the police that Tina's teen daughter accused her of threatening to kill the girl's dog. This had triggered her ex-husband's request for a change in the custody arrangements. Tina adamantly denied ever threatening to kill the dog. I asked her why her daughter would lie about such a thing. Tina said she lied because she wanted to spend more time with her father, adding, "I never choked or threatened the dog."

I told Tina that I had reviewed an old child abuse report—part of the extensive discovery compiled by the defense attorneys—that had been filed by her daughter's teacher years ago. The teacher had observed Tina verbally abusing her daughter in the school parking lot. Tina reacted by saying the teacher was incompetent and her anger problems were resolved; she had undergone "anger management training," a probation requirement after an early DUI arrest. She said this with no sense of irony.

***

The doctor who examined Tina hours after the stabbings described her as dissociated. Was Tina in such a mental state at the time of the crimes? After running a number of tests, he found no medical abnormalities and concluded that her loss of consciousness was not due to a medical condition but psychological in nature ("psychogenic"). I queried her further about possible conditions that might have contributed to Tina's reported amnesia. She had no history to suggest she suffered with undiagnosed sleep disorders. She denied ever having had a problem with sleepwalking (somnambulism), for example. I saw nothing in the record to indicate a vulnerability to dissociate; what I did see was a lot of evidence for psychological denial as a style of coping.

Was Tina dissociated during the crimes, or did she become emotionally disconnected from her stream of awareness and numbed after the stabbings as she absorbed the enormity of what she had done? Either way, it seemed like she should have *some* memory of the hours after the crimes, especially given the statements she made at the hospital. She denied any awareness of the crimes or of intense resentment or rage at the victims leading up to the crimes.

A review of all the records, including the audio and video recordings of interviews with Tina's friends and Bentley, made clear the stressors she was coping with before the stabbings. She had by then lost custody of her daughter. It was significant that her last DUI occurred after an altercation with Bentley and during a time when she was in the throes of a custody battle. Her ex-husband successfully claimed that she was unfit and emotionally instable. Tina angrily expressed resentment at Bentley, believing he caused her DUI charge, which contributed to the loss of custody of her daughter. She even broke off the relationship with Bentley for a couple of months but couldn't stay away, telling herself that she forgave him.

We explored these issues several times during our encounters, with me wondering if Tina's resentment toward Bentley continued until the night of the crimes. I was curious if she resented his relationship with his daughter, given that she lost custody of hers. She blithely denied any connection between her bitterness over the custody issue and the crimes, saying, "I was past it." I read aloud what Bentley told police she had said as she stabbed him ("You ruined my life.") I asked if losing custody of her daughter had been weighing on her. I asked her to again consider the possibility that this had something to do with her fury at Bentley. In an irritated fashion, Tina reminded me that she could not recall what had occurred that early morning or why. I asked her to speculate what she could have meant by such a statement. Exhaling, she said, "I have no idea."

***

Tina was as dismissive and uninterested in revisiting her early life with me. Nonetheless, I pressed on and developed as much understanding as I was able about her roots. She was never close to her parents, who themselves never got along, though, Tina said, they were never violent. Her father always worked and "wasn't around much." She was sure he had affairs. Her stay-at-home mother was "more like a child than a mother" and very insecure. Her mother now suffers with dementia, but Tina continues to be resentful of her past emotional neglect. She had one older sister who committed suicide when Tina was in her late teens. When I asked how she dealt with the loss, she said, "Basically, I guess I ignored it. . . . We all did." She rhetorically asked, "Why would she do such a thing?" She then became irritated, saying, "It has nothing to do with anything. Why does that matter now?"

Insisting that her childhood was fine and not germane to her current plight, Tina described herself as self-sufficient and "self-disciplined" during her early years; she was average in school. She characterized herself as "a little shy" during that time in her life, but she had girlfriends, and by her teenage years, she had boyfriends. After high school, she took some college classes but was more interested in making money and working. Eventually, after several positions in a variety of areas, she migrated to the financial industry and worked in a midsize accounting firm.

Tina's only criminal history included three DUIs. She had no documented history of previous aggression or violence. She was divorced, her marriage having lasted about five years. It ended in disaster and a contentious divorce, with both parties accusing the other of violent behavior toward the other. She had one child from the union.

Throughout, Tina was, at best, disinterested and distracted in revisiting her past, viewing it as a waste of time. She asked, "Can't we just go on now?"

***

I administered several psychological tests to identify problems with Tina's intellectual capacities. I didn't observe cognitive symptoms of behaviors of concern (e.g., word-finding difficulties, tendency to perseverate) during our interviews, but given her memory complaints, I conducted some basic testing. If issues were identified, I would then conduct an extensive neuropsychological examination. Tina completed the Wechsler Adult Intelligence Scale Fourth Edition[1] (WAIS-IV), which is a verbally administered test of a person's overall intellectual ability. Although she complained that the testing was "useless," she did well; she was within the average range in all domains, including her verbal and nonverbal abilities. Importantly, she was average in her working memory and concentration capacities—even though she was distracted during the process and didn't seem to be invested in giving it her best shot.

I administered sections of the Wechsler Memory Scale, Fourth Edition (WMS-IV), which is specifically designed to measure a variety of memory functions. Given that she complained of recall lacuna, I was especially interested in Tina's cognitive capacity for immediate and delayed verbal recall. I was also interested in her ability to recall details of short stories presented to her verbally and to remember the details over time. Again, she was without any deficits in these domains.

I usually supplement these instruments with tests to help assess a defendant's effort or to determine whether the defendant was faking memory problems or willfully abandoning recall. Tina performed adequately on the cognitive test, and she seemed to be exerting adequate effort, even while complaining about the testing process.

These were good signs, suggesting that she wasn't faking a memory impairment. Still, the test results didn't rule out the possibility that she recalled more of the crimes than she admitted.

I administered instruments to help diagnose various mental disorders and her personality style. The results were informative. One was the Psychopathy Checklist to help assess whether Tina had psychopathic traits, which include heartlessness, a tendency toward cruelty and the remorseless use of others, as well as an antisocial lifestyle.

Tina's scores on the Psychopathy Checklist were consistent with my clinical observations; she was free of psychopathic traits. She didn't have a criminal record to speak of, other than her DUIs. She could lash out in anger, but she wasn't cold blooded. She didn't use people in a calculated fashion.

Another psychological test I administered was the Minnesota Multiphasic Personality Inventory-2-RF, a widely used instrument to examine mental disorders and to identify personality style and disorder. The MMPI-2-RF also has many additional scales to help conclude if the test taker is honestly answering the true-or-false questions.

Tina's validity scales on the MMPI-2-RF were interesting in that she minimized her emotional problems. When it's in the defendant's interest to appear disturbed, the results tend to show an exaggeration of mental illness. There was no evidence she that was overstating her symptoms: on the contrary, the validity scales suggested she underestimated her emotional disturbances.

Tina presented herself as well adjusted, without even minor faults. She was in denial of that which made her look bad or feel uncomfortable. This was consistent with my observations of Tina from our interviews.

The most predominate of her clinical scales was the one measuring paranoia, which was within the clinically significant range. Tina generally distrusted others and was cynical in her attitude, believing people were mainly out for themselves. Although she overtly appeared nonplussed in her demeanor, the testing revealed a deep sense of demoralization and dissatisfaction with her life. This likely undergirded her cynicism, as well as her elevations on scales suggesting tendencies toward low frustration tolerance, an easy dislike of others, and a proclivity for substance abuse and aggression with impulsive behavior. She could excessively ruminate to the point that her thinking becomes distorted.

The testing results helped to clarify the meaning of Tina's matter-of-fact, blasé attitude, even as she faced assault and murder charges. Though her everyday functioning was normal—she could work and relate to others in normal ways—her self-centered ruminations and distrustful ways surfaced destructively in her intimate relations with close friends, lovers, and family. Tina showed a proneness to paranoia and an intolerance for unwanted realities, which she simply dismissed.

***

Tina killed a child and nearly killed her lover. It's not that she was remorseless; as I said, she was not psychopathic. She could be cruel, but the cruelty stemmed from chronic emotional frustrations and uncontrolled emotional reactions to feeling injured, not from a cold, calculating cost-benefit analysis.

Most striking was Tina's extreme denial about what she had done and the pending consequences. For instance, she repeatedly asked me to remind her attorneys to bring the paperwork necessary to renew her driver's license. I told her that her license renewal was the least of her problems. She acted as though she didn't hear me. "Just ask them to bring the paperwork," she said. She wasn't psychotic in that she did not display any blatant perceptual distortions. But she lived in a state of primitive denial,[2] disavowing that which was too painful to face. A degree of denial or self-deception is fairly normal. However, in Tina's case, even while facing such a serious crisis, she maintained a disconnection to its emotional implications. It suggested that any reckoning of her behavior could be emotionally overwhelming to her. The extent of her denial was a measure of her need to protect herself from psychological dissolution. And it was an expression of her rather significant psychological arrest.

Although Tina was not psychotic—she had no delusions or hallucinations, no perceptual distortions—she wasn't fully in reality either.

***

Tina's degree of denial and disconnection from her emotional life, together with the brutality it wrought, affected me. Her fractured psyche seeped in, leaving me with a sense of desolation and a strange sense of foreboding. For instance, the night after one of our long sessions, I dreamt of hearing sounds coming from the kitchen of my house. With trepidation and a racing heart, I walked into the kitchen area but couldn't find the source of the noises. I woke up with my heart pounding. It took an hour to get back to sleep. The next morning, when I walked into my kitchen, my attention went to the knife block on the counter. I felt a strong urge to put it in a closet, out of sight. I didn't.

I understood the dream as emerging from Tina's emotional life having insinuated itself into mine, prompting a dream-state of menacing danger and helplessness. It helped me to viscerally grasp her inner state of chronic and fearful suspiciousness, helplessness, and reactive rage, which distorted Tina's relationships, none of which she can articulate because it's not allowed into her awareness.

***

Tina's deep denial allowed her to avoid self-scrutiny and pain that comes with it. Such self-deception had a maliciously paradoxical effect on Tina's coping ability, and it compromised her grasp of reality. To better understand what I mean by such a level of denial, imagine answering your front doorbell to a police officer who informs you that your loved one, who had just left the house to go to work, is dead, killed in a car accident ten minutes after walking out that same door. Your first reaction is *no, that can't be, he just left, we kissed good-bye a few minutes ago. It's a mistake.* It's not yet real, not yet a psychological reality—until you're forced to face the factual reality that your spouse is gone forever. When you finally do absorb reality, despair and longing metastasize into unbearable agony.

Tina's coping style was to avoid reality—psychic and factual—at all costs, for as long as she could.

***

I concluded that Tina suffered not from a major psychosis but from a mixed personality disorder, with paranoid and borderline features[3] as well as alcohol abuse. Individuals with her personality type are prone to misperceive the actions of others as personal slights and to develop brooding resentments that may turn into states of emotional confusion and surprising fits of anger or even rage. A basic distrust of people and a defensive coping style created misperceptions whereby she viewed the world and people in black-and-white ways. Technically, it's called a splitting defense[4] and is used as a way to avoid intensely confusing emotions as well as the complexity of reality and relationships. This is a defining defensive mechanism for someone with a borderline personality. We all function in this way sometimes, during moments when we're drained or threatened, but we get clarity when calmer. For Tina, it's where she psychologically *lives*. Her misperceptions and rage reactions become so extreme that, for brief periods, her view of reality becomes distorted.

***

I met with Tina's lawyers midmorning on a Wednesday at their office. Traffic was light, but I arrived about ten minutes late. I missed the freeway exit even though I'd been to the office before. My anxiety was in the driver's seat. That happens when I'm delivering bad news. Tina's legal team had retained me privately, so my findings were confidential and protected by doctor-patient privilege; only the defendant and her attorneys had the right to know my opinions. Under such circumstances, I sometimes come to conclusions that the lawyers don't like, but this case felt different. On one hand, Tina had significant psychological problems, but I concluded that her dissociation from the crimes was likely partial. She was not purposefully deceptive about her recall and motivations regarding the assaults, but her personality and style of defense clouded her forthrightness. With such an opinion, it would be dicey to use me at her trial, even if my testimony was only to document her psychological problems. What if, say, the prosecutor during cross-examination asked me if I felt Tina was being *totally* honest in her recollection of the events that night?

As I drove to the attorneys' office, I felt a pang in the pit in my stomach, knowing I would disappoint them with my conclusions. When I was first retained and given a cursory summary of the facts, I said it seemed like Tina might have a mental-state defense (such as lacking intentionality) or an insanity defense but the devil is in the details. Still, I knew her lawyers felt Tina was literally out of her mind when she committed those brutal acts.

Soon after arriving at their office, I was ensconced with two attorneys, a paralegal, and a staff member in their impressive conference room/legal library. The office suite had the usual professional looking appearance. The conference room told a different story, with its impressive mahogany table and cushy, comfortable chairs. The lavish surroundings made the burden of delivering disappointing news seem more difficult, as though I'd be stepping out of line by not delivering the expected. Maybe that's the point of such an opulent milieu, to wield influence. I decided the best way to handle the situation was to jump in. I leapfrogged past the small talk, informing them I could not conclude with a reasonable degree of psychological certainty that Tina was insane or that she lacked intent on the night of the assaults. The air in the room became heavy and dense like the table between us.

I discussed Tina's psychological conditions, which included alcohol abuse and a personality disturbance. Her most serious problems stemmed from her mixed paranoid and borderline personality disorder, with symptoms including the distrust of others—especially those with whom she is close—mood instability, and her suspiciousness and vulnerability to aggression and rage. In addition, her absolute refusal to face uncomfortable realties in her life and her susceptibility to misperceive others' behavior and motivations were liabilities extreme enough to create reality-testing problems. She did not have a schizophrenic-like psychosis, but her emotions, perceptions, and thought processing could become distorted to the point where she misperceives emotional reality and has a distorted view of her relationships.

Further, I told Tina's team that her claim of complete dissociation from her deadly actions was difficult to accept. The psychological testing results showed she was not faking a memory deficiency, but her memory for events was selective. She had recall of the evening's activities before going to sleep. After her arrest, she made comments to the medical staff at the hospital and before the police took her to jail that suggested she had at least fragmented images of the events. She asked a medical staff member about the condition of the victims, yet she repeatedly claimed complete dissociation at the time of the assaults. Consistent with the scientific literature, my experience with people who have had violent episodes is that they may become depersonalized during the act, with an out-of-body-like experience but not complete unawareness.[5]

Dissociative disorders are controversial if not resulting from biological factors. Some experts argue that dissociation of violent behavior may occur in the context of extreme trauma.[6] Under such circumstances, it has been argued in court that a "reasonable person" could possibly dissociate from his or her actions.[7] Tina's situation was different, though. She was not under acute stress or in a state of agitated passion. As I said, her last memory before the assaults was of watching television with Bentley.

Her denial of even fragmentary images or memories of the violence, despite her partial recall of surrounding events, together with the complex nature of Tina's psychological testing results gave me doubts about the veracity of her claim of *total* dissociation. I wondered if she was also hiding the reasons for so much rage toward her boyfriend that rose to a murderous crescendo.

When I concluded my summary of the results of my evaluation of Tina, it was clear from the collective reactions of the legal team that they were taken aback. There was a period of awkward silence, which I ruptured by acknowledging their disappointment and letting them know it was a difficult evaluation to complete and even harder to conclude. I wanted to go into the devilish details to help explain my thinking. The lead attorney suggested we take a ten-minute break before resuming.

***

After the break, I explained my thinking about Tina's case in more detail. I told the team I based my opinions not only on my interviews with her and the testing results, but also on my digestion of all the additional reports and interviews with others. During our interviews, Tina avoided responding to many of my questions or gave evasive answers. For instance, I had had a phone interview with Joanne, Tina's friend and colleague. Tina had suggested I call her because she had commiserated over the years about her relationship problems with Bentley. Joanne told me that about six months before the crimes, Tina had nonchalantly commented at dinner, "Maybe I should kill myself and Bentley" because she couldn't take the "on again, off again" nature of their relationship. When I reminded Tina of this conversation with her friend, she dismissed it, saying she was drunk. This, after she had repeatedly denied alcohol abuse. I told her that Joanne mentioned that she, Tina, drank too much when she was depressed or unset. She reiterated her denial, without even attempting to rationalize the contradictions. I had already told the attorneys of Tina's rigid defensive style: here it was in action. I went a step further, saying that her denial was so extensive that it didn't function as a protective coping mechanism, but as a reality-distorting liability.

Tina also denied ever being violent with others, although the record showed otherwise. For example, I told them about the dog incident with her daughter, who also alleged that Tina had verbally abused her during her childhood. Tina simply denied this, saying her daughter was under the influence of her ex-husband. She minimized an observation made by a teacher alleging that she verbally abused her daughter.

A user-friendly explanation of personality style was in order to help the group better understand the reasoning behind my conclusions. Tina compartmentalized her emotions into good and bad ones, as she did with people. For example, she had difficulty understanding Bentley's commitment to her while still having loyalties to his daughter. If she wasn't first on his agenda, he was not someone managing conflicting emotional demands; he was betraying her. Such a divided emotional experience protected her from having to manage complex emotions involving herself and others, but at great cost. Her self-esteem fluctuated, depending on the status of the emotional tie to those on whom she depended, like Bentley. When in a dark place, for instance, she considered killing herself and Bentley. This immature defense, this splitting, is characteristic of borderline personality. Since Tina didn't have the emotional maturity to manage complicated feelings, she compartmentalized until she couldn't. Her denial and sequestering of her pain worked hand in hand with her splitting defense to shield her from emotional turmoil until the buildup became too much to bear. Then she exploded.

Tina also had a paranoid dimension to her personality revealed in her concerns about Bentley, believing he was "plotting something" against her. Her psychological testing results also suggested that, especially when stressed, she will get suspicious of others and employ the use of projection[8]—another dysfunctional, immature defense. She tends to project disowned emotional parts of herself onto others. (This is likely what happened to me, which contributed to my bad dream. I didn't share this with the lawyers.) This combination of denial, splitting, and projection allowed Tina to maintain emotional stability with a distorted sense of reality and righteous rage. The distortion and rage radiated out to those she perceived as causing her pain. Thus, Bentley and his daughter were likely targets.

The evening of the assault, she and Bentley watched TV after dinner. His daughter was in her room. They continued drinking wine as they watched TV. She couldn't estimate how much wine they consumed. Her last recollection before the attacks was being awakened from the couch by Bentley's daughter and going to bed.

I concluded by telling the group that, based on the evidence, it was likely that Tina had worked herself into an angry, fuming emotional state during the day, powered by her distorted sensitivities regarding Bentley and a growing distrust of him. She could not end their relationship but felt used or peripheral. She finally acted this out in a homicidal rage fueled by her distortions and likely the alcohol that she had consumed. I reiterated my suspicion that she had at least a foggy memory of the stabbings, basing this on several comments to medical staff soon after her arrest, which implied some recollection of the assaults; her defensive denial, which was likely unconscious (resulting from splitting and projection); and her seemingly willful evasiveness, such as her disinterest in pursuing the significance of her comments at the hospital soon after the stabbings. She did not have a history of dissociative states associated with extreme violence nor of neurocognitive deficits associated with fugue states or explosiveness. Furthermore, she appeared to me unwilling to delve into her recollections and face the gravity of what she had done.

***

Tina was charged with first-degree murder and attempted murder with premeditation and deliberation. Her defense team called me as an expert witness during the guilt phase of the trial. In California, insanity trials are bifurcated. The guilt phase come first: if found guilty of the charged offenses or lesser charges (e.g., manslaughter), it's on to the insanity phase, in which the defendant may be found to be sane, with the guilty verdict affirmed, or not guilty by reason of insanity. In Tina's case, the defense team knew the jury would find her guilty, though they hoped for an offense less serious than premeditated murder, which comes with a life sentence.

The defense team also had Tina evaluated by another expert who concluded that Tina was insane at the time of the crime. They used me in the guilt phase of the trial to help the jury see someone so disturbed that it interfered with her self-control and that she did not premeditate the attacks. They used their other expert in the insanity phase.

I testified that, although Tina claimed amnesia, she likely had a partial memory after the crime, based on the evidence. Her long-term mental health disorders—including depression, alcohol abuse, and personality deficits—all combined to cause her to be unstable, conspiratorial, and volatile, a dangerous mixture that led to the crimes. I gave several examples of our exchanges and reviewed the psychological testing results, which confirmed that her emotional instability and paranoia were extensive enough to distort reality.

During cross-examination, the prosecution had me confirm that although Tina was vulnerable to transient distortions of reality, she did not have delusional symptoms characteristic of a major mental disorder such as schizophrenia. This was an important point for the prosecutor to establish in preparation for the insanity phase of the trial. She knew juries rarely find defendants insane when they are not convinced that the defendant has a documented history of suffering with an illness like schizophrenia. [9]

Surprisingly, I was not questioned in any detail about Tina's claim of complete amnesia. Such queries might have been preempted by my already expressed observation that she likely had a clouded memory. Instead, the prosecutor wanted to establish that Tina had premeditated the crime, posing questions that emphasized Tina's history of aggression, her statements to medical personnel soon after her arrest, and her prior thoughts of killing herself and Bentley.

After establishing Tina's previous aggressive behavior and incriminating statements, the prosecutor questioned whether this led to the reasonable conclusion that Tina's vicious attacks were consistent with her history and that she had full awareness of what she was doing at the time of the crimes. If the jury believed those facts to be the case, then Tina would be guilty of premeditated murder and attempted murder. In response, I affirmed her emotional instability and her history of aggression but emphasized her impulsiveness, her overall emotional arrest, and her reality distortions. Taken together, it left Tina saddled with a defective capacity to regulate her emotions. In particular, I emphasized her vulnerability to

brief periods of reality distortion, which disrupted her conscious awareness and judgment. Individuals with Tina's severe personality problems
can become very destructive yet can function well. I reiterated that the
results of my evaluation, including the psychological testing results,
showed she was not calculating or unfeeling.

The jury had to decide how fully aware and in control of herself Tina
was during the stabbings.

After the guilt phase of the trial, the jury found Tina guilty of second-
degree murder. After the insanity trial phase, they found her sane.

***

I spoke with the lead attorney after the insanity trial. He wondered if the
heinousness of the crimes affected my opinion regarding Tina's sanity. I
admitted that the crimes affected me, but I didn't think they had influenced my forensic opinion. But that brief exchange rattled me. It forced
me to reflect further about my work with Tina and wonder if the nature of
the crimes, especially the brutal slaying of a young girl, had affected my
forensic opinions about her. The scientific literature has documented that
female murderers are viewed differently from male murderers, sometimes
with greater disdain.[10] Did I fall prey to this bias?

More than 90 percent of those incarcerated for murder or manslaughter are males.[11] Still, women who end up serving time in prison are
subject to more intense scrutiny and shame.[12] And those women who
have committed violent acts of murder are held in particular societal
contempt, as they are perceived as violating their basic nature.[13] For
instance, in one study reported in the journal *Psychiatry, Psychology and
Law*,[14] the authors analyzed the sentencing remarks made by male judges
in murder cases involving heterosexual partners. They framed killings by
men in far more forgiving terms than killings by women. The judges
frequently emphasized a man's suffering and anguish at being left by his
wife. Here are examples of how eight judges sympathetically described
the plight of males at the time of the killings:[15] "suffering from severe
psychological distress and . . . acted as a man stressed and depressed,
rather than as one in control." When the judges sentenced women, empathy was lukewarm. A judge described a woman murderer as a good
student, though pejorative references to character were frequent, such as
her "inability to pay her household debts" or that the crime revealed a

"lack of concern for [her] children's wellbeing." The judges' messages seemed to imply that even "good men" kill because of anguish and deep emotional turmoil. Meanwhile, women who kill are wicked. The message: violent men can't help themselves but women can and should.

In another study, reported in the journal *Women's Studies International Forum*,[16] the media portrays homicidal women, more than men, with sensational imagery and as incapable of rational decision making. Apparently, it's not as irrational for men to kill; it's viewed as a by-product of masculinity.

Other studies that look closely at the context of gender difference in homicide belie the biases by judges and the media and draw a much more complicated picture. Research results in several journals such as *Homicide Studies*[17] found that most women who kill an intimate partner do so out of self-defense, whereas men kill out of jealousy or rage due to an intolerable loss.

I thought about all these issues as I was coming to my conclusions about Tina and after the trial. Was I biased like some judges and the media? Did it affect my opinions about her? I don't think so. Tina may have felt Bentley caused her problems, but she had a paranoid personality style and couldn't see how she was driving their relationship problems and her estrangement from her daughter. I concluded she was in a state of rage when she committed the crimes, not psychotically disordered and incapable of knowing that what she was doing was wrong. She assaulted out of unbridled rage, not self-defense. I've evaluated many women who have committed horrific acts such as murdering their children. These cases have been emotionally impactful, leaving me at times with emotional numbness and vertigo. Yet I had concluded that some of these women were out of their minds.

Was I gender-biased toward Tina? Did I see her as a feminine form of daimonic evil, albeit unconsciously? Did Tina's less-than-sympathetic character influence my forensic opinion regarding her sanity?

I find comfort in recalling that I've examined many, many violent and unsavory characters over the years, male and female, and believe I've given as honest and objective forensic opinions as possible. But, I suppose, I can never be sure.

5

THE CASE OF THE BODY SNATCHERS

Horror is the removal of masks.—Robert Block, author of *Psycho*

It was late afternoon when I met Mr. Parks, the father of Andrew, a twenty-five-year-old charged with first-degree murder of his stepbrother. It was not long after the killing. Both parents had been scheduled to come, but Andrew's stepmother didn't make it. She was too devastated and immobilized. Mr. Parks arrived from his work as a superintendent for a midsize construction company. He wore jeans and work boots with a heavy red shirt atop a black t-shirt. Tall and wiry with a full head of salt-and-pepper hair and slight paunch, he was in good shape for a man in his sixties. The product, I figured, of years in construction. We greeted one another in my reception area. He was polite, straight faced, and restrained, with a serious air. On the way to my consulting room, I noticed his gait was erect and his pace measured, which harmonized with his overall countenance. Together with his physical stature, Mr. Parks projected the image of a poised and toughened individual.

It was all belied by his dark grief-stricken eyes.

Mr. Parks sat quietly with a folder of papers on his lap, unmoving. I began the interview by explaining the purpose of the interview, which was to gather personal information about Andrew and to learn about his son's emotional condition just before the homicide. He interrupted me. "You did this. You." I was at first stunned into silence. I reminded myself of his recent trauma and certain despondency. Just more than a week ago, his family was shattered; his stepson dead and his wife forever traumatized, with his son the agent of the family's existential devastation. I finally uttered, "Okay. What do you mean?" Mr. Parks replied, "Your kind. Mental doctors. My wife pleaded with them to not release him. They told her *she* needed medication. *She* was overreacting." It turned out that Andrew had recently been released from a psychiatric hospital just before the killing. Mr. Parks went on, "We tried all kinds of help . . . private hospitals, the county hospital." Andrew would be admitted on a seventy-two-hour hold as a danger to himself or others but discharged soon after. He'd tell the staff that he was better, free of his crazy thoughts. "We told the doctor, 'I know my son. He's not well. He's still paranoid.'"

Provided with a psychiatric appointment for continuing care, Andrew wouldn't follow up, at least not regularly. He refused other services such as a day treatment program or visiting with a case manager or therapist. Even when he made an appointment with the psychiatrist, he rarely showed up. Because of his unreliability, his treating psychiatrists prescribed long-acting antipsychotic medications requiring that Andrew show up only once a month for an injection. He sometimes missed monthly appointments, became psychotic, and ended up rehospitalized. The cycle continued until the killing.

Before he began receiving psychiatric care, Andrew was spending long periods of time in his room, sometimes not eating. More and more, the craziness was surfacing. Once, he came out of his room and announced, "I'm giving my life to Jesus." Another time, he asked Mr. Parks, "Can you tell the future?"

Andrew was first hospitalized at the age of twenty-one. One evening, Mr. Parks heard Andrew shouting in his room. He was by himself. His father went to see what was going on. Andrew was talking to himself, pacing. He had pulled out his toenail, and blood was all over the bedroom rug. Up until then, the family had hoped the "crazy talk" would go away with time. Then he became self-destructive. Mr. Parks decided Andrew needed to get help.

Between the years from his first breakdown to the murder, Andrew became more and more strange. He told his stepmother, "The angel Gabriel visited me in a dream. He told me my future. I will suffer and go to heaven. It's a thousand tears." Another time he told Peter, his stepbrother, that God spoke to him. "It's spiritual warfare. He doesn't want me to murder anyone." At times in the middle of the night, he'd shout "into empty space," Mr. Parks said.

***

Andrew's first hospital stay was his longest, about a month. He was diagnosed with schizophrenia, paranoid type. It's a grim diagnosis, one that entails a variety of symptoms, the most serious of which are distortions in perceptions and thought processing. Andrew's burden included hallucinations and distorted beliefs. Solidly convinced that he received messages directly from the Lord, his predominate psychotic symptom was religious delusions. After months of treatment, including psychiatric medication, Andrew seemed, according to Mr. Parks, "a little better." He was subdued and less imposing about his connections to God. But still preoccupied, with a poverty to his relationships, he didn't talk crazy, but he didn't express much of anything, verbally or emotionally. His personhood was flattened. The psychiatrist attributed it to a combination of his medications and his illness. Hopefully he'll get better over time, the family thought. At least he's not saying crazy things.

As time passed, Andrew began talking about his love for God. Mr. Parks and his wife, both born-again Christians, strived to believe the best: that he was simply expressing his faith in God and personal connection to the Almighty. At least he wasn't making outlandish claims about God or uttering nonsensical verbiage, like before.

Over time, "he'd get worse." It started with the mumblings, which grew louder until the bizarre grandiosity returned: "I'm a prophet of Jesus" or "I will suffer and go to the heavens. . . . I will be raptured."

The cycle became a familiar one. The crazy talk and religious delusions. The isolation and the not eating, "fasting for the Lord." Not sleeping and howling in his room until the family couldn't take it anymore.

After returning home from a hospitalization, Andrew would be a little better, then slowly descend into his delusional world, with or without his psychiatric medications. He'd be rehospitalized, soon to return home. It was wearisome and increasingly demoralizing.

The difficulties managing Andrew sharpened after Mr. Parks's construction company lost a major contract, along with a sizable portion of his income. The family moved from a rented condo to a smaller apartment. Andrew and his stepbrother Peter now had to share a bedroom. Peter was a year or so younger than Andrew, but they were never close. At first, when Mr. and Mrs. Parks married, they seemed to get along. Over time, not so well. Sharing a bedroom became a point of contention,

especially as Andrew's mental disturbance blossomed. Peter found Andrew's behavior "annoying." His weird religious pronouncements were
inexplicable and alarming. A junior college student and budding visual
artist, Peter's work and quiet time were disrupted by Andrew's agitation
and "crazy talk." Andrew always complained about his stepbrother's music.

***

After Andrew's most recent hospitalization, just before the stabbing, Mr.
and Mrs. Parks concluded that their living arrangements had to change.
They were at their wit's end with his psychotic behavior. They decided to
place Andrew in a board and care home, which is a privately run residen-
tial care facility that's licensed by the state to provide twenty-four-hour
care and supervision to adults with mental illnesses. In the meantime, to
give Peter "some peace and space," they decided to have Andrew move
out of the bedroom and sleep on the couch. The morning after they made
those decisions, Mrs. Parks decided to give Andrew the news. Mr. Parks,
as usual, had already left for work early in the morning.

Andrew didn't take it well. He looked at her and, without saying a
word, turned and went to the bedroom, where he stayed for the remainder
of the day with the door closed.

When Mr. Parks returned home in the early evening, Andrew came
out from sequestration. He was tense, with the look of a man scorned and
insulted. He had obviously been stewing the day away. In anger he asked
his father, "You agree with this?!" Mr. Parks replied, "Yes I do." The
possibility of board and care placement had been considered at family
meetings during Andrew's many hospital stays. Mr. Parks had always
been reluctant to do so. "Let's see how things go," he would tell the staff.
Now, he told Andrew, "It's time."

Andrew had never been seriously violent. He was verbally aggressive
at times, usually when his psychotic thinking was on the rise. Once, Mr.
Parks became concerned after hearing disturbing muttering coming from
his room. He knocked on Andrew's door and was met with a shrieking,
"Get out. Leave me alone!" There were a few acts of irrational physical
aggression. After his first hospitalization, Andrew's grandmother took
him shopping for clothes to celebrate his discharge. As they walked to her

car, he slapped her across the face. She was dumbfounded, and he quickly apologized.

Still, the family was not concerned about him being violent. It was more about how he was so disruptive to their home life and peace of mind.

Though Andrew and Peter had verbal arguments, there was never even an insinuation of violence. When Peter couldn't tolerate Andrew's "crazy talk," he'd leave. Mr. Parks thought Andrew was jealous of Peter. It was true that the family enjoyed Peter's "normal . . . happy life" and his creativity. Though sometimes self-absorbed and thoughtless "like any kid," Peter was never a problem. He was usually busy with his friends, his work, and school. He and several artist friends had plans to open an art studio in the future. Peter wasn't imposing and he enjoyed his life, whereas Andrew was burdensome. Peter was easy to be around and livened the home up. Andrew no doubt noticed.

***

The stabbing occurred on a Friday, about two weeks after his release from the hospital and pending the changes in Andrew's living arrangements. Mr. Parks had scheduled a weekend visit to a board and care home in the area. That morning, he took Andrew to work with him, something he occasionally did to give his wife and Peter a break from the pressure of having Andrew around. He usually gave Andrew a simple administrative task or some money so he could hang out at a local shopping mall. This day, Andrew got into an argument with one of Mr. Parks's helpers. "They almost got into a fistfight." Mr. Parks was furious. He gave Andrew some money and told him, "Go to a movie." About an hour or so later, Andrew called. He was with the police. They found him sitting on a curb talking to himself. When asked by an officer if he was okay, he responded, "God doesn't want me to see the movie." Mr. Parks left his work site, picked up Andrew, drove him home, and went back to work. At that point, no one else was home. Peter had a morning class and Mrs. Parks had left the house to speak with a tenant in the apartment complex.

Peter returned home from school in the afternoon. It was then when the stabbing occurred.

Mr. Parks received a frantic call from his wife. She returned home and found Peter on the floor and Andrew gone. Peter was still alive. He told his mom he and Andrew got into an argument. Andrew walked out of the bedroom, came back and stabbed him, and left.

Mrs. Parks immediately called 911. Incredibly, before an ambulance arrived, Andrew returned to the house. Enraged, Mrs. Parks told him to get out, which he did. Peter was taken to the local medical center where he was pronounced dead. He had two stab wounds, one in the chest and one in the stomach area.

The police found Andrew sitting in a doughnut shop two blocks from the house, alone, where he was arrested.

***

Andrew's early life was uneventful, at least until he was eight years old. It was then that Mr. Parks and Andrew's mother separated. His mother had a history of recurring depressions and psychiatric hospitalizations. Between bouts of dark moods, she leaned on alcohol more than medication to cope. She decided, at one point, to visit her sister who lived in the Midwest and who also was an alcoholic. What was to be a brief sojourn morphed into longer stay, then a relocation. They eventually divorced. Andrew missed his mother, but he adjusted and began to accept that she was not returning. "Maybe we were both relieved," Mr. Parks speculated. During the first few years, Andrew visited his mother and seemed to enjoy their time together. Returning from those visits, he'd be a little sad, but Mr. Parks didn't notice any real change in his behavior or emotions. Nor did Andrew seem to have a problem accepting Mr. Park's new wife and his younger stepbrother Peter.

The problems with Andrew surfaced early in adolescence. By his junior year of high school, he was spending more and more time alone, detached. He was never the extroverted type, but now he was different. He had little interest in engaging with anybody. He stopped attending school regularly, he didn't do homework, and his grades suffered.

Mr. Parks began to notice Andrew's "weird little behaviors . . . fidgeting . . . opening cabinets." His grand claims began; for instance, he was "destined" to have a "big important job," even though he was having difficulty completing schoolwork. He became preoccupied with religion and talked of how "God made me special." He dropped out of high school but somehow completed his continuation school assignments and received a diploma. He tried holding jobs, usually at fast food outlets, but they never lasted more than a month or so.

After it became clear that Andrew was mentally ill and after his multiple psychiatric hospitalizations, he applied for Social Security disability. To the family's surprise, he was initially denied. But after several more attempts and with the help of a social worker, he was finally approved to receive Social Security disability income. Placement at a board and care facility would have been financially prohibitive otherwise.

By this point during our interview, Mr. Parks was grim faced and spent of the ire that arrived with him. He softly commented that he, his wife, and Peter were looking forward to the day Andrew was placed in a board and care facility. He'd be receiving care, and they could go on with life.

After Mr. Parks left, I sat at my desk looking out the large window before me, one of two that frame my consulting room. It was late in the afternoon and the sun was setting. It's my favorite time at the office. By then, with sunlight fading, the floor lamps radiate a golden hue. The shadows, created by the day's passing, are softly suspended around the room and project a balmy coziness. That's how it feels when I conduct my evening psychotherapy sessions. But not tonight. As the early evening transitioned to twilight, it was different. I was left with a dark, foreboding mood, an awareness of life's unfairness and harsh unpredictability.

***

Andrew's lawyer, Tony Scott, requested I interview Andrew, review all the records, and confirm Andrew's diagnosis of schizophrenia. That was the easy part. More difficult, he wanted to know if Andrew's mental disorder compromised his ability to know right from wrong (insanity) or, if sane, whether his mental illness blurred his ability to form the intention to kill. In other words, was his mental illness a mitigating factor to a first-degree murder charge, which requires evidence for malicious deliberation before the killing?

With "mental state at the time of the offense" evaluations, it's best to interview the defendant soon after the offense to get as close as possible to the psychological state around the time of the crime. What was Andrew's mental state at the time of the killing? Did he have the psychological capacity necessary to meet the mens rea, the "guilty mind" requirement under the law; did he purposely intend to kill with premeditation and deliberation? If so, was he aware that it was morally and legally wrong? What, if any, mitigating factors are in play?

But I couldn't begin the evaluation: Andrew was transferred to a state hospital for treatment after having been found incompetent to stand trial. A pretrial public defender declared doubt about Andrew's competency. Two forensic psychologists agreed.

After about four months of treatment in a state hospital, Andrew was declared competent and returned to jail to face his charge. Shortly after returning to jail from the hospital, he trashed his cell and began screaming at a deputy about "days of judgment." And two days before I was scheduled to begin the examination, Andrew made a serious suicide attempt.[1] Employing a common method among inmates, he tied together bedsheets and tried to hang himself. After treatment at a local hospital, he was placed on suicide watch and was unavailable to be interviewed.

It took several weeks before he was cleared for visitations. By now, it was almost six months after the homicide, not an ideal situation given the questions I needed to answer. In any event, I was now about to begin my evaluation of Andrew.

***

As I sat at the attorney/bonds reception area of the jail, awaiting notification of Andrew's arrival from his cell, I made small talk with the attorneys, probation officers, and another shrink who were also waiting for their defendants. In the background, there's the clamoring of opening and closing jail gates, shouting deputies, and the cling-clang of shackles being dragged by the ankles of defendants moving to and fro. Finally, after about an hour, I get the call. "Lettieri, booth A," the deputy shouts in a matter-of-fact style. Andrew has arrived. I walked toward the rickety iron gate that slowly opens, allowing me to enter the secure section of the jail. From a distance, I could see Andrew sitting in a locked booth, waiting. I'm struck by his diminutive size. Such a violent act from such a small body. I feel that familiar mix of emotions that surfaces when I'm about to greet an inmate who committed an act of raw violence. I'm about to encounter someone who acted on primordial impulses that are beyond the usual human experience yet so much a fundamental part of our nature. Strangely, I actually feel more real.

I've seen Andrew's mug shot and photos of him taken immediately after the killing. As is typical of defendants or victims immediately after such traumatic occurrences, he looked ghastly, crazed. In person, Andrew looks younger than his twenty-five years. I can't see his face completely, as he's gazing down at the table in front of him, covering it with thick black hair. His shoulders were hunched as though he was trying to hide. My first thought was that he was probably overmedicated and that he would be difficult to engage.

I greeted him, but almost immediately, Andrew's bizarre thinking herniated forth. His speech was rapid and tense as though he needed to express something lest he'd explode. "They're forcing me to take them" (antipsychotic medication). "It's taken away the good voices. They tell me I'm going to heaven." As I listened, he veered into the supernatural. He rambled about angels, the sinfulness of inmates having sex with each other, and angels informing him of his eventual ascension to heaven. After several minutes of cathartic release, he seemed less overwrought, a bit relieved to simply have someone listen to his concerns and thoughts. During a pause, I took the opportunity to begin explaining why we were meeting, my obligations to him, and the questions his lawyer asked me to address.

Andrew understood, but he was obviously preoccupied and ensconced within his own ruminations, chomping at the bit to further release himself: "I'm going to commit the perfect sin. I'm not gonna have sex with another inmate. I hear God directing me. I need to hear His voice. If I don't take the poison, they'll take my clothes away." He seemed to be saying that if he did not take the "poison" (i.e., his medication), the jail staff would again place him on suicide watch. After he attempted to hang himself, Andrew's jumpsuit was taken away, and he was given a paper gown. He didn't want to take his medications, but he didn't want to be placed on suicide watch again.

He was also revealing his sexual preoccupations ("perfect sin"; "I'm not gonna have sex with another inmate") and his need to hear the voice of God to deliver him from the urges of temptation. He complained about "my enemies, the deputies . . . nurses." I listened quietly, nodding and taking notes. Interestingly, he seemed comforted by my note-taking, pausing at times to give me time to write. I had the sense that, by documenting his thoughts, I validated them to him.

I suggested we table any talk about his medication for now, as I wanted to get to know him. Andrew didn't respond, but he didn't continue his rambling either. He looked about with a distant, faraway gaze. I took his silence as agreement.

I asked Andrew about his living circumstances at the time of his arrest. That was a mistake. He immediately launched into a psychotic tirade, this time focusing on his family. "My parents, they're evil demons. They're fallen angels. The one who died, he's a fallen angel. It's a sign to commit murder. Technically, I acted in self-defense." The more he spoke, the more his thinking became unhinged. "I agreed to eternal suffering to be successful on this earth . . . a home and a new car. A girlfriend, an earthly success."

It quickly became clear that asking Andrew open-ended questions was fruitless; his thoughts were too mangled and disconnected from reality. During the remainder of that first session and the next, I asked him specific, concrete questions. No guarantee, but such queries pull for more reality-based responses. Had you worked recently before the arrest? How many times have you been hospitalized? When did you receive your high school diploma? How old were you when your parents separated? During this early stage of our relationship, I stayed away from questions about the quality of his relationships with family, the events leading up to the homicide, and what was going on in his mind at the time of the killing.

Over the course of our sessions together, Andrew slowly improved—somewhat. His complaints about the medications continued. He had to be coaxed into taking them from the jail mental health staff. But he stopped refusing them and he was more coherent. His speech was less pressured and his thoughts seemed slightly more organized. Still, his religious preoccupations continued, as did his distorted thinking. "I work for God. My father committed the perfect sin by making me take medication." Though still complaining about the medications, he did so with less force. And he was more interpersonally responsive, less dominated by his strange inner thoughts and machinations. He appreciated, for instance, my simple displays of empathic reflection. I remarked how I understood why he missed hearing God's voice, as it was comforting to him. He accepted my support without a crazy follow-up response. His psychosis had less of a hold.

It's not uncommon for someone with long-held delusions to improve very slowly. Antipsychotic medications work fairly well in targeting hallucinations but not so well with delusions, which take more time to fade.

Fixed beliefs, especially those involving God and religion, become rooted within the self-concept and provide a way to live in the world. Unlike auditory hallucinations that are experienced as coming from outside the self, delusional thoughts are part of one's mind and not easily accepted for what they are, rank and insidious forms of distortion and self-deception. Giving up a long-held deluded way of thinking is experienced as a personal loss.

In Andrew's case, the hallucinations were inseparable from his delusional beliefs. Not hearing God's voice weakened his conviction of specialness. With God as his light, he was inoculated from depravity. His delusions have been weakened, I thought, but remained active and operational. He worked for God and was special. Others, like his father, were transgressors. As would become apparent, so were his other family members.

***

Though less psychotic, Andrew continued to be digressive with illogically connected and frequently bizarre thinking. "For seven years I've been suffering. God showed me my failure. He showed me his power. I was in a fetal position. . . . He opened me up to the heavens. I had this dream. I woke up and I was confused, but then I knew it was from God." He went on, "After a dream, I met Cassie. She turned me into an evil person, a big sinner." I asked him to tell me more about that. She "turned me into a stoner. I got worse and worse. I don't even remember, but I saw my future. I even saw this encounter between you and me. But I couldn't stop fornicating. . . . I was watching pornography, masturbating, God chastised me. God made it obvious to me." I asked what he meant, what exactly was made obvious. He ranted about the canard of mental illness: "There's no real thing as crazy. I've been around schizophrenics and bipolars. It's all fake . . . fake actors."

Religious delusions were key elements in the madness of Andrew's inner world. And the spiritual madness was indivisible from his bizarre beliefs about his family. Consistently, as his psychotic rambling picked up speed, his kin became implicated in one way or another. "My family, God took them away from me." I was puzzled and asked what he meant. I pointed to the obvious, that he had been living with them until his arrest. Again, "God took them away from me. They were raptured." He explained how his family's "good spirits" were taken into heaven, their bodies appropriated by demons. It happened two years ago. Since then, "They've been plotting against me. You don't know the extremes that I've gone through, my parents plotting against me. They wanted me to go to hell." He went on, "I couldn't take it. I don't know why I didn't take their lives. I don't know why I didn't take my stepmother's life. She has internal hate for me." I asked if Peter hated him as well. He responded, "They wanted me to go to hell. They had eternal hate for me." He bizarrely added that, after the stabbing, he heard his stepmother's voice say, "I'm proud of you."

**

I decided it was time for Andrew and me to baldly explore his extraordinary inner world and its calamitous consequences, Peter's killing. We had developed a good rapport over the course of about six weeks of lengthy interviews. Andrew had improved and, I felt, was now as stable as could be expected. Further progress with his reality testing ability would be slow and unpredictable.

Andrew was expressing his usual disdain for his family and their evildoing nature but with less of a vile edge. I told him I wanted to talk with him about the morning Peter died. My understanding, I said, was that he was already at the house when Peter arrived home. In a matter-of-fact fashion, Andrew described how he took a kitchen knife and stabbed his stepbrother twice. He watched Peter stagger and fall. There was no exchange of words after the stabbing, no strident exchange or emotive altercation leading to the deadly assault. He called his family "extremely wicked people." He wanted to kill his stepmother and father as well. I asked why he didn't try to do so. His father, Andrew said, is a strong man. Peter fought back in an attempt to grab the knife from Andrew. "It's a hard thing to do. He struggled," Andrew said.

Very soon after, as Peter lay there, halfway between the bedroom and hall, Andrew left the house and returned not long after. By then, Mrs. Parks was home, next to Peter. She looked up and shouted at Andrew, "You did this!" She was alternating between comforting Peter and shouting at Andrew. "Get out. Get out!" He left and went to his local coffee shop a few streets away, sat, and had tea.

Andrew abruptly shifted from the events of the killing to a personal lament. "I can't trust anybody." His father was "evil. He kicked me out." I asked if he had been upset over the planned visit to a board and care home. That topic set him off. Glaring at me and with unusual directness, he growled that Peter got the bedroom. "That led to the killing too." His thought process crumbled under the weight of his emotional intensity. He descended back into incoherence and religiosity. "God was putting a lot of guilt on me for everything, I don't know. I was supposed to do something for God. I don't know what. I was angry at my brother. . . . He wanted to send me to hell. It doesn't matter who I killed. I could have killed my dad and my stepmother. Everybody wanted me in hell."

I queried Andrew about his thoughts as he sat in the coffee shop after the stabbing. He didn't know if Peter was alive or dead. "I knew I was going to prison. It's not fair. They're all demons," he said, referring to his family. I asked if that was what made him stab Peter. As might be expected, he responded obliquely and paradoxically; first, "It was an act of faith," then, "It was a sin. I knew it. I acted in self-defense."

As he sat at the coffee shop sipping tea, Andrew contemplated running away, strangely enough, to South America. I asked if he'd ever been there or if he speaks Spanish. Negative to both. He sat there lost in delusional thinking.

***

Andrew had already been diagnosed with paranoid schizophrenia. I concluded that he also suffered from Capgras syndrome, which is a subtype of the delusional misidentification syndromes.[2] It almost always occurs in the context of a major mental disorder such as schizophrenia and is characterized by a specific kind of delusional thinking. Generally, a delusion is defined as a false inference about the world or other people that is rigidly maintained in spite of incontrovertible evidence to the contrary. There are a number of various delusional misidentification syndromes, such as the syndrome of subjective doubles, in which a patient believes there are individuals walking around the world who look and act exactly like the patient. With Capgras syndrome[3] (named after the physician who first described it in 1923), one has a fixed delusion that an identical-looking imposter has replaced another, usually a family member. In Andrew's case, he believed demons had replaced his entire family, with his "real" members having been raptured to the heavens years earlier. It's as if he were living in a horror movie such as *Invasion of the Body Snatchers*. Only with Andrew, it wasn't military personnel whose bodies were appropriated by soulless "pods," but the bodies of his own family members hijacked by demons.

Another layer of complexity included the fact that Andrew believed he was influenced by God at the time of the killing. This added a wrinkle in Andrew's psychiatric illness, further complicating my understanding of his psyche, which in turn would affect my medical-legal decision making. During one of his discursive ramblings in response to my query about his thinking at the time of the murder, Andrew referred to himself as a "prophet who suffers God's will. I was supposed to be a man of God. I'm giving my all to Christ." He added, "God changed my heart. He made me do it. . . . I'll suffer on earth." Did he psychotically believe he was doing God's will when he murdered Peter? And now, for following the word of God, he'll "suffer on earth" like a martyr? Did his delusions about his family and divine influence interfere with his ability to understand and appreciate the wrongfulness of his homicidal behavior? Did he believe he was acting at the direction of a transcendent God?

I pondered the implications of Andrew's mental state when he stabbed Peter, with his delusions of demons and divine influence. In California, as in many jurisdictions, the legal standard used by forensic psychologists and psychiatrists for opining whether the defendant is insane at the time of a crime is guided by a version of the M'Naghten test.[4] Named after a famous eighteenth-century judicial decision made in England, it requires that, at the time of the crime, the defendant suffered from a mental illness. The mental disorder must have been grave enough to (1) interfere with the defendant's ability to know or understand the nature or quality of his criminal behavior or (2) to have compromised the defendant's ability to know or understand the legal or moral wrongfulness of his behavior. An inability to fulfill either of those two prongs qualifies a mentally disordered defendant for the insanity defense. In actual practice, most defendants know or understand the "nature or quality" of their behavior unless they suffer from a serious and fairly obvious medical or neurocognitive condition. Consider a person, for instance, who has an epileptic fit while driving and killed a pedestrian. Under such circumstances, he acted without awareness and purposefulness.

Recognizing whether a defendant lacked an understanding of the wrongfulness of his actions can get complicated. It's clear that most people, even under the influence of a severe mental disorder, understand it's legally wrong to kill. If a person truly believes he is morally justified in killing someone, is it justified? In *People v. Stress* (1988), the California Supreme Court ruled that, in the case of an insanity defense, morality is legally understood as the generally accepted social standards of society, not "those standards peculiar to the accused." In Andrew's case, did messages received from a Christian God qualify him to be excused from murder if he actually believed it was so divined?

Some states have an addendum to the insanity defense called the deific-degree doctrine.[5] It concerns those who believe they have been commanded by God to commit a criminal act. Such a delusion allows for the insanity defense to be considered and for the wrongfulness prong to be broadened. The idea is that a command from God subsumes a defendant's free will and extinguishes the ability to know the difference between right and wrong. Such a defense was used in the nineteenth century after President James Garfield was assassinated.[6] The killer claimed to be an agent of the deity when he shot the president. His defense team argued that their client believed he was doing God's work when he assassinated the president. Though the jury found the defendant guilty of murder, the deific-degree doctrine was established as a possible element to be considered in some jurisdictions when insanity is claimed. It also highlights the influence of the Judeo-Christian tradition in criminal law.

California criminal law does not recognize the doctrine per se, yet a delusional belief about a divine command requires an analysis of its implication regarding a defendant's comprehension of moral wrongfulness, especially the *moral* dimension. Believing one has received a deific command decree can obscure an understanding of moral righteousness, as God is the ultimate moral arbiter.

***

Throughout the course of my interviews with Andrew, I listened carefully to his assertions of putative deific communication. True to form, Andrew regularly contradicted himself. He spoke of his family as doppelgängers, demons living in his parents' and brother's bodies, and of a deific command to kill them. "I can hear God direct me. . . . [I]t happened because of the will of God." On the other hand, "God doesn't want me to murder anybody." Or "God chastised me" for the killing. I tried to understand when he received each of those messages and which type of message was delivered before and after the killing. His responses were confusing and contradictory: "The day I did it, I acted in foolishness. Besides I'm going to heaven."

To help tease out my understanding of his moral liability, I wondered aloud with Andrew why he didn't attempt to kill his father and stepmother. I reminded him of his claim that, like Peter, they were doppelgängers, his "demon parents." Again, his responses were ambiguous, not always fully irrational, but not totally incoherent either. He hated "my stepmom demon," but he could not say why he didn't try to kill her. Regarding his father, "It would be hard to do it . . . [the] struggle." And, "I love my dad." Did he *rationally* decide not to harm his father, even when in the throes of demonic madness? Though psychotic, was he still able to make legal and moral choices with a reasonable degree of rationality?

***

I completed comprehensive psychological testing on Andrew. He clearly suffered from a psychotic disorder but with a complex mental functioning that was atypical. The results, I hoped, would add to my developing understanding of the contours of his illness and his motivations. Sometimes, the results could clarify the extent or limits of a defendant's emotional control and reasoning, moral and otherwise. In addition, I wanted to obtain objective measures of Andrew's tendency to exaggerate his symptoms. In medical-legal situations, particularly those with high stakes, a defendant might deny or embellish psychological symptoms or outright malinger in an effort to sway the evaluator's opinion. In Andrew's case, there was no doubt of his mental illness. But his contradictory claims and promptings, his selective targeting of Peter and not his stepmother or father, his clear bitterness over losing his bedroom to Peter, and his impending placement out of the house all demanded further scrutiny. The stakes could not be higher: Andrew was facing life in prison if convicted of first-degree murder.

Given all of this and the overall strangeness of his psychological symptoms, including his Capgras syndrome, I thought it important to consider the possibility of neuropsychological disorder. The diagnosis of schizophrenia is associated with changes in cognitive functioning caused by the disease, such as reduced gray matter volume in the cortex and hippocampal areas of the brain.[7] Capgras syndrome in particular has been linked with neuropsychological dysfunction.[8] Fortunately, neuropsychological testing had already been done at the state hospital where Andrew was sent after having been found incompetent to stand trial. The testing was completed by a postdoctoral psychologist in the forensic training program there.

The result was consistent with someone who suffers from chronic mental illness. Andrew's testing results revealed several intellectual deficits that were not present during his developing years, based on his father's memory and the school records I reviewed. The years of having been on powerful antipsychotic medications had taken its toll. His overall IQ was in the low 80s, considered low-average, at about the twelfth percentile. His word reading and reading comprehension were average, as was arithmetic. A skill like word reading is not degraded by a neurocognitive condition and is an indicator of his premorbid functioning, which was average.

The neuropsychological testing revealed Andrew's cognitive deficits to be in the areas of concentration, short-term memory, and language expression. He was below average in executive functioning, a higher level of intellectual ability that enables an individual to initiate and maintain goal-directed behavior under new and even novel circumstances.

The testing results made sense. Andrew's thinking disturbance, the fundamental characteristic of schizophrenia, interfered with his use of language, his ability to rationally organize his thoughts, and his capacity to manage and guide his behavior. But his cognitive abilities, though below average, were within the mildly impaired range, not severely so.

I administered a number of psychological tests,[9] including those that provide a measure of validity, accuracy, and truthfulness of symptoms expressed by the defendant. This was important for a number of reasons. Almost always in criminal forensic situations, with the defendant facing the loss of his freedom, the possibility of faking symptoms is real, either by grossly exaggerating or fabricating them. The motivation arises from the hope that a mental disorder will help to mitigate penalty. It's estimated that between 15 and 18 percent of defendants malinger psychological symptoms in criminal cases.[10] Some studies report high estimates of symptom distortion, up to 66 percent in forensic settings.[11]

Although clearly psychotic, Andrew's symptom picture was quite bizarre and contradictory in nature. It's possible to be both mentally ill *and* exaggerating or faking symptoms.

First, I conducted a brief structured interview designed to identify an exaggeration of psychotic symptoms.[12] With the Miller Forensic Assessment of Symptoms Test as a guide, I questioned Andrew about the specific forms of his psychotic symptoms. Individuals suffering from bona fide mental illness do not endorse most of the extreme or rare combinations of symptoms presented during the interview, usually less than six. Andrew endorsed seven of twenty-five.

Given this result, I had Andrew complete the Structured Interview of Reported Symptoms.[13] Similar to the Miller instrument, it's more comprehensive in nature and includes 172 questions and follow-up probes. Again, the results were equivocal as to whether Andrew's symptoms were genuinely honest or exaggerated to some degree.

I continued the psychological testing, hoping for a scent of guidance. I administered the Personality Assessment Inventory (PAI).[14] Unlike narrowly focus symptom validity instruments, it's an omnibus measure of psychopathology that includes multiple validity scales as well. Andrew's validity scales were instructive. He endorsed a larger number of psychotic symptoms than usual, even compared to those with genuine psychosis. What's unique about PAI is its specialized scales that help clarify whether the test taker is consciously presenting himself in a distorted manner or if he actually *perceives* himself in the manner reflected in his results. In other words, whether the clinical scales of the testing are influenced by overt attempts at deception or by the way he actuals sees himself. The results revealed Andrew's atypical psychotic presentation was a reflection of his self-perception, albeit distorted, and not dissimulation.

The PAI clinical scale results confirmed that Andrew's disturbance in thinking was broad and pervasive. He has significant persecutory ideas about others seeking to harm him. The results were consistent with someone who is chronically saddled with magical-like thinking and disconnected from reality with sensory-perceptual disturbances. The testing also highlighted Andrew's suicide risk, which was of course consistent with his relatively recent history. The results were similar to individuals who feel overwhelmed by the stressors of everyday life. As might be expected, his scores were consistent with one who *perceives* a lack of family support. He has little trust in people, and he harbors cynical beliefs, such as that others are out for only their interests.

The testing results resonated with my clinical observations and intuitions. Andrew was full of psychotic-level contradictions and about-faces. He clearly suffered from an unusually complicated and severe form of psychopathology, and his family members were targets of his darkened and deformed worldview. He both exaggerated and minimized psychiatric symptoms. He was floridly open, but with a distorted self-perception. God commanded him to kill yet chastised him. He knew it was a sin to kill. His father was demonic but beloved, his thinking flush with paradoxes. "I'm going to go crazy if I commit a perfect sin." He had moments of lucidity, yet his mind was ceaselessly imperiled by religious preoccupations and delusional perceptions. He'd be unusually agitated, rapidly shaking his legs such that the entire booth shook, only to abruptly calm down and talk for a few moments like a normal human being.

There was, though, a consistency to Andrew's functioning. He was unfailing in his inconsistency. The psychological test results, though complex, uncannily mirrored his in-person behavior. I certainly couldn't conclude that Andrew was faking his mental illness or even exaggerating it. The testing results reflected the bizarre and psychotic contradictions that were Andrew's inner world, his crazed and chaotic thinking and his corrupted emotional experience and self-perceptions. All without a fleeting quantum of self-awareness.

Now it was time to pull all the accumulated forensic information and forge an understanding of Andrew's mind at the time of the killing.

***

Andrew's lawyer, Mr. Scott, was considering various legal defenses. His client was seriously deranged. "He rambled in riddles," he told me. This was *after* months of psychiatric treatment at a state hospital. Mr. Scott knew Andrew's state of mind was an issue in play. To be guilty of first-degree murder—the charge Andrew was facing—requires the state to prove beyond a reasonable doubt that Andrew killed with malice aforethought, meaning it was both intentional *and* premeditated and deliberate. Did Andrew go through a thought process something like this: "Should I kill Peter? Yes. What about the consequences? I don't care. I want to." With Andrew's psyche so riven and aberrant, was he capable of such wanton calculation? Could a mind so frenzied with deranged thinking execute a cold-blooded killing?

Mr. Scott had asked me to investigate his client's mental illness and how and if it influenced his criminal conduct. Was he insane? If not, were there other psychological considerations? Was he capable of carefully planning out the crime or was it the product of a wantonly crazed impulse? And what about his ability to premediate and deliberate?

I figured Andrew's attorney was hoping to argue an insanity defense. But if I didn't find him insane, did his mental illness warrant a partially accusing defense, one that could reduce his degree of culpability[15] from the first-degree murder charge?

                                        ***

I came to the conclusion that Andrew was psychotic at the time of the killing, together with a number of caveats and "buts." He believed Peter's body was possessed by a demon, with his "real" stepbrother raptured to the heavens. He was not faking his craziness. And he claimed to have killed at God's behest. Then again, he had religious delusions and misidentification beliefs for years, yet he had not been provoked to kill. Why not, and why then? Though he believed his parents' souls had also been raptured, their bodies possessed by demons, he hadn't attempted to kill them. Why? He couldn't explain the pass he gave to his stepmother. And his response to my query about his father troubled me. "It would have been difficult to overpower him" was an accurate observation, given his father's physical stature. Though he spoke of his father with ill will at times, he clearly felt warmth as well. His affection for his father compared to his resentment and antipathy for Peter factored into the killing choice, even though both were demonic doppelgängers.

During one of my queries into his thoughts and feelings before the stabbing, Andrew tensely blurted, "They kicked me out . . . that led to the killing too." Then his thinking went off the rails. He rambled irrationally about God's messages to him about his family. Curiously, the divine dispatches about killing Peter were contradictory. "I believe it happened by the will of God" immediately followed by "God doesn't want me to murder anyone." Throughout our time together, he voiced these kinds of contradictory messages about deific messages, frequently in succession.

It's quite useful to pay close attention to the contiguousness of thoughts as they are expressed. Their close association tends to unwittingly reveal some dimly felt, unacceptable emotional conflicts and the unconscious ways of avoiding awareness. For instance, a patient with an inability to accept his resentment toward his wife might say, "My wife is so nasty. But I love her. She's so great with my kids." Here, the patient struggles with ambivalent feelings toward her. He *undoes* an undesirable sentiment by immediately employing a favorable observation ("so great with my kids"). Her positive qualities may be real ones but are used here to deny his conflicted emotions.

Andrew, it seemed to me, was exposing an ambivalence toward his homicidal impulses and doing so in his usual deranged manner. I asked if, at another point before the killing, he felt it was wrong to kill his stepbrother. "I always knew it was. I did it. I acted foolish. Besides, I'm going to heaven." Andrew's inner struggle before the killing ("it happened by the will of God. God doesn't want me to murder anyone"), though expressed in deviant form, revealed an effort to restraint his homicidal impulse and again signaled an awareness of its wrongfulness.

During our last session, Andrew asked for help. He hoped I would recommend hospitalization rather than prison, a very rational request. By then, he slowly had been stabilizing, and I saw his request as a reasonable one and rational. But he had some rational thinking immediately after the killing, as well, when he considered fleeing to South America. Though unrealistic, it was a measure of practical reasoning that floated about in a sea of psychic turbulence.

***

To opine that Andrew was insane at the time of the killing, I would have to have first concluded that he suffered from a mental disorder or defect during the offense. That was a no-brainer. He has a long history of paranoid schizophrenia, and he had been discharged from a psychiatric hospital shortly before the stabbing. He suffered from Capgras syndrome and neuropsychological deficits as well. At the same time, Andrew understood the nature and quality of his actions at the time. He knew that he had a knife, a potentially lethal weapon, in his hand when he stabbed Peter and that he was inflicting grievous harm. He was conscious and sentient.

What about the wrongfulness prong? Did Andrew understand that the killing was legally or morally wrong? Did his deific degree and delusional beliefs about Peter lend a moral justification for his action? During a number of occasions in the past, I had testified that a defendant was insane due to a deific decree in one form or another. One psychotic man stabbed his father in the heart after seeing the devil in his father's eyes and hearing God's voice tell him to "smite him to death in My name."

But Andrew's case was different. Yes, he was psychotic and he received messages from God. But the messages were mixed, some admonishing him against homicidal conduct. At the time of the killing, he was railing with bitterness and resentment toward his family, especially Peter, to whom Andrew lost the bedroom, and he was about to be placed in a board and care facility. Andrew was not only losing his bedroom, but the privilege of living at home.

Andrew's brooding anger and resentment, his ambivalent deific messages about the killing, and his thinking and behavior immediately after the stabbing (realizing he would be going to prison; considering leaving the country) together led me to suspect Andrew had at least a rudimentary understanding of the wrongfulness of his action. His was driven, I thought, by deranged motivations, but also by some all-too-natural daimonic urges.

***

I concluded that Andrew was sane when he killed his stepbrother, that he knew it was legally and morally wrong. His deific messages were mixed, yet he followed the deadly directive that was likely propelled by fuming, nonheavenly impulses.

The M'Naghten test for insanity, the legal standard in California, is referred to as a "cognitive test." It requires that a defendant's mental illness impair the rational awareness of his action and its wrongfulness. Volitional deficits—insufficient self-control—does not apply. If Andrew were tried in a state with a different standard, I would have come to a different conclusion. Many states have adopted the standard proposed by the American Law Institute, for instance.[16] With it, a person is judged insane if, due to a mental disorder, he lacked a substantial capacity to appreciate the criminality of his conduct or to conform his conduct to the requirements of the law. It takes into consideration a volitional vulnerability.

Andrew was clearly vulnerable to loss of emotional control at the moment of the killing. His mind was fractured by delusions, and he was burdened with neuropsychological deficits, reeling from having been displaced from his bedroom and facing a looming change in residence. With a mind chronically in chaos and with such limited psychological resources to manage stress, his capacity to contain his ambivalent impulses and virulent rage was ravaged and his decision-making ability corrupted.

I told Mr. Scott that although I could not conclude Andrew was insane, I didn't believe he killed with premeditation and deliberation. That would require an intentionality formed after he coolly weighed the reasons for and against his actions. It would mean that Andrew murdered after having completed a process of measured thought and reflection. Andrew's severely fissured mind preempted such purposeful and mature psychological functioning. In essence, I was suggesting he was capable of second-degree murder, not first.

**

I was privately retained by Mr. Scott. Two other experts appointed by the court also evaluated Andrew. One concluded he was insane, one sane. Mr. Scott had me testify during the guilt phase of the trial, while the other experts did so during the insanity phase.

My testimony during direct examination focused on Andrew's severe mental disorders and the limitations of his neuropsychological functioning. The cross-examination was mild by the usual standards of a murder trial. The prosecutor focused on Andrew's growing resentment of the victim and his calm behavior afterward. He was suggesting to the jury that the murder was the result of Andrew's resentment but that he did it with calm deliberation.

After the guilt phase of the trial, Andrew was found guilty of second-degree murder. By the same jury, he was then found not guilty by reason of insanity after the insanity phase of the proceedings.

**

When the jury was surveyed and questioned by Mr. Scott after the trial, they said expert testimony was not very helpful in coming to their decisions. They were swayed by his clearly documented history of mental illness. In particular, they were influenced by its severity and intractability, even so many hospitalizations. The jurors decided he was "so sick" and irrational that he couldn't understand right from wrong. Interestingly, when researchers survey people about the insanity defense, a majority express a great deal of dissatisfaction about it and mental health defenses in general. The public generally feels it is used by criminals to avoid their just deserts. In fact, the insanity defense is employed at an extremely low rate, less than 1 percent, and rejected by the trier of fact 75 percent of the time.[17] Those 25 percent that are found insane usually have an unequivocal history of severe mental illnesses.

That certainly was the case with Andrew. During my testimony at the guilt phase of the trial, I presented evidence on the severity of his mental disorder and described it as a neuropsychiatric condition. However, given the restrictions imposed by legal procedures, I wasn't allowed to opine on the "ultimate cause"—about how his illness directly influenced the murder. That's left to the jury members to decide, given my expert description of his mental conditions. I suspect that the sanction against directly speaking about Andrew's state of mind at the time of the murder left the jury less than satisfied during the guilt phase of the trial. Each attorney asking leading questions designed to emphasize their perspectives also could be confusing. Then comes the insanity phase, in which the jurors are confronted with two more experts who arrived at two divergent expert opinions. Each independently made sense; taken together, it's babble.

With all of this, the jurors concluded in Andrew's case that the insanity defense was not a "get out of jail free" card. They didn't see him as a smarmy defendant getting away with murder. He wasn't just another violent criminal trying to weasel out of his just reward. Andrew wasn't an abstraction to them, but a flesh-and-blood person. And with their commonly held humane sense, all twelve saw a very disturbed young man.

I was glad—even relieved—that Andrew was found insane. I couldn't come to that conclusion given my technical understanding of the law. Was I too restricted in my decision? Did I follow the letter of the law too closely and miss its spirit? I don't know. But I didn't believe he was a cold-blooded murderer exercising an evil privation. His deadly misconduct was the result an impetuous urge delivered by a ravaged psyche.

In the next chapter I examine an individual whose malevolence came naturally from a rational mind.

6

HEART OF DARKNESS

Tall, Charming, and Psychopathic

The belief in a supernatural source of evil is not necessary; men alone are quite capable of every wickedness.—Joseph Conrad

In some ways, Randall was an ordinary thirtysomething. He joined the marines in his late teens, determined to serve his country. Secretly he wore contacts to conceal his poor vision during the entrance physical examination. When his liability was revealed during training exercises, he was sent packing, having enlisted under false pretense.

He wanted so much to be a marine. Randall imagined himself in that impressive dress uniform, in combat, fighting for his country. Now, all he had to show for his efforts was the marine crest tattooed on his left shoulder. I was told by a family member how he loved the thought of being a combat soldier. And how he loved showing off his tattoo, even though he served for less than a month.

Just the same, Randall could claim to be one with a desire to serve and be a part of something. It was a thirst that seemed to develop early. Raised a Catholic, he was an altar boy who talked about entering the seminary and becoming a priest.

He eventually settled into a more traditional lifestyle, one that was ostensibly fulfilling, at least on the surface. At the age of thirty-three, Randall was married and living in a condo with his pregnant wife and two-year-old daughter. Hardworking, he was recognized in his employer's monthly newsletter for his sales prowess. So impressed were his superiors, he was selected to run a seminar for new employees on how to "close the deal."

Randall is the tall, dark, and handsome type. Coupled with an easy smile and amiable way, it wasn't hard to understand why he was liked by so many, especially women. His physical good looks, his ease of expression, and charismatic ways all adjoined into a sales talent that seemed preternatural. He was destined for great professional things. And with his beautiful wife, young daughter, and another child on the way, he seemed to have it all.

So it came as quite a shocking jolt to all when Randall was arrested and charged with murdering his pregnant wife and daughter. Before the call from his attorney, I had heard a headline on the radio about a suspect being arrested for killing his family. I've worked on many similar-sounding cases: a husband or boyfriend goes berserk at the thought of his partner leaving and, in the heat of blazing passion, kills. Though provided with only the most basic details by the attorney during that first phone call, I was stunned by its grim heartlessness. If true, Randall was alleged to have killed his family and to have disposed of the bodies. Before the arrest, he had filed a missing persons report with the police. He and his wife Emma had been separated for about six months at the time. He claimed she was vindictive and aimed to prevent him from having contact with Kara, his daughter, and the upcoming newborn to punish him.

His wife's body was later found in a shallow grave in a national park within driving distance of Randall's apartment. Kara was missing. Forensic evidence from his wife's condo revealed blood traces of two victims. The blood samples matched those of Emma and Kara.

Randall was arrested about three weeks after he reported his family missing. Remarkably, during the interim, he had thrown a party at his apartment for coworkers and neighbors. On the day of his arrest, he and a current girlfriend were on their way to the airport for a vacation in New York City. He was detained at Los Angeles International Airport.

As is usual in cases like this, my immediate reaction is like everyone else's: more visceral than clinical. Something like, "That can't be. How can anybody do something like that?" My gut responded with jolting horror. What happened? Randall's pregnant wife was dead, and the blood evidence seemed to confirm that his young daughter was as well. Three pulsating hearts, violently extinguished forever, two just commencing their journey. The spiritual is not within my province, though I understand why others may see such malevolence as beyond human depravity and stemming from some kind of supernatural evil. For me, it derives from an all-too-earthly derailment and distortion of psychological being. It's at the dark tip of Jung's shadow, at the wicked end of the daimonic spectrum.

The forensic evidence accumulated was unimpeachable: Randall murdered his pregnant wife and daughter. And blithely carried on with his life.

Randall had exposed a face of radical human evil.

***

Randall's lawyer asked if I could get eyes on him "ASAP." The alleged killings had occurred recently, so there was an opportunity to evaluate the seriousness of his psychiatric symptoms that may have contributed to his behavior at the time of the killings. I rearranged my schedule so I could interview Randall later that week. I had not yet reviewed any records nor had I spoken to anybody who knew him or his deceased family.

Although I knew what he looked like from images on TV and in the newspapers, I was surprised when the deputies brought Randall to the interview booth at the jail. He was knockout good looking, standing about six feet, one inch tall, well-built, thin but muscular. His hair was straight and coal black, in contrast to his light blue-green eyes. Adding to his appeal was his soft voice and easy smile. This man was born to be in sales, I thought. At first blush, he radiated trustworthiness.

Randall was expecting my visit. He greeted me by name and thanked me for coming to see him. He was eager to talk, like someone wanting to clear up a misunderstanding. At the same time, he was subtly evasive. When I asked about his living circumstance before the arrest, his easygoing attitude sharpened as he shifted topics. With a clipped cadence, he complained about how his dead wife "stressed me out." He described her as "basically vulgar . . . mean . . . violent." He told me of his business successes, all interrupted by his wife's "craziness" and now the arrest.

This pattern—oscillating between chummy and acid—continued throughout the interviews until I dug into the mystery of his wife's murder and his missing daughter. Then came the stonewalling.

***

During our first encounter, I explained to Randall that our interviews were confidential. We would be meeting several times. This day, I wanted to learn something about his past and any problems he had during the lead-up to his arrest. I also wanted to know how he was holding up. In cases like this, when the accusations are disturbing and heinous, I find defendants are frequently agitated and depressed—even suicidal—or guarded during the early period of their incarceration. And when there's media coverage like in this case, there's a sense of having already been judged as evil. But all this didn't faze Randall. With a self-possessed easiness, Randall talked about himself and his life with a special emphasis on his romantic prowess. Before his arrest, he had been living in a condo with Hollice, his most recent girlfriend. They planned to marry as soon as his divorce was final. He continued work as a salesman but had been transferred to an office in a different county. They had started an affair before Randall separated from Emma; Hollice was one of multiple women he slept with during his marriage to Emma. He clearly enjoyed telling me about them. With a well-honed braggadocio, he described how women are drawn to him, how several ex-girlfriends "stalked me" during his marriage to Emma. It was a problem during his previous marriages as well. At the same time, he attributed his philandering to his frustration with Emma's emotional instability.

Randall has two other children from two affairs he had over the years. The mother of one was "stunningly beautiful." When he first saw her in a bar, "I decided she's got to have my child." She was "too crazy" to marry, though. He has no contact with their child or his son from another affair.

His first marriage was to Consuela, a woman eight years older than he. She had three children when they married. This marriage "was as good as it gets" for the first few years. But Randall's work in sales meant he was frequently on the road. "I got a lot of attention from women." Though he "loved the boys," his stepchildren, he resented the money it cost to care for them. Eventually, his affairs and resentment destroyed the marriage.

Veronica was Randall's second wife. It was short-lived and blew up after Maryann, the mother of his second child, informed Veronica that she was pregnant with Randall's baby—and that she conceived the night before Veronica and Randall married.

Randall simultaneously complained and bragged about having been stalked by ex-girlfriends who, at times, confronted his wives with the affairs.

Returning to his relationship with Emma, I made the obvious observation that his cheating behavior didn't seem tied at all to Emma's emotional issues, as he had been having affairs throughout his adult life. Randall explained his motivations. "It's kind of . . . one woman has one great thing, another woman has another great thing."

The first few hours of our initial session focused mostly on Randall's philandering; despite my efforts to widen the discussion about his life, he circled back to his mesmerizing influence on women. He was undaunted by his immediate plight, that he was in jail and accused of murdering his pregnant wife and child.

The picture emerged in my mind of a narcissistically absorbed man even before Randall offered his chilling explanation and rationalization for his actions regarding the events surrounding the murders.

***

Usually I spend time early in the examination process exploring in some detail a defendant's life history. This helps in a number of ways. It places the person's recent travails in context and gives us time to become comfortable with one another. Since Randall was so comfortable—inappropriately so—talking about his heterosexual relations, I decided to begin my examination of his relationship with his wife and his view of what happened to his dead family.

Randall and Emma met at work and soon after began dating. He was living with another woman at the time. Emma was "hot and infatuated with me." Three months later she was pregnant. Before Kara's birth, they moved in together.

Soon after Emma came home with the infant, her behavior changed, Randall said. Always the possessive type, she became more "hormonal. She acted weird." Randall described her as "hyper . . . paranoid." Having stopped working to stay home with their newborn, Emma incessantly "called me . . . checking on me." If he came home late, she became hysterical, accusing him of cheating. I said that it made sense, given his history with women. He agreed but still felt she was "insane." Emma threatened to slash her throat if she found he was with another woman.

"She was always talking about death." He hoped it was "a postpartum thing" and she would eventually "calm down."

That was not to be. With a cold-blooded stare, he said, "I found out she had psychiatric hospitalizations for suicide attempts." Emma's mother told him so that he'd appreciate her mood changes since the baby's birth. Immediately, "I had second thoughts about getting involved with someone like that," Randall said with a whiff of disdain.

Emma's "insane jealousy" became chronic, he complained, as did her desperate pleading for his reassurance of love and loyalty. Emma's medical doctor attributed her behavior to postpartum depression and prescribed medication. He recommended that she get help with the baby. Her mother began visiting to help out with the baby. But, Randall said, Emma's relationship with her mother was fraught since childhood. He described her mother as "a bitch" and complained that she wanted money for the help she provided to her daughter and grandchild.

Over time, Emma was less emotionally unhinged, but the possessiveness continued. "I couldn't take it anymore." He told her, "I want to work it out, but on my own." Randall moved into his own apartment but continued to financially and, in his view, emotionally support Emma and Kara, now almost two years old. He had been giving Emma's mother a weekly stipend and increased it, so she could spend more time at the house.

Surprisingly, Emma at first accepted the move. But when he invited her to a housewarming party he threw at his new apartment, "Her behavior was out of whack." She abruptly became enraged at him, "screaming in front of my friends. She locked herself in the bathroom, screaming and crying." Randall broke into the bathroom and said Emma "looked crazed. She threatened to kill herself," as she was hitting herself in the head with a glass.

He had everybody leave so he could calm her down. He called Emma's mother, who was babysitting, told her what happened and that he'd be taking Emma to her. While on the phone, he claimed Emma went out on the balcony of his apartment and threatened to jump. After he pulled her back into the apartment and told her he was taking her home, she again threatened to kill herself and Kara too. He called the police, but not 911. I asked why he did not call 911. "I don't know." (There is no record of any call made to the police.)

That night, after he took Emma home, her mother stayed until morning and then took Emma and Kara to her house for a few days.

***

During the course of a year or so, Randall described Emma as having become more emotionally stable. Her "hysterical episodes" continued but lessened. She was prescribed psychiatric medication but refused any other kind of treatment. It helped, he said, that he visited Kara on regular basis.

Toward the end of the first year of their separation, the three of them—Randall, Emma, and Kara—had a Saturday excursion to Disneyland. Over that weekend, Randall and Emma had sex on both nights. She got pregnant.

After telling me this, Randall apparently noted my puzzled look, given the history he just provided. He responded, "She was calm for a while. . . . You're right, I was irresponsible."

During Emma's pregnancy, Randall moved in with Hollice, unbeknownst to Emma. While on a trip with Hollice to San Francisco during this period, he received a call from Emma. "That's when the fucking nightmare started." She found out about Randall's living arrangements and "blew up." She again threatened to kill herself and Kara. Randall called her mother and begged her to go to the house and stay with Emma. He told her about the phone call and her daughter's threat.

I asked if he called the police. He did not. He called only her mother, figuring that Emma would calm down. Emma had made these threats so many times that he had become "numb" to them. He was more angry than worried.

When he returned to southern California, Randall went to visit Kara and see how Emma was doing. "She was in one of her hysterical moods." She called Hollice a "whore . . . bitch" and pulled out a knife, put it to her neck, and threatened to kill herself. Randall was furious, he admitted, but he tried to stop her by removing the knife from her hand. In the process, "I got stabbed in the hand." The cut was serious, he claimed, damaging a tendon in his left hand. Before he was able to take the knife, she had stabbed herself in the shoulder and throat. She was bleeding but not badly. After taking the knife from her, Emma collapsed on the floor weeping. I asked if he called 911. He responded, "I was gonna call 911, but I didn't." He went into Kara's room to see how she was doing. "She wasn't there." He saw spots of blood on a dress draped on the bed. With an incredulity difficult to conceal, I asked why he didn't at that point call 911. He didn't know. I asked if he questioned Emma about the blood and Kara's whereabouts. No, he did not. He couldn't say why. I asked if he called Kara's grandmother, thinking maybe she was there. He did not. Again, he couldn't say why. "I wasn't thinking," was his response. He left and returned home.

I told Randall his nonreaction to such a grave, possibly tragic situation was strange. He agreed. "My only defense," he said, was that he "wasn't thinking." A moment later, he offered a second explanation, saying he was accustomed to Emma's drama and underreacted.

Two days later Randall went to the hospital seeking treatment for his hand, as it was not healing properly. He told the medical staff at the hospital that he had cut himself in the kitchen. He lied because he didn't want to get Emma in trouble. Several days later he went to the house to see how Emma and Kara were doing. Nobody was there. He did not call the police. I asked if he called to speak with Emma's mother. He said that he did not. "I wanted some space from all the problems."

***

During my next few interviews, I focused on developing a fuller understanding of Randall's personal life before returning to discussion about the crime. He was raised by his mother, grandparents, two uncles, Bill and Andy, and Aunt Martha. He never had contact with his father, who married and has two other children. His mother, seventeen years old when he was born, married a man when Randall was ten and moved in with her husband, leaving Randall with his grandparents. "I didn't like her husband," he told me. With his grandparents, aunt, and uncles, "I was the center of attention."

Randall talked about his early life in glowing terms. His grandparents adored him. He was an average student, although he could have done better, he said, if he were interested and applied himself. "School was boring." He loved sports and made friends easily. He was never abused. In high school he ran track. "I had lots of girlfriends." He was always popular in school and at his church.

After high school, Randall registered at the local junior college and took some classes in business administration. Uninterested, he dropped out and joined the marines. "I wanted to do something exciting . . .

daring." He was discharged because of his vision problems, after which he reenrolled in junior college and worked a part-time job in the payroll department of a paper goods business. He wrote a couple of bad checks that added up to about $700. Randall's supervisor found out and called the police. He was arrested, spent a day in jail, and was placed on probation, which he completed. Other than this one misdemeanor, he had no other record.

That was his only "blip . . . I had a great upbringing." He loved being in sales, his profession throughout most of his adulthood. And he "loved" his last job before the arrest, selling time-shares for an international hotel chain. He traveled frequently and regularly spoke in front of large groups. The challenges of persuading others to buy—"converting them"—was thrilling. He especially got a rise out of "closing the deal" with skeptical clients. And he was exceptional at it.

I reflexively ripple with skepticism when somebody describes his or her past with glib and binary memories and images, whether endlessly wrenching or infinitely idyllic. Randall claimed no distress caused by a neglectful mother or longings for an absentee father. He was ceaselessly adored. No drug or alcohol problems, ever. He loved his work and was a top-performing salesman. Save one thoughtless slip and misdemeanor conviction, his rectitude and normality was conspicuous. Until now.

Though smooth and beguiling, Randall was blind to his one-dimensional self-image.

***

I was able to consult by telephone with Randall's family members who lived out of state. Randall's grandmother was unavailable, as she suffered from mild dementia. His grandfather was deceased. But I got a fuller picture of his developmental years from his uncles. He was indeed the apple of his grandmother's eye. As a child, they recalled him as being carefree and friendly most of the time. He wasn't apt to share very much about his everyday concerns, but he wasn't exactly low maintenance. He had a temper and a tendency to brood. Over what, Uncle Bill couldn't say or recall. During middle school, his grandmother was called several times to help deal with his bullying of other children. And his temper led to more than the usual number of schoolyard brawls. Schoolwork came easily to him, and teachers liked him, so they were surprised when a "mean side" revealed itself.

Uncle Bill told me that Randall frequently lied, sometimes for no apparent reason. In high school, he ditched classes, but adamantly denied doing so, even when his absence was clearly documented. He lied about the friends he was hanging with, though the family never restricted him.

Of all his family members, Randall was closest to his grandmother, especially during his younger years. But as he got older and eventually moved away, their relationship changed. Always respectful and not exactly cold but a little too "casual" in a way that was bothersome. For instance, it bothered Billy that Randall seemed strangely unaware of or indifferent to her memory problems when he was in town on a business trip and visited.

As an adult, Uncle Bill thought of Randall "as sort of a grifter. And I'm his advocate!"

***

After several interviews and telephone conversations with his uncles, I met with Randall's attorney, Michael Everly, and his associates. I told them my initial thoughts. He was clearly not psychotic. I could not, at that point, see any mental health issues that might be relevant to his defense. Given the charges and quality of evidence against him and my initial encounters with him, it appeared to me that he has a severe personality disorder, possibly psychopathic in nature.

Mr. Everly wasn't surprised. Randall was not being forthcoming with his attorney. He described Randall as strangely "indifferent" during their meetings, even when he outlined for his client the legal process and the consequences. Though he was having an independent expert review the physical forensic evidence, it looked powerful. Still incurious, Randall calmly asserted his innocence.

Mr. Everly asked me to continue the evaluation. His legal team didn't ask me to give an opinion regarding any specific legal issue (insanity, for example). It was unlikely that I would be used as a witness at any future trial, given my developing opinion of Randall's personality. The attorneys gave me free rein to delve into the issues surrounding the death of Randall's wife and the whereabouts of his daughter. The hope was that I would develop an understanding of their client that would help them crystalize legal options or a plea deal. In other words, something in Randall's history, psychological makeup, or a dysfunction that could at least be mitigating.

If the district attorney's office decided to pursue capital punishment, Randall's attorneys would have an opportunity beforehand to present evidence from his personal history and psychological status that would contravene a recommendation of a death sentence. They were preparing for such a contingency.

Mr. Everly was frustrated by Randall's evasiveness and seeming indifference. He apparently distrusted his own legal team or at least was being cautious with them. This is actually not uncommon. Many defendants, especially those who are repeat offenders, disadvantaged, or socially marginalized in some way possess a basic distrust of the entire justice system, of which their attorneys are part. They sometimes share more with their cellmates than with their attorneys. Randall seemed different; he had no criminal history to speak of and portrayed himself as a "pillar of the community," one who typically has faith in its institutions and their representatives. His lawyers wanted a better understanding of "what makes him tick." Maybe then they could gain his trust. I had my doubts.

I continued the examination with Randall, which included an exploration of the circumstances of Emma's death and Kara's whereabouts.

***

During the months and interviews following my meeting with Randall's attorneys, he continued his complete denial of any involvement in Emma's homicide or awareness of his daughter's fate. I reviewed some of the most damaging evidence with him, such as the blood spattering that was found in Emma's bedroom, along with alleged attempts to clean up the crime scene. There was also evidence that the bodies were stored on the outside deck of his wife's condo for a week. During that period, he had friends over to Emma's apartment to watch a football game. He admitted doing so, saying he was still paying for the condo and his fiancée was hosting a bridal shower for her girlfriend.

When the opportunity presented, he would, in one way or another, make the case for himself—that he was innocent—and implicate Emma, the victim, in her own death. "Look, I have no idea what happened. . . . She was constantly talking about death."

Randall never mentioned Kara, his missing daughter, unless I brought her up. What he *didn't* say spoke volumes. He had little concern for his missing child. It reminded me of Uncle Bill's troubling observation of Randall's indifference to his grandmother's dementia.

***

In between our meetings, I received additional reports and documents from Randall's attorney. A supplemental police report indicated that two days after Randall visited the hospital to have his finger sutured, he purchased a tarp and sundry other materials from Home Depot. Emma's body was found in a shallow grave in the desert by a weekend camper, wrapped in a tarp. Its location wasn't far from a resort hotel where Emma, Kara, and Randall occasionally went for weekend getaways. Another report described the circumstances of his arrest, his detainment at Los Angeles International Airport. He and his fiancée were on the way to New York to meet her family.

The police spoke with Emma's neighbors after Randall's arrest. They spoke with Randall's colleagues from work. Most neighbors had nothing to say, but a few told police that they frequently heard yelling and verbal threats flying about from both parties. None witnessed any violence. Some of his coworkers described Randall as "smooth" and dishonest. One claimed that he sold a franchise to unsuspecting clients who "lost all their life's savings." Several men whom he worked with suspected he had a drug problem, mostly methamphetamines and alcohol, given his sometimes frenzied behavior during business trips.

Subpoenaed records from Randall's employer revealed several sexual harassment claims against him by female employees, none of which were sustained. One employee, a man, claimed Randall was regularly inappropriate with women. He surmised that the harassment claims were found to be unsubstantiated by human resources because Randall was valuable to the company; he was a high-producing salesman and earner for the company. No civil lawsuits were filed.

A police forensic report included an interview with the property manager of Emma's condo. He told detectives that his cleaning crews discovered blood beneath the carpet in the unit.

An investigator working for Randall's attorney flew out of state to interview various members of Randall's family and acquaintances. An ex-girlfriend accused him of "pinning me against the wall" and putting a gun to her head. She filed a restraining order against him, which the investigator confirmed. She also accused him of episodically abusing methamphetamines. Another ex-girlfriend accused him of having a "bad temper . . . Jekyll and Hyde."

His uncle Bill seemed more piqued at Randall than he was when we spoke. He called Randall a "pathological liar." By this time, more evidence had accumulated, pointing to Randall's guilt.

Randall's second wife refused to be interviewed. His first wife confirmed that his philandering caused the breakup. "That's all I have to say about him."

***

With time, Randall lowered his guard a bit with me. We explored the circumstances of his arrest. Most striking was his sense of victimization. Continuing to deny any wrongdoing, he casually dismissed the forensic evidence. He admitted to buying the tarp wrapped around Emma's dead body, but said, "I left it at her house by mistake." He complained of being unjustly targeted by the police because of his prior illegal check-writing conviction. "If only people could *forget*." He quickly corrected himself "if only they could *forgive*."

Randall's slip of the tongue revealed a wish that "people" would follow his lead and indulge in fantasized denial of the undeniable, making everything okay. He then launched into a mini-tirade about crooked politicians who "get away with murder." He oddly referenced Charles Manson, saying, "He never killed anybody."

Randall was revealing his unconscious identification with daimonic malignancy.

At another point, Randall told me he wanted to take the witness stand if his case went to trial. In a stunning display of a narcissistic belief in the virility of his charm and influence, Randall commented, "Everything is marketing."

***

Given Randall's tendency toward duplicity, I administered specialized psychological tests that are designed to not only assess his psychological makeup, but measure his degree of honest response to the test items. He completed the Paulhus Deception Scales,[1] a brief yet nuanced instrument that measures the level of a person's deliberate impressive management and self-deception tendencies. I administered the Rorschach Inkblot Test.[2] Inherently ambiguous, the examinee simply looks at the ten ink-blots, some colored and some achromatic, and shares what he sees. With the use of true-or-false questions about psychological symptoms used on most psychological tests, it's easier to portray oneself as either healthy or severely ill, thus necessitating the use of validity measures. With its am-biguous content, the Rorschach is difficult to purposefully project an image of normalcy or aberration. And it provides a penetrating look into a person's psyche. The complex scoring system includes a number of deter-minants, such as form quality and content of the perceptions, use of color, and the movement and reality-based nature of the percepts. Are people moving? And if so, how? Dancing or fighting? Are emotions expressed directly? Overall, the instrument yields a rich understanding of a person's inner life and emotional depth.

Given the time it takes to score and analyze the Rorschach, I don't usually administer it in forensic settings. And due to its complicated scoring method, it's open to criticism during trial. I felt it was warranted here, given Randall's skills at misrepresenting himself.

Probably the most important instrument I administered was the most recent edition of the Hare Psychopathy Checklist[3] to estimate Randall's psychopathic and antisocial tendencies. I scored him on twenty items related to behaviors and traits usually associated with psychopathy (de-gree of glibness, lack of empathy, for example). A scoring manual de-scribes each behavior/trait in detail and includes an associated rating from zero to two. The highest rating possible is forty, with a score of thirty or higher usually considered to be diagnostic of psychopathy.

And finally, I also administered my standard omnibus measure of psychological functioning, the Minnesota Multiphasic Personality Inven-tory-2-RF.

On the Paulhus Deception Scales, Randall showed little effort to make a positive impression but scored high on self-deception. One sees this pattern in narcissistic individuals who are indifferent to others' thoughts and feelings and who have little awareness or interest in their own inner emotions or the mental activity of others. Socially, this surfaced in Ran-dall's self-assurance and his natural tendency to self-promote. With his excessive self-absorption and limited self-awareness, there's no room for doubt or hesitation: he wants what he wants, and he deserves it.

Randall's MMPI-2-RF test results were valid, and the scales measuring his response style were interesting. He denied emotional problems. He saw himself as well-adjusted, confirming the Paulhus Deception Scales results.

The clinical scales of Randal's MMPI-2-RF were elevated on measures of antisocial behavior, paranoia, and mania. He has not incorporated the standard societal values, and he resents authority, as he likes to be in control. Indifferent to the feelings of others, he tends to be socially controlling, impulsive, and self-absorbed. He's unable to form warm and secure attachments with others. His degree of elevation on the mania scale was not to suggest a bipolar illness, but an individual who is stimulus seeking and a high-risk taker. His extroversion and high-energy style could be charming and charismatic, albeit in a shallow and superficial form.

What was surprising was Randall's elevation on a score that measures paranoia. He was not paranoid in the sense that he suffered from overt delusions; his score reflected an inner state of distrust and guardedness, with a propensity toward hostility and resentfulness hidden behind his benign persona. He likely projects his manipulative motives onto others, fueling his interpersonal distrust.

The Rorschach results were intriguing. There was no evidence to suggest he was prone to hearing voices or experiencing outright delusions. Although he had no thinking disturbance, he was capable of compartmentalizing unwanted perceptions and subjugating facts to fanciful hopes. This allowed him to secure a temporary relief from worry or responsibility, but it also distorted his perceptions of people and situations. And himself. He didn't show a range of emotional concerns that's typical in adults with full and complicated lives. He had an intellectual way of minimizing the impact of feelings on him and a strong escapist tendency.

Though clearly narcissistically oriented in his style, the Rorschach results revealed him to be paying insufficient attention to himself, to be avoiding self-focus. It's a common way of preempting emotional discomfort, as introspection could be dangerous; it may cause a face-to-face encounter with discomforting features of the self. So he avoids reflection and reacts to his immediate experience based on how he feels, not what he thinks. This likely makes him appear spontaneous, which is part of his social attractiveness. But his impoverished inner life and self-absorption preclude a capacity for intimacy. His interpersonal ties are glib and shallow. Randall's not impulsive per se; when threatened, though, he has the potential to erupt. It's a type of vulnerability that's not unusual among narcissistically oriented individuals; when the slick veneer gets pierced, an underlying emotional immaturity becomes apparent, sometimes in the form of rage reactions.

To score the Hare Psychopathy Checklist, I had to collate an extensive and disparate amount of personal information on Randall. The process helped to solidify my thinking about him.

The instrument has two-factor scales that measure two dimensions of psychopathy. One is related to the degree of antisocial behavior/lifestyle, displayed by a history of poor self-control and parasitic lifestyle, as examples. The second dimension is defined by interpersonal dysfunction/callousness, displayed by a lack of remorse or empathy, cruelty, and a manipulative style, to name a few characteristics. It includes twenty items, each scored from zero to two. A total score of thirty or greater is considered within the range of psychopathy.

Randall's total score of twenty-nine was below the threshold for classification as a psychopathic personality based on this instrument. What's most telling is not his total score, but the factor scores. His score was relatively low for the factor measuring his past antisocial behavior and lifestyle. Compared to prison inmates, his score placed him in the eleventh percentile, meaning about eighty-nine out of one hundred males in prison scored higher. That's because he did not have much of a documented criminal history or lifestyle. On the interpersonal dysfunction/callousness factor, however, which measures emotional cruelty and cold-heartedness, Randall scored at the ninety-seventh percentile when compared to prison inmates. His score was a reflection of his glib and manipulative style, his grandiosity and lying, and his degree of empathy or compassion.

My assessment of Randall was clear. I saw him as dangerously psychopathic in nature.

***

When I met with Randall's legal team, they were unsurprised by my conclusions. I had been giving the lead attorney regular updates as the assessment process unfolded. I told them that his complete denial of any crime forestalled and eliminated the need for an examination of his mental state around the time of the killings. The only mitigating factors were his lack of extensive past violence and his limited criminal history. Nonetheless, they asked me to continue seeing him. Cases like this could take years to adjudicate, and they hoped my input would help them manage Randall and their relationships with him as the evidence accumulated. They hoped to eventually present him with viable legal options.

At this point, I suggested a two-pronged approach to managing Randall. He's socially pleasant but narcissistic in his interpersonal style. He's guarded, calculating, and distrustful. To preempt these psychological traits from rupturing the attorney-client relationship as time passed and tension rose, I advised his lead attorney to meet regularly with Randall, keeping him updated on the information flow and the legal process. Most defendants complain that their lawyers don't see them enough or share what's going on and where they are in the legal process. It would pay dividends to have regularly scheduled contact with this defendant, to keep him informed, and to listen and consider his input. Feeling part of the process, he would be less suspicious and angry. And hopefully over time, more straightforward.

At the same time, the team must manage Randall's manipulative and self-deceptive ways. Tactful confrontation would undoubtedly become necessary at some point. For instance, if he continued to insist on being a witness at his trial, a direct description of the overwhelming evidence against him could be necessary to convince him to consider available options. Such a confrontation would hold the possibility of success if some degree of trust has been established.

I employed a metaphoric phrase used by family therapists to describe their process when working with difficult families. After first working on establishing rapport and some measure of trust ("joining," in the therapeutic vernacular), the therapist proceeds to alternately "rub their backs while kicking their asses."

***

Incredibly, Randall's case took a bizarre turn that had nothing to do with him directly. The criminal attorney for an inmate held in the county jail where Randall was also incarcerated subpoenaed records from the county jail, exposing serious and illegal conduct by the sheriff's department and a potential cover-up by the district attorney's office. The explosive jailhouse documents revealed that deputies systematically planted informants (a.k.a. snitches) in nearby cells of high-profile defendants to elicit damaging information. It's unconstitutional to do so, as the inmates were all represented by counsel. What made matters worse was that deputies whose signatures were on many of the documents had denied the existence of an informant system during pretrial testimony. In other words, they lied under oath. To top it all off, the informant was a repeat offender facing murder charges and had been used prolifically in other cases. He received special treatment in jail and a "sweetheart deal," according to the criminal attorney whose client had been targeted.

The law requires both prosecution and defense to exchange complete information about the facts of a case. It's a way of leveling the playing field. It appeared that the district attorney's office and the sheriff's department colluded to obfuscate and delay sharing certain documents with the defense, lest the jailhouse informant system be exposed. The trial judge finally issued an order commanding the prosecution and sheriff's department to immediately turn over all relevant documents to the defense and eventually recused the entire district attorney's office from the case.

Randall was not one of the inmates targeted by the informant program. But an ongoing investigation into the scandal revealed more official malfeasance. Records showed that a number of inmates, including Randall, had their confidential attorney-client telephone calls recorded. As these scandals hit the headlines, the attorney general's office in California became involved. In an effort, I suppose, to mitigate damage to the reputations of the officials involved and to contain the damage to the cases against the inmates, deals were made.

Before the outbreak of the latest scandal, the district attorney's office hadn't yet made a decision to pursue the death penalty for Randall. Afterward, the prosecutors offered him a deal: plead guilty to two counts of first-degree murder and life in prison without parole.

Randall accepted the plea. Kara's body has not been found.

In March 2019, Governor Newsom of California ordered a moratorium on the death penalty.

***

Was justice served? Was Randall's plea deal a righteous one, especially given its circumstances? One can easily be outraged at his escape from a just reward, capital punishment. After all, the evidence was strong that he wiped out his entire family, including his pregnant wife and young daughter. On the other hand, some psychological scientists and neuroscientists argue that psychopaths lack a fundamental capacity for moral reasoning, exempting them from criminal responsibility.

To note again, as the law currently stands, a person is not criminally responsible if, at the time of the crime, his irrationality disrupted his ability to form the necessary mental state at the time of the crime. I'm guilty of murder, for instance, if I stab and kill my neighbor on purpose, knowing it's wrong. I'm legally excused if I irrationally thought he was coming to kill me and my family and I believe I acted in self-defense. It's argued that psychopaths, though not irrational, are burdened with an inability to incorporate moral reflection into their behavior. Their inherent fearlessness and low emotional arousal disrupt the internalization of conventional norms and the development of emotional control and empathy.[4] A moral reasoning process typically levies the "brakes" on bad behavior, which fail with psychopathy.[5] Even children with psychopathic tendencies fail to show the expected negative emotional reactions when viewing nasty or unethical behavior, demonstrating the fundamental deficits in moral reasoning and judgment.[6]

A particularly interesting body of research has emerged that suggests psychopathic callousness and fearlessness are specifically influenced by a capacity to deflect attention and disregard unpleasant physiological and emotional responses.[7] This accounts for the psychopath's easy willingness to tolerate someone's suffering. James Blair, a noted neuroscientist, proposed a neurocognitive mechanism that normally responds to the stress cues in others (fearful faces, for example), and automatically inhibits aggression and enhances empathy.[8] He labeled it the violent inhibition mechanism. It may be disordered in individuals with psychopathy by their ability to miscue the pain of others via inattentiveness.

As it currently stands, an irrational state of mind at the time of a crime is the central deficit considered as a possible excusing psychiatric condition. In some jurisdictions around the country, an inability to conform one's behavior to the requirements of the law is also a possible excuse. The psychopath's misconduct, though, isn't a function of poor self-control or irrationality, but the result of an inherent defect in its biological-based moral machinery. These scientists believe the legal system should consider this condition a mental disorder like other potentially exculpating mental disorders. Even Stephen Morse, a leading legal scholar who has been critical of the growing lists of psychological excuses for criminal culpability,[9] has written that the moral reasoning deficits accompanying severe psychopathy should be considered legally excusing.[10]

In many states, like California, psychopathy is not currently considered a psychiatric disorder that meets the requirement of a mens rea defense. The Model Penal Code, which is employed in many jurisdictions around the country, explicitly excludes criminal antisocial conduct as a basis for a mens rea defense like insanity.[11] It's these kinds of legal restrictions and statutes that researchers and some legal scholars argue are behind the times, scientifically.

Joshua Greene and his colleagues[12] presented an interesting, even radical, perspective on the basic determinants of all behavior. In an influential article, they argued that everything in nature is mechanically driven in a fashion dictated by the laws of physics and determined by preexisting conditions. The vicissitudes of behavior derive from and are functions of the brain. Psychopathy is a neuropsychiatric disorder, a byproduct of which is a hard-wired impairment in moral reasoning.

These researchers are *not* arguing that criminals should be found not guilty and freed. Psychopaths convicted of serious crimes need to be isolated and controlled. Nonetheless, this emerging neuroscientific view considers psychopaths as less culpable due to their brain-based condition.[13]

***

The "hard" neuropsychiatric position that psychopathic individuals should be legally excused for their criminal conduct raises questions beyond science; it calls for a closer examination of morality and, more specifically, the difference between immorality and mental illness. Is psychopathy a disease of the mind, like schizophrenia, or a form of our basic nature that allows for varying degrees of immoral conduct? Should all psychopaths be excused, or should a legal exception be made for the extremes of the extreme? How to discern the difference: a Hare Psychopathy Checklist score somewhere between thirty and forty demarcating illness and wickedness?

The earlier study I cited on psychopathic children found that they were *more likely* to grow up with lacunae in their moral reasoning. However, these gaps in rectitude and the potential for cruel misconduct were not expressed by all these children as they reached maturity. The connection between immorality and callousness wasn't causal; not all of them became psychopathic criminals. Psychopathy isn't a condition like diabetes, which results when the body's immune system destroys insulin-producing beta cells of the pancreas. A malfunctioning pancreas *causes* type 1 diabetes. In everyone, without exception. Not all psychopaths cross the line and act criminally or with acute malice.

It's not clear whether psychopaths are incapable of internalizing social norms or, more accurately, reject conventional morality and are inclined toward living by a different set of moral rules. Psychopathic inmates have no problem following the mores of jail culture. They accept the rules set by those with whom they identify. If the "shot caller" (i.e., the inmate with the most status) on a cell block sets a regulation—for example, morning exercise for all on the block or a contract on an alleged snitch—the compliance rate is quite high. Peter, a psychopathic individual I discuss in detail in a later chapter, was already serving time for a number of serious felonies when he stabbed another inmate to death, an alleged pedophile. It was his duty. That's part of the jailhouse ethic; pedophiles are to be attacked at every opportunity. It's a moral code, albeit unfaithful to traditional norms or higher moral obligations (e.g., "Thou shalt not kill"). It's utilitarian in nature; it's calculated; it's rational and serves one's own best interest, wherein the ends justifies the means.[14] Psychopaths appear to place value in loyalty,[15] albeit when it's serviceable. It's a kind of *practical* moral reasoning found in individuals with psychopathic personalities.[16]

Psychopaths account for about 25 percent of the prison population, whereas antisocial personalities, distinct from the psychopath, account for about 40 percent.[17] That's not a distinction without a difference. Antisocial types are defined more by a history of criminal behavior and impulsiveness, without cold cruelty and interpersonal ruthlessness. Think, for instance, of Randall's Hare Psychopathy Checklist factor score differences; his minimal antisocial factor score yet elevated interpersonal ruthlessness score.

Beyond the prison walls, psychopathy is present in about 1 to possibly 3 percent of the general population of the United States.[18] Where are they? To paraphrase a popular book by Martha Stoud,[19] they're living next door.

Referred to as successful or corporate psychopaths, these individuals are found in the worlds of business, the professions, and in politics.[20] Interestingly, in these domains, the personality traits of self-centeredness, self-assurance, aggressiveness, and even meanness are not infrequently perceived as evidence of self-confidence and are valued as someone who thinks strategically[21] and "get things done." Here, a utilitarian bent is viewed as an asset. A narcissistic executive with a malicious undertone may be viewed as a commanding extrovert with a healthy dose of self-esteem. At least for a while.

It seems clear, then, that psychopathic traits per se do not preclude self-discipline, to think consequentially and get ahead. Many of those with psychopathic traits are capable of functioning well in society, and some have reached its apogee. Some employ their utilitarian sentiments to make cool-headed decisions that are necessary and service the good, whereas many others make cold-hearted, self-serving judgments. Some successful psychopaths break the law. Their behavior accounts for a large portion of white-collar crime.[22] And some become wickedly violent, like Randall. But not all.

The range of behaviors among individuals with psychopathic person-alities—criminal or not—is wide and varied, from the violently criminal to that of the calculating professional. As in any group, it's characterized by diversity of style and nuance of expression, not mechanically predeter-mined as a result of an orderly unfolding biology that corrupts a capacity for moral reasoning. Studies have found successful psychopaths to have above-average moral reasoning and cognitive functioning,[23] the area of the brain that contributes to moral decision making. It takes more than a defect in neuropsychological machinery to undermine moral decision making and propel one into criminally wicked conduct. If not simply a defect in moral reasoning, then what?

***

As I said, Randall fit the successful psychopath model, at least until the time he killed. He clearly has a problem with his moral reasoning, which allowed him to perpetrate such violence toward his wife and child. Like many successful psychopaths, he has a well-functioning brain, with at least an above-average executive ability, given his apparent cunningness and success as a salesman. When we spoke about his relationship with his wife and her death, he blamed Emma for deceiving him and making his life miserable. Then, in an apparent attempt to construct an alibi, he makes a cold, calculating decision to kill his daughter. It's not that his decisions were devoid of a moral reasoning dimension; he employed a self-referential form of darkly deformed utilitarianism.

The psychological testing results tell us something about Randall's cruel logic and decision making. In line with the recent evidence about psychopathy, Randall's Rorschach responses revealed his ability to compartmentalize undesirable information and a proclivity to avoid attending to emotionally laddered stimuli as psychological coping strategies. This is a defining part of his psychological makeup, of his personality. It's as fundamental as his style of reasoning, moral or otherwise. He's protected from the discomfort of facing the full emotional consequences of his actions. Psychopaths know right from wrong, but they're insufficiently motivated to make the moral decision.[24] Disconnected from the emotional press of guilt or remorse that usually drives moral decision making, Randall was free to deceive others, and likely himself. He was free to construct a story he could tell himself, which in part he revealed to me, with themes such as "she made my life miserable," "she deceived me," "she's always talking about death." His ability to morally "miscue" and deflect, combined with a self-serving utilitarianism, led to the killing of his pregnant wife and, likely, his daughter. It allowed him to engage in a thought-out, sustained attempt to cover up his efforts.

A mental illness like schizophrenia doesn't automatically excuse one from criminal conduct, unless the disorder caused derangement and irrationality at the time of the crime. Psychopathy in general—and Randall in this case—showed a capacity for immorality that ranged from everyday deceptions to an unconscionable degree of malignancy. Randall's deficit was selective and circumscribed within the moral domain and emerged from the totality of his personality makeup. His powers of reason weren't defective. They were used in a solipsistic fashion to rationalize away morality. This, it seems to me, reflects a daimonic immorality, not mental illness.

***

All behavior derives from multiple causes, including hard-wired neuro-anatomy, innate temperament, and the quality of early caretaking rela-tionships, to name a few of the important ones. But not one of them is determinative, and biology isn't destiny. A person's entire life history and identity gets processed through the brain and is not of it. The neuroscien-tist Robert Sapolsky, though an advocate of psychopathy as a legally excusing mental disorder, admitted he can't explain why some at neuro-risk don't go down the psychopathic path.[25] From the aerial and abstract scientific perspective of group statistics, it's impossible to see the mé-lange of trees among the forest.[26] Moral decision making and reasoning are emergent from the fruits of a person's unique history and lived experi-ence. The outcome, a personal identity with a unique personality, is to a large extent unpredictable and certainly undetermined, even by biology.

It's likely that many individuals with similar biological makeup to Randall's serve others. The fearlessness and natural boldness that leads to psychopathy in some allows others to employ their nature for ennobling causes. Some enter the high-risk professions.[27] Consider airline pilots and air traffic controllers who have been described as exhibiting a tough poise. It derives from a lower-than-average sentimentality and warmth,[28] likely an emotional system that's similar to many successful psychopaths.

Unfortunately in Randall's case, he embraced the far reaches of his malevolent potential, disavowing his humanity.

7

TILL DEATH DO US PART

All things truly wicked start from innocence.—Ernest Hemingway

I fondly recall listening to Tom Jones sing one of his hit songs, "Delilah," and mingling with friends at a bar or singing along in my car. I was in my twenties, and I loved the name Delilah—it's sexy and exotic. With Tom Jones's deep, powerful voice and the song's pulsating rhythm, I couldn't help but become energized and elevated.

That was before I began my career as a forensic psychologist. Until then, I never *really* paid close attention to the lyrics for "Delilah." Here's a verse: "She stood there laughing / I felt the knife in my hand and she laughed no more."

My innocence, like my youth, is bygone. Now when I hear the song, it evokes all kinds of tragic recollections. Like that of Stu and Nicolette, a couple who had been living together for a year or so in what only could be described as a relationship fated for failure. The police had been called by concerned neighbors on several occasions after hearing yelling and threats. The threats mostly came from a male voice. No domestic violence charges were ever filed. The source of their problems were many: economic, temperamental, and sexual. Nicolette—another sexy name — was in her mid-thirties, previously divorced with no children. According to her younger sister Elizabeth whom I interviewed, Nicolette not only had a sexy name, but a sensual style that instinctively caught the eyes of men. She was funny and feisty. She had a flash temper, but just as quickly she could crack a mischievous smile. I saw photographs of her. She wasn't beautiful, but with her long, reddish-brown hair, soft features, and glittering eyes, I could imagine her attention-grabbing persona. She was taller than average, curvy, and slightly overweight, not the type of body one sees walking the runway at a fashion show. But she had good looks and an attitude that made her desirable. And she was bright and facile with words, skills no doubt honed in her job as a paralegal for a large corporate law firm.

Stu was almost four years younger that Nicolette. He had the California look, with light eyes and blond hair. His sinewy frame made him appear taller than his nearly six-foot height. He was self-employed and ran a small, struggling contracting business. He had a son from a previous relationship, but he didn't have much contact with the boy, who lived out of state with his mother. There was no real attachment between the two. Though he paid child support, Stu resented that it added to his financial difficulties.

At the same time, he felt guilty about his meager involvement with the boy. Stu came from a broken home with a cold, absentee father. Stu and his son's mother were high school sweethearts. She got pregnant not long after their high school graduation. He told himself that he'd be unlike his father. His relationship with the boy's mother quickly crumbled, as did the promise he made to himself.

It was evident that, in most ways, Nicolette and Stu didn't fit well together. She was professional and outgoing by nature. Congenial, spirited, and quick-witted, Nicolette frequently used her skills with language to control conversations or dominate an argument. Her sister Elizabeth clearly implied this to me, adding that Nicolette could be demanding when ramped up.

Stu had the looks that attracted a woman like Nicolette, but the divide between them was great. Her extroversion was matched by his phlegmatic style. Expressing himself with words didn't come naturally to him: he was much more the type to do something to make himself feel better than to talk about it. And he surely wasn't much interested in hearing about Nicolette's law office machinations and gossip. It was an alien world to him. More subtly, though, the vicissitudes of Stu's life had weakened his soul. He had been something of a heartthrob during his high school years, but his social status was short lived, with a premature entrée into the stress and responsibilities of fatherhood. This fate was atop a psyche with the scars common in young men who came of age in a latchkey, fatherless home. His mother was overburdened and financially strapped. She provided as best she could, financially and emotionally.

His youthful looks belied a sense of burden and weariness befitting an older man. By the time I met Stu, he had a languid presence. He projected a passive resignation that was deep and formed long before the homicide. It masked a quiet bitterness and sense of failure.

Elizabeth told me that Nicolette was attracted to Stu because he seemed to be, at least early in their relationship, the "strong silent type." There is, I thought, a softness to Stu's presence, the more positive dimension of his halting approach to life. Over time, it became clearer that he was the brooding type. Stu's emotional repression made him less interested in sex than may have seemed the case from his youth and appearance. This frustrated Nicolette, as her sex appeal was an important part of who she was as a woman. When they argued, she overpowered him with words and logic. As her sister noted, Nicolette could wield language like a spike; her verbal potency struck with great force, greater than Stu could match. He was left to submit, but his brooding would worsen. He'd become more distant and indifferent, which made matters worse. Nicolette would become exasperated.

Stu was outmatched and humiliated. His nonresponsiveness was both defensive and passively offensive. Nicolette in turn was left yearning for something she couldn't get from Stu. She was habitually peeved and occasionally infuriated. Ironically, before the killing, Nicolette was the one whose self-control seemed precarious.

They finally decided to separate. As Stu packed his bags and prepared to leave, an argument erupted in the kitchen. Who knows how it started this time—the last time. As Stu tells it, Nicolette again began berating him for his lack of sexual interest and ability. He couldn't say why, but at that moment, at the end of the relationship, "I lost it." In a New York minute, all the repressed brooding came to a head. Without a memory of reaching for a knife that must have been on the kitchen counter, he stabbed Nicolette in the chest. She collapsed and lay on the floor, motionless. There wasn't much blood, as he recalled, and he didn't remember any sounds, only an oozing grunt from her dying body. His most vivid recollection is of this strong woman collapsing like a rag doll. She was lifeless, lying on the kitchen floor with her eyes open and vacant, her face blank. The taunting was over.

***

Stu was first charged with second-degree murder. The coroner had informed the district attorney's office that the location of Nicolette's chest wound was almost certainly mortal. The prosecutor felt this was evidence that Stu purposely aimed to kill.

At the request of his defense attorney, I conducted an evaluation of Stu that included a detailed personal history and some psychodiagnostic testing. Stu's life was free of violence during his childhood and adolescent years. He had limited criminal history, including a weekend bar fight a few years before he met Nicolette, for which he had accepted a plea of misdemeanor assault. He told me he was just protecting himself but decided to accept the plea because "I just wanted to move on." He had one drug conviction for possession of cocaine when he was nineteen years old.

Stu's psychological vulnerability, his emotional makeup, stemmed from having been raised in a fractured, unsupportive home. Temperamentally, he was passive and prone to mild anxiety in the form of rumination. He was full of self-doubt, which together with his passive temperament made him defensive and caused him to withdraw from conflict. But he didn't have a history of extreme violence.

The psychological testing results were expectable. Stu's responses to the questions in the Personality Assessment Inventory, which I described in an earlier chapter, were straightforward and honest. Clinically, he scored as mildly anxious and depressed, with a doleful personality style. His emotional struggles were long term in duration. There was no evidence for propensity to violence.

I completed the HCR-20,[1] a guide for estimating the potential for violence. It includes twenty items identified by research to be strongly associated with the risk of future violence, such as past violence, personality style, diagnosis, and relationship style. Based on the scoring of those twenty items, an individual is placed within a low-, moderate-, or high-risk group for potential violent behavior.

I concluded that Stu was at the low end of moderate range of risk. He wasn't a characteristically violent person. However, he had an assault charge, a conviction for drug use, as well as limited self-awareness and access to social support networks. Maybe most important, he was burdened with regrets and resentments due to broken relationships, which created a lower tolerance for frustration. And there were the domestic violence calls to the police.

Stu's attorney, John Hennery, asked if I thought my testimony would help jurors lean toward manslaughter rather than second-degree murder. I wasn't sure. Those prior domestic violence calls to the police were problematic, as was his past assault conviction. I had additional concerns; though not a violent individual, Stu had problems managing intense emotions, which made him vulnerable to poor control in close relationships.

Mr. Hennery was in negotiations with the prosecutor, Susan Duncan. She had interviewed Elizabeth, who presented a sympathetic perspective on Stu, even though she was shattered by the death of her sister. Understandably, prosecutors are responsive to the perspectives and wishes of the victim's family members. It was unusual, I'm sure, for Ms. Duncan to hear anything positive about an offender who killed a loved one.

Weeks before the trial was to begin, the district attorney's office decided to offer Stu a plea of low-term, second-degree murder. In this case, Stu would not have to face the possibility of a conviction at trial and a potential life sentence in prison. Ms. Duncan told Mr. Hennery that if he wanted a manslaughter offer for his client, her office would proceed to trial and let a jury decide.

Stu accepted the plea, and the judge signed off on it. He was sentenced to fifteen years in a state prison.

***

Though not exactly straightforward, Stu and Nicolette's tragic ending wasn't as legally or forensically complicated as many murder cases. The same could not be said of the homicide involving Simon and his wife, Joy. After more than forty years of marriage, Simon strangled Joy to death, the result of one of their regular early morning rows. Joy, an alcoholic, was intoxicated, as usual. Simon hadn't slept for days, kept awake by his wife's hectoring.

Strangling the life out of someone is qualitatively different from stabbing someone to death. It takes time to kill with your bare hands, leaving open the question of whether Simon had time to cool down, at least to some degree, and stop the strangulation before death occurred. The prosecution charged Simon with first-degree murder with malice aforethought, meaning with premeditation and deliberation. The precise definitions and times required for deliberation and premeditation can vary depending on the circumstances.[2] A decision to kill can be reached quickly. Did Simon have enough time to stop strangling Joy before she expired but simply decide to keep going? Or was he acting in a moment of rash impulsiveness? Had he thought about killing her beforehand and decided now was the time?

By filing a first-degree murder charge, the district attorney's office had decided the killing was purposeful and not the result of Simon's having been in a highly charged state, which would warrant the less serious charge of voluntary manslaughter. Reducing murder to manslaughter is considered only when the facts indicate that a victim was killed under conditions of extreme provocation such that the killer was in a highly charged state, in the "heat of passion." Just as important, the time between the provocation and killing must be of a limited duration, such that a "reasonable person" would not have had time to "cool off" and regain composure.[3] And simply being enraged isn't enough: it must have been to such a degree that it impaired the killer's ability to exercise everyday reason and forethought.

Simon was facing twenty-five years to life in prison. Already in his early seventies, even a minimal sentence was tantamount to life in prison if convicted.

***

I first interviewed Simon about one week after he was arrested, which occurred on the day of the murder. This was helpful because I got to see his emotional state at a time quite proximate to the killing. In later interviews with his daughter, she described him to me as a "broken man" at the time of the killing. That was apt, and much like my first impression of Simon as he entered the attorney-bonds section of the jail for the interview. In the medical and police reports I had read before meeting him, Simon was described as six feet tall and of average weight. That wasn't my first impression; he looked like he had shed about six inches. Hunched and bony, his tempo slow and hesitant, he struggled to carry the weight of screeching leg irons as he meandered down the hallway toward the interview booth. Finally, he shuffled into the narrow booth. Without me asking, the escorting deputy removed Simon's handcuffs, a signal that he wasn't worried about this murderer's potential for violence. Simon gave his escort a weak smile and a thank-you. His withered frame accentuated a distended torso. He had thin graying hair, unwashed and bedraggled. His jail jumpsuit was soiled. He looked like a lost soul who'd given up.

Simon was on special observation at the jail at the time of our first meeting, meaning he was viewed as a danger to either himself or others: they clearly saw him as a potential danger to himself. He had not yet been prescribed medication.

Belying his age and appearance, Simon's speech was surprisingly rapid, almost like a man "on the move." This struck me as incongruous with his overall weary appearance. It was my first observation of Simon's mood disturbance. During later interviews, he was prescribed mood-stabilizing medications. But now I was able to observe his mental condition as it was around the time of the killing.

During that first visit, he was not psychotic. Simon had no auditory or visual hallucinations, nor did he have any crazy delusions. He was "revved up" and on edge, he said, from the constant background noise that's part of life in jail. Though edgy, he was easy to interview. He told me he felt calmer than he'd felt in months, maybe years. He was sleeping better and eating well. He didn't understand why the psychiatrist placed him on observation, as he was not suicidal. He felt his concentration had improved, maybe because he was sleeping again. His thinking was clear and organized with no hint of psychosis. He later was prescribed Prozac, an antidepressant, and Zyprexa, an antipsychotic that's also used for patients with agitation.

Although weakened and edgy, there was a strangely peaceful quality to Simon's demeanor. His smile was soft, and his brown eyes were active, as though he was enjoying taking in what he could, even encaged in his new quarters. There was a touch of mirthfulness. "I'm the old man in here," he smirked.

As the interview progressed, I began the process of readjusting my first impression of Simon as "broken." Maybe what I was faced with was a man who had been psychologically crumbling for a long time but was now relieved. Perhaps he hadn't given up, and his bedraggled demeanor was the upshot of a sense of relief, a letting go of a weight he'd been carrying for a long time.

As usual, I began the examination process by asking Simon about his life and his past and giving him time to get a feel for me. In most ways,

Simon's personal history was quite unremarkable and normal. He was raised in a traditional family in North Carolina that included his parents and three older brothers. His mother stayed at home and his father worked as an executive in an engineering firm. He recalled a happy childhood, albeit with some persistent but low-grade anxiety. It wasn't incapacitating or even recognized as a problem at the time. Simon was easily distracted at school, but again it didn't create academic or behavioral problems for him. He generally did well in school and attended college, studying engineering. He graduated with a degree in electrical engineering but lost interest in the field. He realized that there was more money in sales and management, which is the direction he took and the areas where he spent most of his professional career. He had been retired for years at the time of the killing.

Simon had no prior run-ins with the law. He was free of past episodes of aggression that would portend a potential for eruptive violence. He never used illicit drugs, not even in high school or college. For many of his employment years, he drank, but in his early years, at least, he didn't abuse alcohol. Although he began drinking during his college years, it was never a problem. He seemed proud of never having received a DUI, as did several of his friends. As time went on, with the traveling, business dinners, and late-night socializing on the road with clients and colleagues, his alcohol consumption increased and eventually turned into a major problem.

It eventually infected his wife, Joy, as well.

Simon was without mental health problems until his forties. "It came out of the blue." After an unusually long business trip, he returned home in a full-blown manic episode. Announcing to the family that he had the divine spirit, "I told them I was gonna dictate the Bible." He was briefly hospitalized and diagnosed with a manic episode and late-onset bipolar disorder. He eventually came to understand that he had had manic-like symptoms (technically, hypomania) most of his adult life. But at that point it was a shock "to be so nuts. And the Bible . . . I'm agnostic!"

He couldn't recall the medications prescribed at the hospital. In any case, he did not follow up with treatment. But Simon's awareness was heightened, and he and Joy recognized the need to watch for a reoccurrence of his mania. Eventually, his children assumed the role of monitoring and informing him of any manic-like behavior. Interestingly, he had not received standard treatment for his mood disturbance until after his arrest. He continued to view it as an insignificant factor in his life.

During my subsequent interviews with Simon, we explored his marriage and relationship with Joy. They met on a blind date and dated for about two years before their marriage. Early on, when raising their children, the marriage was quite good, Simon recalled. But when the kids went off to college, "We were looking at each other, not the kids." In retrospect, he realized they had grown apart and were very different. Simon was introverted and Joy more social, with lots of friends. This created tension that became apparent after he retired and they were home together for long stretches of time. He didn't want to socialize the way she did. They solved the dilemma by drinking together. With the perspective of hindsight, Simon realized how his career, with its demands and travel requirements, helped to inoculate them from the limitations of the marriage.

It was after his retirement that they began using alcohol heavily together. By then, Simon had been drinking heavily for years, but when on the road, not so much at home. He didn't view his drinking as a problem. It was almost a job requirement. Joy had been no more than a social drinker until that point.

Several years into his retirement, Simon and Joy were both alcoholics, Simon said. For a while, their routine was to begin having cocktails sometime after 3:00 p.m. Over time, they gave each other the green light to start drinking earlier and earlier. Their drinking got so bad that it ruptured their relationship with their two children and grandchildren. Simon was especially close to his daughter, who refused to visit after one especially nasty exchange between him and Joy. It transpired in front of their daughter Martha's two kids. John, the youngest of his children, soon followed suit.

About five years before the homicide, Simon and Joy both decided to stop drinking. They sought treatment at a local hospital but were told they didn't meet the requirements for an inpatient hospitalization. The facility recommended its outpatient treatment program. They decided to seek consultation with an addiction specialist instead. He prescribed antianxiety and sleep medications to help them decrease their drinking. He recommended Alcoholics Anonymous.

Simon was serious about discontinuing his drinking, realizing it was destroying his relationship with his children and grandchildren. Joy didn't feel the same urgency. She never stopped drinking. At this point in the interview, Simon's demeanor altered; he appeared to be drifting into a painful place. Looking away, he shifted a little and folded his hands. His face tensed, a reaction to disturbing private thoughts. After a few moments, he looked up and confessed, "I caused Joy's alcoholism. I introduced her to drinking." She had never been a heavy drinker until the later years after his retirement. And he was the one who began the routine of drinking every evening. He was able to stop with the help of occasional AA meetings and contact with his sponsor. What motivated him most was a strong desire to reconnect with his children. Though he spoke to Martha regularly and John occasionally, both refused to visit with the grandchildren. With his sobriety, the situation improved somewhat. The children began to visit for brief periods during the day, sometimes with the grandchildren. Joy would not drink before or during Martha's or John's visits. Simon was especially grateful for the increased contact with Martha. They had had a special bond since her childhood.

Reestablishing the psychological bonds with both children helped enormously, he said.

Joy continued to drink heavily, more so as time went on.

By the time of the homicide, Joy was completely estranged from the kids and "raging at me" most of the time. The children used Simon's cellphone to keep in contact, never the house's phone. "They didn't want to talk to their mother."

Simon recommended I speak to his children. "They could fill you in on the family issues." I agreed. But next, I told him, we'd delve into the circumstances of Joy's death, and he would be completing a number of psychological tests. "Okay," he responded.

I ended the interview with the impression that Simon was someone who had nothing to hide, no masked motivations. My sense was that he had no agenda other than to answer my questions and to describe the circumstances of his family life and marriage. I hoped his candor and openness continued when we explored his antipathy and state of mind on the day he strangled Joy to death with his bare hands.

**

Joy started drinking about 3:00 p.m. on the day she died. Her routine was to imbibe all night and sleep the day away. On the last full day of her life,

"She was in the worst place I have ever seen her," Simon said. He had been working on their finances after having suffered a loss on an apartment investment. He hadn't paid the previous year's taxes, hoping to be able to pay the current year from extra income derived from the investment that ultimately failed. He felt stressed and trapped; he couldn't come up with a solution to his financial dilemma. Joy had been nagging him for months to "deal with the tax situation." Now, late in the afternoon, "She's berating me for my stupid decisions" regarding their finances. She followed up with a litany of additional failures. "You never complete anything," like painting the bedroom or renewing his driver's license. Simon admitted these were accurate and true criticisms, but he was chronically distracted and fatigued "by her . . . drinking . . . her tirades."

Joy repeatedly called him a "stupid fucking asshole" for causing them financial woes. Simon described her as being in "an alcoholic rage. . . . [S]he almost attacked me physically. . . . [It] went on and on . . . the worst ever." At one point, she walked down the stairs, took the photograph of their two children from the wall, and threw it down the stairs. Though furious, he said to her, "Let's stop this." He continued to monitor her to make sure she did not fall and injure herself as she had done in the past.

It wasn't difficult to keep an eye on her. "She was following me around in a rampage." All this was happening, he related, while he had been in a sleep-deprived state for at least a month, kept up by Joy and his ruminations about financial worries. During the week before the killing, "I was totally exhausted, emotionally and physically."

After beginning her early afternoons drinking, Joy became increasingly irritable and talkative. This had been their pattern for years. The only time he got adequate sleep, Simon said, was when Joy was briefly hospitalized for one reason or another. During the last five years, she had been detoxed in a hospital on multiple occasions, only to be released and to continue her drinking.

The month or so before the homicide, Simon noticed that Joy's drinking had gotten worse. Maybe, he thought, because of concern about their finances.

Joy's drinking pattern was the same on the evening of the killing, only worse. She was consuming more than her usual amount of Jack Daniel's. She "latched on to the financial problem . . . stalked me all night," provoking a fight, complaining, and threatening.

The killing occurred about 1:30 a.m. Simon recalled making an at-tempt to sleep at about midnight after leaving Joy in the downstairs living room. She had been "raging at me" and blasting the TV, one of her standard evening badgering tactics. It was, Simon said, her way of con-veying bitterness and anger when she was intoxicated. He had lowered the volume on the TV before going to bed.

She followed him upstairs but not before ensuring the TV's volume was again thundering. She entered their master bedroom shrieking. Si-mon left the bedroom and went to the guest bedroom. "I was just trying to get some sleep. Joy followed me around in a rampage," raging and using a variety of expletives to describe his character.

It was in the guest bedroom where the killing occurred. As he turned down the spread, Joy continued screeching expletives. The TV was thundering. "I went into a manic panic," Simon said. He grabbed her by the neck and began strangling her. "I was out of my mind. My head went berserk." He went on. "I was a lizard brain. I grabbed her; she was in front of me. . . . It was like an insane explosion in my head. I lost it . . . lost complete control of everything I was doing." I asked what he was thinking as he was strangling her. Simon couldn't say, nor could he say how long it took to strangle her. He had no thoughts or conception of time. Thoughts "were beyond. I was like a zombie."

I asked Simon if he had had it with Joy and at that point wanted her dead. He said he did not. "It took me about five or six hours to absorb it, what happened," that he had killed his wife. He wasn't sure if he slept or roamed around the house. Before being able to face the dark reality, he picked Joy up and laid her on the bed. He kept looking at her, as though she were about to wake up. He had thoughts like, "Maybe it's a dream; I don't know. My wife is dead? I strangled her? What am I going to do?" He considered killing himself to end the dread and fear. Simon said to me, "I just wanted the yelling, the screaming, throwing things to stop."

When daylight arrived, Simon decided to leave the house. He couldn't say why. If he had had a gun available, he would have shot himself. He got in his car and started driving. He thought about walking in front of a train, hanging or cutting himself. Which of his children should he call? He decided to call Martha, "the supportive one."

Sitting in his car beside a nearby park where he and Joy sometimes took walks together, he texted Martha, who was at work, and asked her to call. A short time later, she called and he told her what he had done. At first, she didn't believe him, thinking maybe Joy was just sleeping. She asked if he had begun drinking again. After he convinced her that her mother was dead, Simon told her he was going to kill himself. She pleaded with him not to and talked him into calling 911, which he did. He was told to go back to his house. As he approached the house, he saw multiple police cars.

Simon was arrested and interviewed immediately after the killing. I watched a video of that interview. The detectives repeatedly asked what was going through his mind at the time. At one point, he told them that when he strangled Joy he thought "I was doing her a favor." I asked what he meant by that statement. He couldn't remember making it. He was in a state of numbness at the time of the interview. As we talked about his state of mind during the killing, he commented, "I just wanted to get rid of the demons. I didn't want to kill my wife."

I asked Simon why he didn't leave his wife if he felt so berated and harassed by her for so many years. He responded by first recalling that he and his wife went to marriage counseling about six months before the killing. After several marital sessions, the therapist met with Simon individually and recommended he divorce Joy because she was an untreatable alcoholic. Her last detox has been about two or three weeks before the killing. Simon took her to the hospital after she had a mild fender bender while going to buy more liquor. "She was on a bender and out of Jack Daniel's. I wouldn't get it for her." He thought about leaving. "I couldn't do it. I had to take care of her." They were married for forty years. He always felt that marriage was forever.

***

With Simon's advancing age, his history of bipolar illness, and his past alcoholism, I thought it best to perform a neuropsychological evaluation. I administered the Repeatable Battery for the Assessment of Neuropsychological Status.[4] It's a brief measure used with older people that assesses a broad range of cognitive tasks. It's less demanding and time intensive than the more comprehensive neuropsychological measures, which can be taxing, particularly for the elderly. Simon was average to above average within all domains, including memory, language, attention, and visuospatial ability.

Simon completed tests to detect symptom distortion as well as forms of social desirability, including the Paulhus Deception Scales and Structured Inventory of Malingered Symptomology, instruments that I described in earlier chapters. His scores provided evidence that he was responding honestly to the questions.

Because he had been under acute stress for a long period before his arrest, Simon completed the Trauma Stress Inventory.[5] It's designed to evaluate acute and chronic symptoms of trauma, including the effects of early and late onset trauma. The validity scores fell within the normal range, suggesting that Simon answered the test items in a forthright manner. His clinical scales indicated he was experiencing feelings of sadness with a sense of hopelessness and diminished self-esteem. They also showed that he tended to be relatively unaware of his needs and feelings and to view the priorities of others as more immediately relevant than his own. This fit with his description of his marital relationship. The overall results were not consistent with someone suffering from a posttraumatic stress disorder.

He also completed the Personality Assessment Inventory, another instrument I have previously described. The results revealed Simon's thought processing was likely marked by episodes of confusion, distractibility, and difficulty concentrating with transient depressive symptoms and possibly a hypomanic tendency.

***

Simon's daughter Martha was eager to meet with me. She and Simon were quite close. They had been speaking regularly during her lunch hour two to three times a week, usually commiserating about her mother's alcoholic behavior. Martha wanted me to know she had had a happy childhood. The problems with her parents began most intensely some years previously, after her mother's drinking became extreme. For a period of time, she refused to visit or take her children to their house; during the year or so before the killing, she'd visit occasionally and briefly without her kids.

She did not recall either parent having alcohol problems or any major marital difficulties during her childhood. Martha described her father as always being "protective" with a good business sense. Her mother was social but emotionally cold, never abusive, during the early years.

Martha noticed her father changing as her mother's drinking became a problem. By the time of Joy's death, "My dad was a shell of a man physically and emotionally." During a visit not long before the homicide, "I was shocked beyond shock to see his physical state. He wasn't the man I grew up with." He was frail and "gray looking."

Several days prior to the killing was the last time she visited her parents, Martha said. She received a telephone call from her father. "Your mother is going crazy. . . . [S]he's berating me." By the time she got over to visit, it was late afternoon and her mother was sleeping. She calmed her father down and left. Martha then described another incident that had occurred a week or so before. Again, she received a phone call from her father, who said that Joy was "raging . . . throwing pictures on the floor and out of control." She counseled her father to call 911, which he did. Joy was taken to a medical hospital when the paramedics found her frail and likely in alcohol toxicity.

Martha left work and went to the hospital. She found her mother in bed with a nurse and her father in attendance. Simon poured a glass of water and gave it to her mother. "My mother threw the glass of water in my dad's face. He just tolerated it." He stared at the floor, looking totally ashamed and humiliated.

On the day of the killing, Martha received a text from her father: "Call me." She texted back, saying she was in a meeting but would call as soon as she could. He texted her back, "Urgent. Call ASAP." When she did, "My dad sounded completely destroyed." His voice had a "confusing tone." His breathing was deep and strained. "Something terrible happened. . . . [Y]our mother is dead. He sounded mentally lost, in shock," Martha said. Simon repeated, "Your mother is dead. I did it."

At first, Martha couldn't believe it, telling him that Joy must have died in her sleep. He said, "No, she didn't. I choked her out. . . . I lost it." He said he was "getting up the gumption to kill myself." By now, Martha was shaking. She still could not believe he had killed her mother. He began crying. "What have I done? I ruined the lives of myself, my wife, my children, my grandchildren." She pleaded with him to call 911. He said he would and hung up. Moments later, he called back and said he was on his way back to the house. By the time Martha got there, he was handcuffed and sitting in the backseat of a police car.

At the end of the interview, Martha told me, "One hundred percent of my life, this human being was such a gentle person. This doesn't make sense. He had a complete breakdown."

Martha brought a copy of her father's diary, which she had found in his home office. He apparently had begun writing it about two years before the killing. After the interview, I perused it.

It included this couplet composed for his wife written three months earlier:

I love you
I will never leave you.
No matter what
Till death do us part

**

When retained by his defense attorney, I was asked to appraise the possibility of insanity as a viable defense. Simon was charged with first-degree murder with premeditation and deliberation. The attorney wondered if his client's untreated bipolar disorder might have caused him to lose touch with reality and not know what he was doing when he strangled Joy.

**

After completing my evaluation, I met with Simon's lawyer and paralegal. I told them that I did not think Simon was insane at the time of the murder. He was not psychotic or unaware of its wrongfulness. During the period of time it took to strangle Joy, he had lost control of his emotions and was in a rage-reaction state. He acted impulsively without any reflection but not with a psychotic, irrational state of mind. He had bipolar disorder, but I didn't see it as a prime mover of the killing.

In my opinion, Joy's homicide resulted from grinding marital discord, her alcoholism, her verbal and sometimes physical abuse of Simon, and Simon's unwillingness or inability to separate from Joy. It left him helpless, emotionally depleted, and humiliated. As an example, I described the water glass incident at the hospital, which happened not long before the killing. It all climaxed in an uncharacteristic and sudden eruption of deadly violence.

They asked if, based on my findings, I thought manslaughter was a reasonable alternative. I believed that voluntary manslaughter was a fair charge given the evidence. Simon had no criminal history, no prior history of violence, and was not an abusive husband. He was credible in his assertion of devotion to his wife, even in the face of her alcoholism and her intense belittlement and hostility. Martha spoke of her father as loving and responsible throughout most of her life, who transformed in later years due to her mother's alcoholism and their toxic and symbiotic marriage. Ironically, his unyielding commitment to the marriage, together with her relentless assaults, his chronic sleeplessness, and his untreated bipolar disorder were ingredients that led to a lethal paroxysm. His daughter confirmed all of it. Both children continued to support their father. The charge of voluntary manslaughter made sense to me.

Nevertheless, I left the meeting thinking that negotiations with the district attorney's office would be a dicey affair. By charging Simon with first-degree murder, the prosecutor, at least early on, was claiming that Simon had killed Joy with intentionality, premeditation, and deliberation. His wife's destructive alcoholic behavior could be seen as evidence of a desire for revenge that had been brewing for a period of time until he took it into his own hands and exacted it.

To be guilty of premeditation and deliberation would have required Simon to have engaged in preexisting reflection and weighted consideration before he decided to kill. I felt assured that Simon hadn't harbored a secret desire to kill Joy. Resentment, yes: Simon was embittered by her abusiveness and treatment of him. Their marriage was in trouble, but so are many. However, their challenges were more intractable and weightier than most. Simon was relentlessly under strain and attack yet tied to their source, Joy. From all the evidence, it seemed to me that until the end he exercised a fraught restraint and devotion to her. Until he didn't.

There was another possible rub. Since the law doesn't require a specific time period between the considered reflection and death, the prosecutor possibly believed that Simon had time during the strangulation period to disrupt his murderous behavior. Such an assertion seemed a bridge too far to walk. It took some time to kill, but by then his thinking and reflective abilities were themselves on life support. He had some measure of culpable intent but not with a premeditated or deliberate facility. His was an intensely emotional reaction. At that point, with his psychological resources depleted, the emotional pull was primal.

***

At the preliminary hearings, Simon's children testified in support of their father. After the hearings and after interviewing others, reading police and court documents, and my evaluation, the district attorney's office agreed to drop the charge from murder to voluntary manslaughter. I suspect that the evidence, including Simon's nonviolent past, his devotion to his wife and marriage—albeit dysfunctional—and particularly the testimony of his children formed the basis of the decision. This was a decent man who had been pushed beyond his limit.

***

Surprisingly, the manslaughter statute doesn't stir a public hue and cry like the insanity defense, which has been mocked as a "get out of jail free card."[6] I would think the consequences of a manslaughter conviction—what the law considers to be just deserts—could create a fuss. After having *intentionally killed* another human being, a nonpsychotic defendant may be sentenced to as little as three years in state prison. Why such a light punishment for someone who purposefully took a life, regardless of the circumstances? Why such a difference in public opinion from the insanity statute? Maybe it's because manslaughter is only partially excusing; the defendant is found guilty of a crime, mitigated from murder. Or maybe it's easier to put oneself in the shoes of somebody who loses emotional control, to identify with that kind of emotional reaction. To understand craziness is less comprehendible. And threatening.

The manslaughter defense does stir controversy in legal circles surrounding the issue of gender.[7] The defense was first established in English common law, a response to the practice of agreed-upon mutual combat by two men, with one or the other declaring a need to defend his honor.[8] The confrontations frequently left one man dead. The killing was intentional, but from a need to defend one's manliness, not out of malice. Though still blameworthy, a manslaughter charge offered a partially excusing alternative to murder. Then and now, it's referred to by the evocative monikers of "heat of passion" or "heat of blood."

The manslaughter statute was later extended to persons who witnessed a spouse committing adultery. Over the years, the law expanded further to include situations in which a reasonable person's passions were inflamed to the point of homicidal fury. The paradigmatic case involves a man who finds his wife in bed with her paramour. Indeed, the doctrine is almost exclusively best suited for men who kill their cheating spouses or paramours.[9] And men kill at much higher rates than women[10] under all kinds of impassioned conditions.

The statute doesn't fit well in situations common to women who kill their husbands after having endured repeated episodes of physical abuse and violence. Frequently, the act occurs in the aftermath of a "cool-down period,"[11] not during moments of abuse. Battered women who kill their abusers often claim self-defense strategy or employ the battered syndrome as a partial excuse (mitigation) for murder.[12] If viewed as being akin to revenge killing, it is legally and morally inexcusable.

What does contemporary science have to say about intense emotions and their regulation? A consistent finding is that all emotions, including anger and fear, continue to fester long after the provoking event.[13] In fact, intense emotions tend to increase over time until a behaviorally relieving discharge occurs.[14] Anger leads to an urgency to take action. Fear is disorganizing and typically leads to avoidance. Anger prompts an automatic sense of confidence, whereas fear triggers uncertainty and helplessness. Besides the emotion reactions, provocation disrupts the accurate appraisal of one's situation as well.[15] It interferes with judgment, reason, and rational decision making.

I focus on anger and fear because they're the most frequent underlying emotions that prompt reactive violence in men and women, respectively. The manslaughter statute takes into account a "heat of blood"–type response more likely to favor men. A woman who had been living with a sense of terror, powerlessness, and accompanying shame is dishonored much like the men for whom the manslaughter law was first devised. Lenore Walker, a leading authority on battered woman syndrome, emphasizes the helplessness of women who are abused and kill.[16] Humiliation and shame, chronic fear, and helplessness are all preambles to rage.[17] In the domestic violence context women find themselves, their emotional reactions are implicit and vaguely conscious at first. Over time, as these sensations become processed and felt, a collage of painful sentiments are recognized, including rage and indignation about having been mistreated and oppressed. Such a slowly mounting yet chronic hurt eventually erodes emotional stability as well as normal decision-making and reasoning abilities. And it creates a need to act. It's a different kind of "heat of blood," more protracted and gradual in the making. Percolating over time, it's without well-defined heating-up or cooling-down periods. Until it pops—which is likely sometime after another episode of abuse and humiliation. It's a reactive violence, not unlike that of a man catching his wife in bed with another.

With the manslaughter statute, the justice system has long acknowledged the brittleness of human beings. Contemporary science and scholarship have revealed the latent emotions that fester beyond an apparent cooling-down period, which may lead to violence. Emotional reactions are likely among women who are abused and kill. Even those with normal dispositions, both men and women, are capable of perpetrating acts of horrendous violence. As far back as 1862, this vulnerability has been legally recognized:

> [I]f the act of killing, though intentional . . . by which the control of reason was disturbed, rather than of any wickedness of heart or cruelty or recklessness of disposition; then the law, out of indulgence to the frailty of human nature, or rather, in recognition of the laws upon which human nature is constituted, very properly regards the offense as of a less heinous character than murder[18]

It's the law's implicit nod to humankind's potential for destructive violence that runs astride basic goodness.[19]

8

BABY KILLER

And I'm a woman made of sorrow.—Euripides, *Medea*

Unfailingly, my dentist is upbeat when he greets me. I usually reserve the earliest appointment. Then there's still time available to race over to the jail, complete a forensic evaluation, and eat something, all before my afternoon sessions with private patients begin. Always kinetic and more than ready for the day, Dr. Sorey can be heard commenting something or whistling as he enters the room to examine me. With a sonorous "Good morning," he greets me with a big smile and a funny comment about my appearance. I'm usually dressed professionally, wearing a tie. "Isn't he looking sharp, Isabelle?" he says to his assistant. "So, what's new?" he asks as he snaps on a pair of purple surgical gloves and begins his inspection of my oral cavity. I'm already antsy.

For at least the last ten years, Dr. Sorey has worn surgical garb as his professional attire. And, as usual, he comments on its sartorial comfort. That's why he's gotten chunky over the years, I think to myself. He's *too* comfortable. Every haven has its cost.

Dr. Sorey's cheerfulness doesn't seem forced at all. I appreciate it, especially so early in the morning. At this appointment, he surprised me with a question. "How do you cope," he asked, "with counseling emotionally distressed patients if you're in a depressed or cranky mood?" He mused that when out of sorts, he is simply quiet and does his work; it's technical and doesn't demand much emotional investment. I was startled by the question. In the twenty or more years he's been my dentist, Dr. Sorey has never been in a sour mood that was apparent to this patient.

Ever the psychoanalyst, I wondered if the question revealed a greater attunement to my mood than I imagined. I happened to be in one of my depressed states that morning. I didn't think it was obvious. I greeted his staff warmly. Dr. Sorey and I engaged in our usual small talk. I didn't think my dark mood was apparent, as I'm skilled by now at camouflaging it when necessary.

If I had to, I could identify a particular reason to make sense of my gloom—a professional disappointment, an argument with my wife or a colleague, politics. I could even draw on my deceased parents and come up with something about my childhood to account for it. But I know that would be mostly a fiction. I know it's something more complicated or, as analysts say, something that's "overdetermined"; it has many and varied roots, psychological and temperamental. It's always been a part of me. During those carefree summer months of childhood when there wasn't very much to worry about or do in south Brooklyn but to play stickball and hang out with friends, the clouds would lurk sometimes. I'd sport a pair of sunglasses, an effort to look cool. If I were too close to the "mood," the shades made it worse, dimming more than the summer sun. Looking cool wasn't worth it. I didn't understand what I was feeling until years later when, in treatment, my analyst commented during one of our sessions, "You were a depressed little boy." Now it seems so obvious.

Was Dr. Sorey more aware of me than I had thought? No, I concluded; he was just chattering away as he probed and prodded.

I decided not to keep my forensic appointment at the jail that morning. My mood was too distracting. This was an evaluation that was going to be difficult and required my full presence.

***

I was to begin an evaluation of a mother who had killed her ten-month-old daughter in an apparent psychotic state. The presiding judge agreed with defense attorneys that an insanity evaluation was in order. He appointed two experts, one selected by the defense, one by the prosecution. I was the defense team's selection. These evaluations are difficult to conduct, professionally and emotionally. I needed to be emotionally present and without distraction.

That morning, I was emotionally off. It was still early when I left Dr. Sorey's office and I already felt debilitated. Not crippled, but not sturdy enough to begin my first encounter with Janice, the baby killer. On my way to the office, I stopped at Starbucks for a cup of coffee. Although Dr. Sorey told me not to drink any hot liquids for an hour, I needed it. That morning, I did paperwork and report editing and prepared for my afternoon's private appointments.

It's not a problem to conduct private sessions with my psychoanalytic patients when I'm in my dark mood. This is especially true of those with whom I already have an emotional tie and have worked with for a while. It's often helpful. I'm almost never despondent, joyless, or apathetic. I've never needed medications. It is more of a dark ache that comes and eventually goes, pain that I cope with. As a psychoanalyst, I work with patients who have long-term, subtle emotional tics and psychic pains. The roots of these sorts of conditions are many and difficult to identify. It's helpful to be a kindred spirit, someone who has dwelled in a similar space. I viscerally empathize with such emotional quagmires. It may indeed be an asset, if not a requirement, to conducting long-term, intensive therapy. That's why psychoanalysts tend to be brooding, depressed types. Who else could or would choose to investigate another's nameless emotional hurt and do so with hope. It comes from a shared pain and commitment to transcending it.

I've noticed this type of brooding identification and commitment to the troubled in some criminal attorneys, more so than in the civil lawyers I've known. To work within the criminal domain requires a tolerance for and some familiarity with a life hewing toward the shadows.

***

After a day and a half of deliberations following the insanity phase of the trial, Janice, the baby killer, was found guilty of first-degree murder, meaning that she intentionally killed her ten-month-old daughter Kimberly. During the trial, the prosecutor argued persuasively that she killed her daughter to get even with her husband. The jurors reached the conclusion that Janice was sane, even after two experts—including the prosecution's own expert—opined that she was insane. Two jail psychiatrists who examined her when she was first taken into custody also testified that she was psychotic.

***

Early one October morning, just as the sun was breaking through, a 911 dispatcher took a call from a frantic woman. "I just stabbed my daughter." I listened to a recording of the call. The dispatcher sounded incredulous. "You did what?" "My daughter," Janice responded. The dispatcher asked, "Okay, with what?" "A knife. *Please*," Janice squealed, "help."

The dispatcher couldn't seem to take in the gravity of what had just happened, which was striking to me. She must have taken many life-threatening calls. This one set her back. She asked Janice several times, "Do you need the paramedics?" "Of course!" Janice screamed. What seemed like a cry of desperation and terror by Janice was later framed in court as evidence of her rage and revenge and as the motive behind the killing.

The dispatcher lost the call. Reconnecting, she told Janice that the paramedics were on their way. Having found her emotional footing, she continued talking to Janice, trying to keep her calm. She asked about the baby's age and name. I could hear the approaching police sirens in the background followed by commands like "Get on the ground!" The phone call ended.

Kimberly was dead before she arrived at the hospital. She could not have survived a penetrating stab wound to the chest. Janice had multiple self-inflicted stab wounds, including deep slashes to her chest. She underwent emergency surgery. It was a week after the infanticide before she was stable enough to be fully interviewed by the police at the hospital.

Janice was interviewed briefly by a deputy sheriff in the ambulance while on the way to the hospital. As she went in and out of consciousness, the deputy asked her questions seemingly designed to establish her guilty state of mind. "You stabbed her, right?" A moment later, "You knew it was wrong, right?" She was either unresponsive or off topic, mumbling something about her husband Richard. "I begged him," she said. The deputy, "So you were mad at him?" After being asked that question several times, Janice momentarily perked up in frustration and blurted out, "Are you listening?" though she hadn't said anything informative. Most of her responses were inaudible or nonsensical. This, it seemed, was the result of her critical condition and psychological disorientation.

Lucid during the hospital interview after her surgery, Janice told the detectives that early the morning of the stabbing, she woke up and went to the kitchen for a glass of water. "I had scary thoughts. . . . Richard was taking my daughter away." The detective repeatedly returned to the moment of the stabbing. Janice recalled being scared and looking at the knife. She illogically responded, "I was thinking . . . young people. . . ."

"What about the knife?" the detective asked. Janice replied, "I didn't want to hurt my baby. I wanted to save my family. . . . [H]e was torturing us." When asked if she stabbed Kimberly to get even with Richard, Janice reacted, "God, no. He wanted it this way. I begged him."

The detective asked about her marital relationship. Janice's replies were contradictory, confusing—and bizarre: "I heard him threaten to put me six feet under. . . . [H]e was gonna hurt me and my baby." A few moments later, "Richard never tried to hurt me." She repeated several times throughout the interview that Richard wanted to take Kimberly away from her.

Janice didn't have any idea how many times she had stabbed the child (once). She had no recall of stabbing herself. At the end of the interview, the detective asked Janice what she would say to a family member about what had happened. Cryptically, she said, "He knew. . . . [H]e knew exactly what my next move was. He knew everything." "Who?" asked the detective. "Richard," she replied.

A week after Kimberly's death, Janice was still hospitalized. The district attorney's office sought her discharge and transfer to the women's jail. The attending psychiatrist at the hospital interviewed Janice and recommended she be placed on a three-day hold for further evaluation. She was psychiatrically unstable and a suicide risk. The police officers at the hospital were adamant; she needed to be in jail. They told the doctor she would be placed in a mental health unit and closely monitored. He acquiesced and wrote the discharge order.

***

Before examining Janice, I reviewed the extensive police and medical reports and interviewed family members.

I first met with Richard, Janice's husband. I wasn't sure he would agree, but Rob Flores, Janice's lawyer, arranged it. Richard greeted me with a sad, soft smile. In his mid-forties, he came to my office from the warehouse where he had completed a double shift. Usually, he works the 4:00 p.m. to midnight shift. He had finished work that morning at 8:00

a.m. and came straight to the interview. He looked emotionally and physically spent. For good reasons, I thought.

He and Janice had been married for about four years. They had known
each other for about seven and lived together in San Francisco for about
two years. Their mutual problems got in the way. He had a drug problem:
"I used meth." And a lot of marijuana. He wouldn't come home some
nights and admitted to several affairs. Janice never used street drugs; her
issues were "unstable emotions. She was okay and happy one day,
then . . . irritable and sad." His drug use made matters worse. When he
didn't come home, she'd surmise he was with a woman. "She would
scream at me. But she never got violent. Not really. Nothing serious,
maybe a few punches in the arm. That's all." Because of her petite size,
she was harmless. The police were called on a few occasions, but neither
was ever arrested. "She was overly emotional, but I made it worse."

Janice decided to leave Richard and move back to southern California
where she had been raised to be closer to her family. Within a year,
Richard entered a drug treatment program. They eventually reconnected,
first over the phone, followed by occasional weekends together. He decided to move to southern California to be closer to her.

Richard hadn't used drugs for more than four years, he said. Janice
continued to be her unstable self but less so than before they reunited.
Until it worsened about six months before the stabbing. Not long after the
birth of Kimberly, Janice's grandmother died unexpectedly of a heart
attack. Having been raised by her grandmother since the age of three,
Janice was devastated by the loss. During Janice's toddler years, her
father had been sent to prison for reasons that were unclear. Sometime
afterward, her mother, a drug abuser, "dropped Janice off at her mother's
and left. Janice really loved her grandmother like a mother." Before her
grandmother's death, Janice talked with her almost every day, even during the years when she lived in San Francisco.

Given the problems with her mood, Richard worried about a postpartum reaction, which didn't happen, he said. But Janice became very depressed after her grandmother's death. At first, he figured it was "normal
grief." Until she became "really depressed. It was weird, even for Janice."
After caring for the baby, she went back to bed, regardless of the time of
day. She didn't want to talk much. Always on the thin side and never a
good eater, she now was looking sapped from not eating. Though never
having voiced suicidal thoughts, she told Richard that Kimberly would be

better off if she weren't around. "I told her that's not true." In the past, she was more like a "split personality," wavering between being angry and irritated or depressed, especially after arguments. This was different.

Though she continued to respond to the baby, Richard became concerned about leaving Kimberly with Janice in the evening when he left for work. He asked her cousin Phyllis to stay with Janice some evenings when she seemed especially fragile. Phyllis told Richard that, despite her problems, Janice was always good with the baby.

Janice continued to deteriorate, Richard said. About two or three weeks before the killing, he got a call from Phyllis. She was at a hospital emergency room. Janice had called 911, terrified, saying, "*Something* was in my house." Paranoid, she claimed that spiritual forces were about to harm her and her baby. The police arrived, interviewed Janice, and took her to a local hospital to be psychiatrically examined. They got Phyllis's number from Janice and asked her to come and take the baby.

The doctors told Richard that his wife had experienced a psychotic break and needed psychiatric care. Janice asked a nurse, "Are you gonna kill me slowly?" She was released after several hours in the ER. That night, Richard woke up to Janice cursing and screaming, "Get out!" The following day, he took Janice to their family physician. The doctor told Richard that she was depressed. She believed their house was haunted by demons. She denied suicidal thoughts. He prescribed Lexapro, an antidepressant, and gave Richard a psychiatric referral.

Richard's parents offered to come down from northern California and stay for a while, but Janice refused. His mother called and spoke with Janice. Alarmed, she soon called Richard, saying Janice sounded "incoherent . . . irrational." When he arrived home, he found Janice crouched in the bedroom closet crying. Janice refused to consult with a psychiatrist, though she agreed to take the antidepressant medication.

The day before the stabbing, Richard was concerned. He overheard a call Janice made to the local Catholic church, asking if a priest could come to her house and exorcise spirits. She pleaded with Richard to stay home from work that day. He told her, "I have to go. I'll call you and check in." He didn't want to miss work again. A week earlier, he had come home from work to find that Janice and the baby weren't there. She had gone to a hotel, fearful of demons in the house. He brought her and the baby home and stayed there with them for the next two days. He didn't want to leave her, but "I couldn't keep losing income." He finally decided to called Phyllis and ask if Janice and the baby could stay for the night. "She's having a hard time." Phyllis readily agreed.

After a few hours at work, Richard called and spoke to Janice. "She sounded fine. Phyllis told me, 'She's fine. The baby's fine.' I was relieved." After work, Richard went home and slept. His plan was to pick up Janice and Kimberly from Phyllis's house the next morning. Instead, he got a wake-up call from the police, telling him that his wife had stabbed their baby and to meet them at the hospital. It was at the hospital that he was informed of Kimberly's death.

"She was a good mother," Richard said. "She put Kimberly first. I didn't have any concerns that, you know, she would do anything to the baby." He was concerned about her "mental condition," her well-being. He worried that someday her depression would become too much for her, and she'd end up killing herself.

***

Since she spent a good amount of time with Janice—right up to the stabbing—I thought it especially important to interview Phyllis. Like Richard, she was ready to talk.

After some introductory formalities, I asked about her observations with regard to Janice's relationship with Kimberly, given the time they had spent together. Her immediate response: "She loved her baby a lot."

Several weeks before the offense, Janice called Phyllis, crying and saying, "Gang members are following me." A few days earlier, she had been paranoid about the police, claiming they were "watching me." Janice was "crying a lot" during this period. She was fearful that her telephone conversations were being tapped. "Pray for me," she asked.

Phyllis noticed a change in Janice after her grandmother's death. It wasn't just depression. She was paranoid. Her behavior was unusual, and it was then that the paranoia surfaced. She frequently made irrational comments, like the one about her phone being tapped. During the week prior to the offense, Janice asked Phyllis to find a Buddhist temple. "Somebody put black magic on me." This seemed especially odd, since Janice had never been a religious person. Phyllis told her, "There's no black magic."

So when Richard asked if Janice and Kimberly could stay with her, Phyllis was happy to oblige, especially in light of Janice's recent behavior. Janice was afraid of ghosts in the house. When they arrived, Janice was weeping, with Richard trying to comfort her before leaving for work. Phyllis had made dinner, but Janice didn't eat much. After dinner, Janice put Kimberly down to sleep, and they talked.

Janice asked Phyllis if she had located a Buddhist temple. "She wanted a big temple. I humored her," telling Janice they'd find one the following day and "remove any black magic." Janice said she would like to move. "My house is weird with a lot of ghosts," but her husband "wouldn't allow it."

The following morning, at about 6:00 a.m., Phyllis was awakened by loud talking. It was Janice on the phone calling 911. She was screaming about stabbing the baby. Not knowing what happened, Phyllis jumped out of bed and went to Janice's bedroom. There she saw Janice with the baby, who was wrapped in a blanket. Janice and the blanket were covered with blood, which was oozing out of Janice's body from self-inflected gashes, and, as it turned out, from Kimberly's body as well. The baby had been stabbed in the chest area.

Phyllis tearfully recounted how she stood there, frozen and whimpering until the police and paramedics arrived. "She loved Kimberly and always kept her healthy and happy," Phyllis emphasized. Janice had "no malicious intent. . . . [I]t's definitely a mental issue," she said. "There's a mental issue in the family. Her mother just left and her father was a "mental case" who spent years in prison.

***

Filicide, the killing of a child by a parent, is not as uncommon a calamity as you may think. A study supported by the National Institute of Health found that about 15 percent of homicide arrests during a thirty-two-year period were of filicidal nature,[1] mostly committed by parents or stepparents. Over the years, a myriad of research studies has identified the motivations of adults who murder children.[2] There is considerable overlap in the findings, and all basically mirror those identified in the 1970s[3] by forensic psychiatrist Phillip Resnick. Based on a review of multiple cases of filicide, he derived a framework that distinguished five distinct yet intersecting groups. The altruistic group includes parents who believe they killed their child for real or imagined suffering. The acutely psychotic group includes those who killed due to some irrational motive. The unwanted child group is viewed as those who perceived parenting as a hindrance. The fatal maltreatment group encompasses parents whose children died as an unintended consequence of neglect or abuse. Finally, the fifth category, the spousal revenge group, is reserved for those parents who kill a child in order to get back at a spouse or partner—to make him or her suffer.

Based on my review of the records and family interviews, I had a strong impression about which categories fit Janice's tragic circumstances. I suspected that she was irrationally psychotic. Until I actually met her, it was no more than a hunch. Though I've been wrong before, I trust my early impressions. Nonetheless, until I'm deep into the evaluation, my first impressions are held in abeyance, along with a consideration of alternate possibilities. For instance, before I actually interviewed Janice and put together all the available information, I left open the possibility that Janice was nursing a chronic bitterness about her life that wasn't apparent in the record, which could have prompted a moment of homicidal rage.

***

I examined Janice during the course of a three-week period. I knew she was slight from the record review. Indeed, at about five foot one in height and weighing maybe a touch more than one hundred pounds, she was childlike in appearance. Her wavy hair was shoulder length, with a brown hue, like her eyes. Mildly self-conscious, she made only occasional eye contact during the early hours of our interviews together. Throughout, her bearing was straightforward in style and deliberate. When necessary, she took time to think before she answered a question.

By the time I began the examination, Janice had been on an antipsychotic medication (Zyprexa) and a mood stabilizer (first the antidepressant Lexapro, followed by Lamictal, then Depakote, according to the jail records). She expressed her thoughts clearly, without apparent distortions in reality. She was glad her lawyer sent me so she could "talk about it. I need counseling for the rest of my life to understand what happened." I told her that the purpose of our meetings was to conduct an insanity evaluation. She understood but added, "I need help figuring out what happened." After obtaining some basic personal information, we posthaste began to explore the circumstances leading to Kimberly's death.

Janice began by describing her 911 call. She had Kimberly in her arms, wrapped in a blanket, and covered with blood. She pleaded for help. "I hoped the voice [that of the dispatcher] was real." I asked her to back up and tell me about that morning before the stabbing. She had awakened early and recalled going into the kitchen. "I was walking back and forth and crying. I don't know why, exactly." She drank a glass of water and stared out the bay window. She felt strange, and for some reason, "I felt I had to protect Kimberly from Richard." She recalled thinking her only choice was to kill herself and Kimberly. Her last memory was of looking at a block of knifes and a pair of scissors that were on the kitchen tabletop. Janice had no memory of picking the knife up or of walking from the kitchen to Kimberly's room. She had no memory of stabbing her. As she had told the police, she remembered looking at her baby and seeing the color fade from Kimberly's face. "I broke out of it. That's when I called 911."

Janice felt terrorized the day before the stabbing. She was convinced "there was something in the house . . . a demon, something supernatural. I thought the house was possessed. Someone put a hex on me." Richard, she thought, was possibly the one. "He was gonna take my baby. I'd wake up in the morning and say, 'Where's my baby? He took her.'" Though she suspected Richard haunted her, she was too afraid that night to be home with Kimberly without him. "That's why I went to Phyllis's house to spend the night. That's where it happened."

After dinner at Phyllis's, Janice put Kimberly to sleep. She and Phyllis talked for a while. "We didn't talk about anything special." At that point, "I felt like I was on drugs . . . nothing seemed real . . . not in focus. It's like talking to you; is it real or am I hallucinating?" She didn't recall when they went to bed, but she slept well, even though she had not been sleeping through the night for a few weeks.

After the police and paramedics arrived, Janice was taken to the hospital. "There were tons of people there. I was screaming, 'They're trying to kill me.'" She had about thirty self-inflicted wounds on her arms and chest requiring emergency surgery. She felt no pain, and she had no memory of doing this to herself. She had no idea if she stabbed herself before or after stabbing Kimberly.

Janice hadn't gotten depressed during her pregnancy with Kimberly nor afterward. She had been "devastated" by the loss of her grandmother. "She was everything to me." Not long after the funeral, "I wasn't normal.

I thought something happened to my daughter. I thought she wasn't my daughter. I cried, 'Where is my grandmother?'

"I wasn't sleeping. I got so skinny. . . . I was strange. I didn't trust Richard; maybe he was doing this to me, I thought." At one point, Janice filed a child abuse report, thinking Richard "did something" to their baby. For several weeks, Janice felt "people had stopped talking to me." She became convinced that Richard "did something to me. I don't know what. I thought maybe he did voodoo or something."

Less than a week before the stabbing, Richard took her to their family doctor. He prescribed an antidepressant and recommended that she see a psychiatrist. "I didn't trust the doctor. I thought he was poisoning me with the antidepressants."

When we met for our second session, Janice told me our time together was more painful than she had anticipated. Though she wanted to talk about what happened, despair followed in its wake. It took her a few days to recover. She realized, "Since it happened, I work at blocking it out." She was afraid of what she might do if she dwelled too long on what she had done to Kimberly.

***

Janice completed the Miller Forensic Assessment of Symptoms Test and the Minnesota Multiphasic Personality Inventory-2-RF (MMPI-2-RF), both of which I have described in earlier chapters.

I didn't need to do intellectual testing, as I could tell from the interview and personal history that she was at least of normal ability and without any cognitive limitations. Never really interested in academics, Janice was nonetheless a good student in elementary school. After high school, she worked odd jobs until she obtained a real estate state license and began her career as an agent.

Sometimes, a close look at an individual's health issues and personal history suggests unrecognized influences on cognitive functioning. Janice, however, had no significant medical history. She had never had any prior mental health treatment. She had not been on any medications for a length of time that would have affected her adversely. She had no record of criminal charges or arrests, save the problems she had with Richard several years before the stabbing. In other words, her history was basically squeaky clean.

The Miller test identifies those who attempt to exaggerate or feign psychotic symptoms. Janice showed no evidence of either. The MMPI-2-RF validity scale score reinforced the Miller, providing further evidence that she wasn't faking her psychotic symptoms. If anything, the scale results reflected an effort to minimize her psychiatric symptoms, as though Janice was trying to put her best foot forward. Still, the results of the MMPI-2-RF clinical scales were those of an individual who was demoralized and suffering from a clinical depression. She was devoid of positive emotions, with a vulnerability to self-destructive thinking. She felt a sense of alienation from and distrust of people. The results were consistent with one who struggles with an unstable mood, but not to the extent of bipolar illness.

I reviewed the results of the testing with her, with the goal of gaining greater insight into her mental life. From a subjective perspective, Janice was most aware of something emotionally missing. She felt different from her past self, without joy, empty. This predated the stabbing, although she couldn't say when her "normal self" disappeared. In terms of her paranoia, it was lessened but still present to some measure. She still believed that she may have been possessed by an evil force or that her house was haunted. "It's possible. I don't know what happened."

I diagnosed Janice with a major depression with psychosis. I opined that she was insane at the time of Kimberly's killing. As a result of her psychosis, she was not aware of the nature and purpose of her actions. Therefore, at the moment of the stabbing, she did not know it was wrong.

***

I testified at both the guilt and insanity phases of Janice's trial. It's important to understand California's insanity statute and how its structure potentially impacted Janice's outcome. A defendant is first tried on the facts of the case and is either convicted or found innocent of the crime. If found culpable, she then moves to the insanity phase, where she can be found sane or not guilty by reason of insanity.

During the guilt phase, my testimony began as usual with the defense counsel, Mr. Flores, asking me to provide my credentials and experience to establish my expertise for the jury. He then asked a series of questions designed to guide me through my examination of Janice's mental state before, during, and after the killing of Kimberly.

After first describing my examination process, I explained that in the six months or so before the stabbing, Janice's grandmother had died rather unexpectedly several months after Janice had given birth to Kimberly. Raised by her grandmother and especially close to her, Janice fell into a depression. It extended beyond an expected grief reaction into a major depression with paranoid psychosis. I explained her symptoms, including her delusions about Richard, black magic, and demonic possession. Eventually, about two days before the killing, her husband took Janice to a family doctor. She was prescribed antidepressant medication but was too paranoid to take them, though she told her husband she would.

I explained how the family described their increasing concerns about her irrational thinking and her emotional instability. Janice at times shifted from depression to giddiness, according to her husband. He'd find her withdrawn, then irritable, and finally she would work herself into a sobbing helplessness and depression. I described her developing paranoia, as I had been told by both her husband and cousin Phyllis. Once, not long before the killing, Janice asked Phyllis to "pray for me." The night before the stabbing, Janice left the house with the baby because she was afraid the house was haunted.

I described Janice's increasingly confused and mentally disordered state of mind until the time of the killing, beginning around the time of her grandmother's death. Her symptoms of depression became increasingly severe with delusions and paranoia. I quoted her. I reviewed the testing results confirming the veracity of her psychotic depression.

Here's where an understanding of California law is crucial. During the guilt phase of any trial, evidence may be presented by an expert regarding a defendant's mental condition that has bearing on her ability to form the alleged mental state required to be found guilty. But the expert cannot give a direct opinion as to whether she did or did not form the mental state in question: that's up to the jury, the trier of fact, to decide after hearing from all the witnesses. In Janice's case, I could present only evidence of her worsening illness until the time she killed Kimberly. I couldn't assert that her mental illness actually impaired her ability to form the intention to kill or whether she did it with premeditation or deliberation. If I did, the judge would likely call a mistrial: that's the degree of import surrounding this distinction. I'd get my chance at opining during the insanity phase, when it is legal to give an opinion about the defendant's state of mind.

The cross-examination began with Mr. Kristel, the assistant district attorney, asking a series of questions about Janice's history. "The defendant was free of a history of chronic depression until the time before the killing, correct?" I briefly described the development of her depression symptoms. A tall middle-aged man with a strong, thundering voice that filled the courtroom, Mr. Kristel asked, "She had never been psychiatrically hospitalized, correct?" "Yes," I responded. "In fact, doctor," questioned Mr. Kristel, "She had only recently been prescribed psychiatric medication?" "Yes," I answered again. "She had no history of memory problems until the stabbing, correct?" "Yes," I answered. The prosecutor asked, "At the time, she must have known what she was doing since she picked up a lethal weapon. She didn't pick up a spoon or hamburger, right?" I again answered affirmatively but added that given her developing mental deterioration and distorted perceptions, her decisions at the time were distorted, which also affected her memory of the events. "It's a little convenient, isn't it, Dr. Lettieri?" No, I said, adding that the evidence, including her psychological testing results and the descriptions of Janice's behavior by family members, affirmed the credibility of her mental problems.

As expected, after two days of deliberation, the jury found Janice guilty of murder. They couldn't unanimously decide (the jury was hung) if she acted with premeditation and deliberation.

On to the next phase.

***

In legal parlance, insanity is an "affirmative defense." This means that it's up to the defense to prove by a preponderance of evidence (which is defined as "more likely than not") that Janice was insane at the time of the killing. During the guilt phase of the trial, Janice had the presumption of innocence. It was the prosecution's responsibility and burden to prove beyond a reasonable doubt (defined as the only logical conclusion based on the evidence) that she was guilty of murder. Now that Janice had been found guilty as charged, it became the defense's burden to prove she was insane at the time of the crime.

During direct examination, the defense attorney, Mr. Flores, asked a series of questions about my findings and conclusions regarding Janice's mental condition in front of the same jury that had found her guilty of murder. In essence, I reiterated much of what I said during the guilt phase. He then referenced a section of my report, which outlined the reasons that lead psychotic women to kill their infants, and asked, "Would you explain to the court what you meant?" A common motivation of psychotic mothers who hurt or kill their infants and hurt themselves is an irrational conviction that they must do so in order to save the infant from a life of misery.[4] It may be an overpowering danger—like an evil spouse or force—to which she's helpless. Death becomes the only option, and she feels she can't leave her baby motherless in such a mad and wicked world. That's why suicidal behavior is so frequently associated with baby killing. Janice and Kimberly's case fit this common pattern. She stabbed Kimberly and herself. When a mother is in such a regressed mental condition, the infant is experienced as inseparable from herself, and what happens to one must happen to the other.

I repeated that during the months before the killing, Janice became increasingly depressed and delusional with a belief that supernatural forces were descending upon her. Richard became a representative of the wicked. During one of her police interviews, a detective asked Janice if she had stabbed Kimberly as an act of revenge against Richard. She reacted with a bewildered, "No. It was him to me." This was again evidence of her delusions, within which Richard became embedded. The killing, bizarrely, was prompted by a wish to prevent a life of suffering.

Finally, the defense attorney asked if, in my opinion, Janice's mental illness compromised her ability to appreciate the nature of her action at the time of the offense. I said yes; her psychotic depression had distorted her decision and conscious awareness of her deadly action.

Mr. Kristel was an experienced prosecutor. His cross-examination was sharp and focused with an eye on his overall theory of the case. He didn't attack every point of my direct testimony, as some of his greener colleagues might. Instead, he addressed the few issues he hoped to shape and fit into his perspective and to drive them home to the jury. I liken the difference in his prosecutorial experience from that of an inexperienced litigator to a surgeon who carefully directs his scalpel, as opposed to a butcher wielding a meat cleaver.

He began his cross-examination by returning to the convenience angle of his challenge to Janice's memory problem. Mr. Kristel asked, "She comes out of it after she stabbed Kimberly and immediately calls 911. From no memory to memory. Why?"

In my professional experience, I responded, this kind of reaction is not uncommon. When psychotically distorted beliefs are finally acted upon, they become perceived in the light of reality with tangible consequences. It's then that the psychotic individual may perceive the craziness of his or her actions. I gave one example from my clinical hospital practice of a delusional man who violently assaulted his roommate. After seeing the roommate on the ground, wounded and terrified, he immediately realized his fear and rage at him had been misplaced. A similar kind of reality awareness kicked in with Janice when she saw the life draining from Kimberly's face.

The prosecution wanted to paint the marriage between Janice and Richard as deeply troubled. Mr. Flores had informed me that Mr. Kristel was especially harsh during his cross-examination of Richard earlier in the trial when he was called as a fact witness. Mr. Kristel brought up Richard's history of drug abuse and sexual liaisons and the domestic violence calls to the police. "He tried to make Richard look like a sleaze-bag and Janice a hysterical witch," Mr. Flores said.

The prosecutor then reviewed Richard's drug problem, which had caused him and Janice to separate in the past. Then, after reviewing subpoenaed records that documented the couple's recent financial problems, Mr. Kristel asked if I agreed that financial stress could cause problems even for a good marriage. I agreed that everyone gets stressed by money problems. He then read from a police report that summarized Janice's statements immediately after the killing. The detective had asked, "Are you sorry?" (for stabbing Kimberly). Janice responded, "Is he sorry!?" referring to her husband. Mr. Kristel asked if I would agree that she sounded "bitter." I said no, she sounded delusional. "That's your opinion, correct?" he asked. I answered affirmatively, based on my training and experience.

In a brief redirect examination by Mr. Flores, he asked if, in my opinion, marital discord was an issue that contributed to Kimberly's death. The emotional difficulties between Janice and Richard predated their marriage. I answered that in recent years, especially around the time of Janice's psychosis and Kimberly's death, Richard was very supportive and concerned about his wife. This was more than confirmed by Phyllis. He had been drug-free for years and working full time. By all accounts, their marriage was a stable one in recent years. Even when paranoid, Janice wanted him around. Though obviously devastated by the death of his child, Richard continued to describe Janice as a good mother who was very mentally ill, and he was supportive of her.

I was the final expert during the insanity phase of the trial. Both experts—I and the prosecution's expert—opined that Janice was psychotic and insane at the time of the stabbing.

***

Women are viewed as generally less violent than men and inherently nurturing.[5] Courts and jurors tend to view violent women in a sympathetic light, ascribing such behavior as the result of external stress or hormonal factors.[6] Though women are very capable of violence—increasingly so in recent years[7]—men are more naturally aggressive. Indeed, most social violence is perpetrated by men. This perspective has been criticized by feminist legal scholars as chauvinistic and essentially a gender-biased standard of law.[8]

Regardless, mothers have been held accountable for filicide acts less frequently than their male counterparts. They've been found by the courts to be more vulnerable than men to biological and psychosocial factors associated with the stress of maternity and caring for an infant. Notwithstanding the social critique, and as I said during my testimony, women who kill their babies are motivated 90 percent of the time by psychotically altruistic reasons. Men are much more likely to kill a child out of revenge toward the mother or as a result of physical abuse.[9] As such, killer mothers are more likely than killer fathers to be found insane or to be convicted of a lesser charge, such as manslaughter, than first-degree murder.[10]

Like many of those mothers, Janice was delusional and in the throes of a psychotic depression. In many ways, she was more of a sympathetic defendant than most. She didn't have many of the characteristics of mothers who have killed their children.[11] For instance, she didn't have a history of drug or alcohol abuse. She was free of a significant mental health history and of past instances of child abuse or neglect. She had no criminal past. She didn't have an extensive history of interpersonal problems suggesting a personality disturbance. At the time of the offense, Janice's marriage was stable, except for the problems caused by her severe depression. She and Richard had financial problems, but he continued to work and to be emotionally supportive as well.

So why was Janice found to have been sane when she killed Kimberly? What happened?

A few factors made a difference, it seems to me. First, and maybe most important, was Janice's lack of an extensive psychiatric history. In my experience, and consistent with the clinical literature, defendants are viewed less harshly if they have an extensive psychiatric history of a major disturbance, like schizophrenia. Janice didn't have a long mental health history nor was she ever psychiatrically hospitalized. I diagnosed her with a psychotic depression, which is a serious and debilitating condition. But I don't think it carries the ominous association that a diagnosis of schizophrenia does with the public.

Some legal scholars make the argument that the law is gender biased and chauvinistic, viewing women as more vulnerable to stress and weaker than men. It's a holdover of the stereotypic perception of women as inherently passive and nonaggressive, despite evidence to the contrary.[12] Scholars argue that such a view is simplistic and binary, fostered by the courts, society, and the media. Women are either "mad" or "bad."[13] If a woman behaves angrily or aggressively, it must be the result of impinging force beyond her control, such as extreme stress or a chronic mental illness. Because such conduct is unnatural to women, she must be out of her mind, mad. On the other hand, if she is not suffering from one of these conditions, she must be a "bad" woman.

I'm not sure I agree completely with this legal perspective of feminist scholars. But the binary argument may shed some light on the jury's perception of Janice as bad, not mad. She was different from the prototypical baby killer who is commonly found to be insane because she didn't carry a schizophrenic or even a bipolar diagnosis. She had no lengthy psychiatric history; her psychosis came upon her only after her grandmother died. With such a history, it may have been difficult for the jury to accept that Janice was so ill and disoriented that she didn't know what she was doing when she killed Kimberly. In addition, she didn't suffer from the litany of psychosocial stressors and disadvantages typically found in mothers who kill their babies and are deemed insane. She had a significant measure of psychosocial support, including her cousin Phyllis and her husband, notwithstanding the image of Richard presented in court. Ironically, this may have eased the way for the prosecutor to convince the jury that Janice was "bad" and killed Kimberly to exact rage-filled revenge.

At a news conference after the verdict was reached, Mr. Kristel told the press that Janice killed Kimberly because "she was . . . angry and selfish . . . a woman desperate to get back at her husband and to get his attention."

I wonder if he actually believed that.

9

A HYDRA-HEADED PASSION

Sexuality, Violence, and Perversion

One sin, I know, another doth provoke; Murder's as near to lust as flame to smoke—Shakespeare, *Pericles*

Before heading home for the weekend, I checked my messages. Bill Bohenski, a private criminal defense attorney, left a long one. I've known Bill for years, since he worked for the county public defender's office. He's a no-nonsense guy with a stark intensity and sharp intellect. Before law school he majored in physics and engineering as an undergraduate. With his fixed eyes and impeccable logic, even a simple conversation sometimes felt like a cross-examination. Not infrequently, he'd end a conversation with a puerile comment or some attempt at joviality followed by a quick chuckle. I suspect he knows, at some level, his listener needs some comic relief.

Bill was appointed by the court to represent a recently arrested defendant. "His head needs shrinking," he said. *Chuckle*. Ray, his new client, was a married African American man in his late twenties. Soft spoken and cooperative, "He doesn't come across like he's crazy," Bill said, but "something's wrong." Ray was arrested for rape. The assistant district attorney said he'd be filing more charges shortly. Ray, Bill explained, was accused of serial rape and murder. In other words, Bill was telling me that his client might be facing the death penalty if convicted. He ended by saying he'd send me the discovery materials, meaning the police records and other documents about the case.

Given the nature of the crimes and the apparent facts, all of Bill's intensity of purpose was going to be in demand.

***

By the time I received the first installment of records, more charges had been filed by the district attorney's office: six rape charges, which included two rape-murder allegations. And Ray was also a suspect in an additional rape and murder.

The case broke open after the police were called to the death scene of a woman in a local motel. They found her partially clothed, with her pants and underwear off. She was on her knees with her torso lying across the bed. She apparently had been raped and strangled to death. This was confirmed by an autopsy.

While searching the motel room, the police found a piece of paper with a phone number that was eventually traced to Ray's cell phone. He soon was interviewed but denied the charges, saying he had never been at the motel in question. However, a video camera had caught a glimpse of him leaving one of the exits. A warrant was issued and his DNA taken. It matched the DNA found in the semen from the dead victim. She was later identified as a young prostitute who had recently arrived from Minnesota.

Originally charged with one count of rape and one of murder, the ongoing investigation and consultations with local police departments led to evidence that Ray had been involved in multiple rapes.

The facts of all the cases were eerily similar. The women were overpowered and strangled until they passed out and then raped. Three of the surviving women filled in details of the attacks. One occurred at a motel where the victim was an employee. As she was preparing a room, Ray allegedly entered and asked for an additional towel. As always, he was very polite, pleasant, and unassuming. She felt safe and unthreatened. Ray thanked her for the towel and left. A moment later, he stormed back in, and, in a burst of ferocious violence, flung her to the ground, and began strangling her. She resisted until she passed out, only to awaken sometime later. She had been raped but lived to tell her story.

This was Ray's modus operandi, or what's commonly referred to by those who investigate rape homicides as his "signature."[1]

The survivors all used similar words to describe their attacker. He was "calm . . . seemed nice . . . polite." The way that Bill described Ray to me in that first phone message. Ray's behavior was consistent: seeming equanimity followed by raw violence and strangulation resulting in loss of consciousness or the death of the victim. And rape. All victims had similar bruises and gashes. They suffered from vaginal bleeding and multiple abrasions on their faces and bite marks on their backs. All suffered petechial aftereffects: broken blood vessels usually in the neck and ears. The surviving victims had ruddy faces with terror-filled eyes.

Eventually the physical evidence, including DNA and fingerprints, implicated Ray, as did three survivors from a lineup. Plus, when the police searched his house, they found belongings from several of the victims. He had taken a laptop from one of the surviving victims, for instance, after leaving her unconscious in a motel.

As the evidence accrued, so did the case against Ray and his guilt. Like hope, primitive denial springs eternal. Ray was relentless in his claim of innocence.

***

After reviewing the first installment of the discovery and before my first consultation with Ray, I called Bill and asked what specific questions he wanted me to address. He was less than clear. At that point, he simply wanted a better emotional understanding of Ray. He reminded me that his client is facing special circumstances allegations and capital murder charges. Special circumstances in criminal law involve conditions under which the crime was committed or specific actions of the accused that merit greater punishment. If possible, Bill hoped to present mitigation at a hearing at which the district attorney's office makes the final decision to seek the death penalty or LWOP: life without the possibility of parole.

***

Driving to the jail for my first interview with Ray, I slipped into a familiar unease that comes about with certain types of defendants and circumstances, when culpability is as clear as the denial is strong. I find a psychotic person who refutes the incontestable more palpable. After all, the person isn't as much in denial as in defiance of reality. Or maybe someone who is simply not yet ready to face what happened and is grappling with the reality of what he or she did. Such a struggle may even mark the presence of a conscience; one needs time to face the developing guilt and shame. I've found this to be the case with some defendants who've committed crimes while under the influence of drugs or alcohol. I'm less patient and less tolerant with defendants who are simply dissimulating, manipulating, or outright lying. It's an attitude that carries liability during a long and complicated forensic examination. I reminded myself to keep my predilection contained and do my job.

How ironic, I thought: it's less challenging for me to interview someone who is psychotically unhinged than rational prevaricators.

Keeping my eye on the ball, I reminded myself of my charge: to assist Bill in developing a psychological understanding of Ray. Bill was preparing for a meeting with prosecutors as they weighed the awfulness of the crimes against the defendant's extenuating factors (e.g., history of having been abused and emotionally neglected) before deciding whether to seek the death penalty. At that meeting, Bill would be given an opportunity to make a case for LWOP. He hoped that my examination of Ray would yield helpful psychological information.

Given the depravity and extent of Ray's crimes, any mitigation would need to be thick and prepotent.

***

Rape is a general intent crime, which means that no specific mental state needs to be established by the prosecutor. Ray's very actions revealed his intent and purposefulness. In addition, the death of three of his victims during the course of the rapes made this a potential capital case. To understand Ray as a person, I didn't have to query him about his thoughts at the time of those offenses like I would need to if, for example, his sanity was in question. But I wouldn't shy away from the issue. If Ray opened up, even a glimpse into his mind-set during the rapes would allow a richer understanding of his psychological motivations and makeup.

As Ray walked toward the interview booth, I immediately thought about the way he had been described by the surviving victims. He meandered down the bending hallways with two escorting deputies, breezily chatting. They hadn't handcuffed him. Small in stature, about five feet seven inches tall, Ray was densely built yet not overly muscular. His gait was casual, and hair closely cropped. Ray was clean shaven and clear skinned, without tattoos on his arms, fingers, or neck that appear on so many defendants. He looked neat and normal in appearance.

As he entered the booth, Ray gave me a smile as he shook my hand. I got a disapproving look from one of the deputies but not the usual "no touching" admonishment. The deputy didn't secure Ray's ankles to the pole beneath his chair with a leg iron to restrict mobility, a typical precaution with very violent inmates. Ray was afforded the standard "PC treatment" for all accused sex offenders: the protective custody of two deputies until he entered a secure booth. But there was an easiness to their monitoring of Ray, given that he was an alleged serial killer and likely capital case defendant. Surprising.

As expected, Ray presented himself as pleasant and ordinary. Nonthreatening in demeanor, his speaking voice so light and low that I sometimes strained to hear him. Eventually, I found this casual breeziness also reflected in the superficial way he shared his thoughts about himself and his life. Over time, I saw it as the product of an abject lack of self-awareness that reflected a psychological development deeply askew.

Raised by his mother and two older sisters, Ray described his childhood in a generic fashion—not exactly idyllic but relatively problem free. Although he had some learning difficulties, he never was diagnosed with a learning disability. He needed the help of a resource specialist in elementary school. (His mother later told a different history of his academic disability). He was free of behavioral or emotional difficulties. He described his mother as "strict" but "a great and loving mom" who worked full time to give her kids all they needed. (His wife later offered a very different perspective of his mother.) Close to his sisters during his childhood and now as an adult, they were like surrogate moms during Ray's early years.

Significantly, Ray made no mention of his absentee father until I brought up the issue. Responding matter-of-factly, he told me about the first time he saw his father coming home from school when he was in second grade. "I'm not sure what his situation was," Ray said. "He was jailed for something."

Although his father occasionally visited, he never lived with the family. "I haven't seen him in years. I heard he's in prison again." Ray didn't mention that his father's early visits were to see his sisters. Or that he ignored Ray, as I learned from my interview with his mother. When I brought this up in a later interview, he brushed it off, saying he was close to his mother and sisters, which was enough for him. He also had an uncle, his mother's brother, "who took me out."

Ray's easy denial extended to his rationalizations about previous arrests. Not long before his arrest, he was charged with forgery—"a misunderstanding," according to Ray. Referring to his employer at the time, he explained, "He gave me a check that I cashed. He said I forged the check." Denying the forgery, Ray couldn't explain what led to the accusation. This was an open case at the time of the rape-murder allegations.

Two years earlier, he had been briefly arrested for stealing a computer from a small accounting firm where he worked as a clerk assistant. He admitted the theft but gave an explanation: "Somebody was offering me money . . . a dumb move on my part." He took a plea deal because "I just wanted to end it."

Having reviewed his rap sheet, I knew the police had made two domestic disturbance calls to Ray's house, where he lived with his wife and two young children, a two-year-old boy and eleven-month-old baby girl. No arrests were made or charges filed. I asked him to tell me what happened. "My wife grabbed me by the neck. She hit me a few times. I called 911. She's stressed out and on psych meds." Ray began to weep and said, "I could never hurt a woman."

***

During our second encounter, we delved into Ray's sexual and marital history. He liked watching pornography, "normal stuff . . . I like group sex porn." He denied unusual sexual desires such as sadomasochism or getting aroused by violent sexual fantasies. He commented how women "always hit on me." Curiously, he complained how "these days" women are "preoccupied with sex. They don't see inside." He reminded me that he grew up in a household of females. I thought he was about to follow up with a claim of how this instilled respect for women in him. Strangely instead, he said, "I have a higher moral ground." When queried, Ray said he "took care a little more" than women when it came to sexual behavior. Unlike most of the female gender, he "looks inside." His devaluation of women was surfacing—and not very subtly.

Women in his life, Ray said, always had been more interested in sex than he, beginning with his older sister's girlfriend who abused him when he was about eleven years old. Four or five years older than he, she was his babysitter for a number of years. They "played house . . . that's what she called it." It first started with fondling. Over time, their activities escalated to intercourse, "about twenty or thirty times." He never revealed this to his family. I asked how this affected him. "I didn't want anybody based on sex. I don't want to show off my body to girls."

Ray said another one of his sister's friends seduced him during his high school years. As he had already expressed but reiterated, "Women are always hitting on me." His girlfriends were always more interested in sex than he.

His wife Tanya, like all women, was more interested in sex than he was, Ray said. She liked sex every day, even after the kids were born. She wanted him to spank her and pull her hair. She liked anal sex. Ray said she took him to strip clubs. He noticed the expression of disbelief on my face about the strip clubs claim. "It's true," he said.

Ray said their marital sex life was normal. Their "best sex" occurred after arguments. He provoked and taunted Tanya by ignoring her attempts for his attention. "She'd get physical with me. It's something I did on purpose . . . get her to attack me. She bites and scratches. She'd grabbed me by the neck to choke me." He admitted that it turned him on, which led to "rough sex. She liked it rough, not me." He did it, the taunting, for Tanya. The roughness was a distraction from her depression and irritability. It was a release for *her*.

Ray's signature rape pattern seemed to me to be the inversion—a mirror image depiction of the ritualistically sexual "dance" he instigated with his wife. During the rapes, *he* was the one taunted and provoked by a woman's sexuality, which he had already explained that females tend to do. *He* then attacks and *he* chokes and bites, which is followed by dangerously rough sex, which is *his* release.

With a Himalayan measure of irony, Ray was consciously oblivious to the parallels between the sexual enactment with Tanya that he instigated and that of the rapist murderer, which he denied was him.

***

After our second meeting, I decided it was time to interview Ray's family members. I was having difficulty contacting Ms. Radcliffe, Ray's mother. She didn't always return my phone messages. Tanya was responsive, but she had problems finding a babysitter for her kids.

I finally got lucky and made contact with Ms. Radcliffe, and we scheduled a time to meet.

Ms. Radcliffe had a long drive from her job to my office. Still, she was a few minutes early. She began the interview by telling me how she always arrives for her appointments on time, "sharp." That's the adjective that popped into my head when I first saw her in my waiting room. She wore a stylish black dress, a multi-toned, purple-dominated scarf that draped around her shoulders. She had matching pumps and a purse. A short, heavyset African American woman, she sat in a noticeably upright manner, military stiff, without much expression. Very official looking, she reminded me of interviews I have had over the years with FBI or DEA agents doing background checks on former patients who applied for high-security positions at their agencies.

Already having had two interviews with Ray, I had his take on his early life. Now I wanted to hear from the "horse's mouth," as it were.

My plan was to begin at the beginning by asking Ms. Radcliffe about Ray's early development and family relations. I prefaced my queries with a few social comments as a way of giving us time to settle in. ("I'm glad we can finally meet.") It didn't help. Ms. Radcliffe simply glared at me with metallic eyes. I later recalled that stare after interviewing Tanya, who described her mother-in-law as harsh and cold.

Ms. Radcliffe was irritated that her son would be in jail during the holidays. (My interview with her was in early November.) "He's already fighting another case," she said, referencing his forgery allegation. Vexed by her seemingly easy dismissal of the gravity of the charges, I reacted in a somewhat prickly fashion, reminding her that the allegations against Ray were as serious as it gets. Instantly, I knew I had blown it. Ms. Radcliffe reacted defensively, reminding me that Ray is African American. She angrily suggested a racial element to the charges. "He's always pulled over by the police for no reason!" Almost instantly, her demeanor tumbled, first to sadness then to anguished terror. When Ray's arrest was announced in the media, "That's when the whole world went upside-down and crazy." She couldn't believe the allegations and still didn't. "It's bizarre and insane. . . . He has been around females all of his life. He's been taught to respect women." I recouped and told her I could only imagine what she was going through. She lost her wary edge, and I my snappishness.

We began talking about Ray's early life. He was raised by her and his two older sisters. His early development was basically normal except for his slowness to talk and communicate. Eventually, he received speech therapy in elementary school. His early language difficulties foreshadowed problems with learning and limited verbal expressive ability and, consequently, his quiet style. "He kept to himself," Ms. Radcliffe said. To myself, I mused that Ray's penchant for inwardness may have formed the basis for the creation of a rich and destructive fantasy life.

Ms. Radcliffe described herself as an overprotective parent and a disciplinarian. This was a necessary requirement for a single parent, she felt. All her children had the same father, but they never really lived together as a family. The children's father would "sometimes come and go" during Ray's childhood years. Frequently unemployed, he lived with other women or ended up spending time in jail, usually for small-time crimes like petty theft or probation violations. Once, he had served a prison term for burglary.

Though never abusive, Ms. Radcliffe wanted me to know that she used physical punishment to discipline her kids. She didn't think Ray was abused in any way. He had some minor behavioral problems in his early years at school, which she attributed to his learning difficulties. He never liked school and would "play sick" a lot. He was in special education classes for delayed reading and language development.

Ms. Radcliffe didn't notice any unusual behavior or emotional problems during his formative years. She spontaneously made the point that he never tortured animals or set fires. He wasn't a bed-wetter.

Almost as an afterthought, she said, "Ray didn't need hugs and kisses" as a child. Stiffening up as if she was summoning the courage to blurt out what needed to be said, Ms. Radcliffe added, "He rejected Ray as his child." She was referring to Ray's father. She never understood why and never asked. "He didn't believe Ray was his child for some reason. He'd call and talk to the girls. Not to my son."

When Ray called his father on the telephone, "He'd be hurt and angry after the conversation."

During the few times he visited the children, Mr. Radcliffe took the girls out, "but he'd leave his son behind." Ray was left dejected and bitter. "Ray learned early how to push your buttons," especially with the females in the house. If one of his sisters was upset about something,

"Ray would find a way to put fuel on the fire" and laugh when she became furious. "He liked to see people get mad."

Ms. Radcliffe's brother, William, was around a lot during Ray's early years. "He didn't help," she said. He told Ray, "You're the man of the house. Control the women."

By the end of the interview, Ms. Radcliffe had managed to circle back to a comfortable state of denial. "I find this whole thing bizarre. He knows to respect them." She wanted Ray home for the holidays.

***

My next session with Ray was about two weeks after I consulted with his mother. He began by talking about how long he had been in jail, echoing his mother's complaints about the unfairness of his detention. They clearly had talked. A folie à deux, I thought. He had been visited by Bill a few days earlier, and the news wasn't good: Ray's DNA matched that found on another surviving victim. With Ray, the weight of the evidence against him only seemed to empower his denial. He dismissed the rape evidence. "Bill said 10 percent of Ray's DNA was missing." During one of our later sessions, after his DNA was identified on one of the murdered women, Ray reacted illogically, saying, "She had drugs in her system." I asked what that had to do with the evidence against him. "I don't do drugs." His logic would twist as needed, so he could remain ensconced in a world of innocence. Throughout, Ray looked for opportunities to assert his innocence, no matter what.

I finally had been able to schedule a meeting with Ray's wife. I hoped to get a better understanding of their life and his behavior, including his sexuality during the years before the offenses occurred. Would such details help to break through his steely defenses in subsequent sessions? Would he be more willing to reveal himself to me? Or would it strengthen his resolve to deny?

***

My time with Ray's wife Tanya was indeed revealing, though it was aborted prematurely. After our initial hour-and-a-half-long encounter, she called and told me that she decided to forego our second scheduled meeting.

Tanya was older than Ray, although she looked younger than her mid-thirties. Jittery and self-conscious, with long brown hair and a tender smile, she telegraphed a soft vulnerability. She immediately expressed ambivalence about our meeting. Worried about "hurting Ray," she at the same time wanted to "tell you some things that will help you understand him." Her voice quavering, she added, "I'm still in shock . . . denial I think" about the allegations against her husband and the consequences to herself and her family.

Tanya described Ray as "loving and kind." He helps in the kitchen, and he enjoys doing family things with the children. "He's never an asshole," she said, "and never violent." In fact, during the episodes of marital discord leading to the police being called, she was the initiator of the aggression, she said. With a long history of depression, she described herself as becoming easily irritated, irate, and volatile when down.

"I knew he was cheating on me," Tanya told me. During the past several years, Ray would leave the house at two in the morning and stay out all night. He "couldn't sleep and wanted to go for a ride," he told Tanya. Or he was just "bored." She accepted his conduct because, "I knew he was never happy." More than depressed, Tanya said, "Ray has a void." He's childlike and frightened to be alone. "He wants harmony at all costs." Interestingly, she described him as "a man with no identity." He was forever afraid of losing her, no matter what amount of reassurance she gave him. This, Tanya was certain, was the result of never having been truly loved by his father or his mother in an unconditional way.

I mentioned that I had met Ms. Radcliffe and she seemed to love her son very much, albeit in an overprotective, possibly dysfunctional way. Tanya first described Ray's mother as an "interesting person." She said Ms. Radcliffe was cold, but, at the same time, she never held Ray accountable "for anything. If Ray forgot to pay his phone bill, it's the phone company's fault." His father completely ignored Ray as though he didn't exist. "The whole family is cold."

Tanya got a "whole lot of criticism" from his family for being nurturing to her children, for being affectionate with them.

She was open about their sexual life. She described Ray as well-built yet very self-conscious and ashamed of his body. He always wanted oral sex more than intercourse. When they did have coitus, it was always from behind; he was too uncomfortable "face to face."

Ray watched porn every day, alone. He especially enjoyed threesome bisexual porn. Tanya told him that she'd watch with him. He didn't want her watching it. She was open to experimentation with a threesome, if that was his fantasy. He wouldn't have it. In fact, he demanded that she dress conservatively. "He had respect for me. He saw me as different from the girls in the porn."

She described Ray as extremely jealous and controlling. She lost contact with friends because he didn't want her seeing them. He told her what makeup to wear and how to wear it.

At the end of the interview, we scheduled another meeting. The evening before we were to meet again, she canceled. "I don't want to hurt his case. . . . I talk too much." She stopped returning my calls.

***

At my next session, I told Ray that Tanya and I had met and asked about his early morning forays. "I was bored," he said, as though they meant nothing. Usually superficially calm and even keeled, he was different that day, even before I asked about his early morning drives. I suspected he and Tanya had talked and he knew she had "talked too much" to me. His voice was smoother than usual, its cadence more deliberate, its volume artificially low. He was exerting a greater than usual effort at self-control. His body movements caught my attention—more accurately, their absence. There wasn't the normal shifting and wiggling that naturally happens while sitting on a hard metallic stool. I sensed a quality of compression. In my mind, I imagined a shaken soda bottle, fizzed up and ready to blow. I asked if he was all right. "You seem tense," I said. "I'm alright," Ray replied.

At first, Ray encouraged me to speak with his family, including his mother and Tanya. I suspected he had a change of mind, at least about his wife, and that he likely talked Tanya into silence, continuing his control of her from jail.

My time with Tanya had been brief but illuminating—and at a cost: Ray's evasiveness and paranoia had been strengthened.

***

Though in extremis, Ray continued drawing from his bottomless well of denial and control. Still, desperation was catching up. He began sending me long rambling missives in between our sessions. He expressed many of his usual complaints about fellow inmates, bad jail food, the unfairness of the deputies, and frustration about not getting enough dayroom time out of his cell. He especially focused on the unfairness of his incarceration. Writing with awkward phrasing and poor grammar, which read like poorly composed legal briefs, Ray repeatedly asserted his innocence. For instance, one of the victims had met her murderer through Craigslist. He denied ever using Craigslist. I had read the probable cause statement written by one of the lead detectives on the case. In summarizing the evidence against Ray, she meticulously tracked the servers and emails connecting Ray and the victim and his repeated use of Craigslist. Ray simply denied it all.

Strangely, Ray perseverated in several letters about how, on the night of his arrest, the news on the radio said police were looking for a red automobile, its driver suspected of kidnapping a woman. When the police arrested him at a traffic stop not far from his house, he told them he was not the alleged kidnapper. He pointed out to them that his car was not red. "They laughed at me," Ray wrote, as though they dismissed evidence of his innocence. He was not only skilled at denying facts that were incriminating, but at fantasizing evidence that was exculpatory.

Becoming increasingly suspicious, Ray asked in one letter if I had ever spoken about him to another inmate whom he apparently saw me interviewing. I reassured him at a subsequent session that I hadn't done that. "I can't trust anybody," he said.

***

Ray completed a series of intellectual and neuropsychological tests. I thought this necessary, given his history of learning problems, his mother's description of him as a slow learner, and my charge to identify mitigating information that might help his defense. He indeed was intellectually limited. He had a full-scale IQ score of 87, which placed him within the low-average range of ability, at the nineteenth percentile. That wasn't so bad. His verbal IQ, though, was 79. That's within the borderline level, at the eighth percentile. These scores were consistent with his academic limitations and explained why he needed special services during his school years. We of course live in a world that requires language skills to navigate and communicate effectively. And language facility is fundamental to the development of self-regulation. Children use inner language to help them follow directions before they really understand why they should. Mommy said, "no, don't touch the stove." Later, as the toddler walks toward the stove, an inner voice yells "No!" and commands him to halt.

Such a process is disrupted in children with language deficits, like Ray. But they don't don't grow up to become murderers.

Extensive neuropsychological testing[2] revealed Ray suffered from mild bilateral frontal deficiencies. For example, on the Wisconsin Card Sorting Test,[3] he was given a stack of cards with designs on them and asked to sort them into different piles, based upon particular abstract principles (e.g., colors, shapes) The principles were to be determined in a trial-and-error manner that provided him with feedback as to the accuracy of each response. After a run of ten consecutive correct responses, the sorting principle would then change, and he had to figure out the new principle. He was lacking in efficient problem solving and in organizing and retrieving nonverbal and verbal information. His frontal deficits added to his psychosocial limitations, especially his immaturity in judgment and, apropos to his case, poor self-control.

However real Ray's neuropsychological deficits, the results placed him within the mildly impaired range. He wasn't severely compromised by his cognitive difficulties.

Psychological testing of Ray's personality and emotional functioning yielded greater insight and added texture to the cognitive testing results. His Minnesota Multiphasic Personality Inventory-2-RF (MMPI-2-RF) pattern of scale elevations represented a complex psychological picture. I expected his validity scales to be elevated to a point that the results might be too distorted to consider. Not so; he was only slightly self-favorable.

The MMPI-2-RF results depicted Ray as an individual with a depressed mood, many physical preoccupations, and a tendency for episodes of agitation and manic-like behavior. He uses denial as needed and lacked psychological mindedness. As a consequence, he had a superficial understanding of himself and others. Individuals with his scale elevations are fearful of sexual intimacy. They have ambivalent feelings toward the opposite sex, possibly as a defensive strategy to assuage the anxiety that comes with feelings of sexual inadequacy. Insecure and with a precarious self-identity, Ray was attention seeking and needy. Because of his fear of intimacy and lack of self-understanding, he was in a state of constant inner tension.

Most significantly, Ray's profile was that of an individual who, when anxious situations created threats to his already frail sense of security, needed to release his building emotional tensions.

Ray also completed the Millon Clinical Multiaxial Inventory.[4] It tests for the presence of mental abnormity generally, with special weight given to identifying and diagnosing personality disturbances. I don't typically use this instrument for forensic evaluations because it overdiagnoses personality disorders, which sometimes might distract from other, more severe psychiatric conditions that are crucial to the legal issues at hand. I wasn't worried about this in Ray's case. He wasn't suffering from schizophrenia or another severe mental illness that was the central driver behind his crimes. Together with the MMPI-2-RF, the Millon could help in my understanding of his personality makeup and disturbances.

Ray's pattern of scores indicated very strong dependency needs and an intense separation anxiety from those on whom he depended. Again, as with the MMPI-2-RF, this was evidence of a fragile self-identity. His profile was similar to individuals who easily feel abandoned, resulting from his insecure attachments with early caretakers. Fearful of losing ties to those with whom he felt bonded, he expressed himself indirectly and, ironically, in passive-aggressive and twisted ways. This finding resonated with Tanya's description of him, as well as his mother's, depicting him as having taunted his sisters in years past.

Interestingly, the Millon revealed a submissive-masochistic side to his personality. He could be self-derogatory and passive in his overt social behavior, possibly reflected in his softer appearance when I first encountered him. But Ray could flip from passive to hostile and sadistic behavior. Similar to the MMPI-2-RF scores, the Millon pattern of "No!" scores were those of an individual saddled with an underlying bitterness and cynicism who is finding it increasingly difficult to control his emotions.

I didn't view Ray as psychopathic, but given his crimes, I completed the Hare Psychopathy Checklist nonetheless. His scores were fairly low, inconsistent with psychopathy. On the interpersonal cruelty factor, he was at the sixtieth percentile, around average for prison inmates. His antisocial behavior factor was low, at the eighth percentile. Compared to psychopaths, including rapist-psychopathy, he didn't have an extensive or versatile history of crime dating back to his teenage years. And unlike psychopathy, his adult history of violence and criminality was widespread and versatile: his sadistic cruelty was sexually linked, readied for and aimed at his rape victims.

In addition, Ray completed the Clarke Sex History Questionnaire.[5] Like the MMPI-2-RF, it's an omnibus test with multiple validity and content scales but limited in its focus to a person's sexual behavior and proclivities. With approximately twenty scales, it probes the various dimensions of an adult's sexual history and behavior, preferences, inhibitions, obsessions, and fantasy life. Ray's scores were compared to a large group of sexual offenders. Scores in the high range are considered significant.

Ray responded candidly to the test items. His highest score, predictably, was on the sexual aggression scale. He was in the twentieth percentile. He admitted to dominant-controlling sexual encounters on at least twenty occasions with various women. When we discussed the testing results, his response was, "They wanted rough sex." He described it as "more passionate."

Ray scored high on the transvestism and child identification scales of the Clarke. As a child, he secretly dressed up in his sisters' clothing. "I don't know. . . . [I]t was fun," he told me. "I wish I could be a kid again." He enjoyed playing with children and indicated he would like to work with kids. He denied ever molesting a child or fantasizing about it.

On the Clarke, Ray reported that he does not engage in sexual fantasizing. I confronted him on this. "It doesn't pass the smell test," I said. I never met a man (especially those who watch a lot of porn) who doesn't, I told him, hoping to loosen his restraint. Finally, after more discussion, he admitted that he did fantasize. Ray imagined "a woman forcing me to have sex with her . . . and oral sex."

I completed the Sexual Homicide Crime Scene Rating Scale for Sexual Sadism on Ray,[6] which is used to estimate the degree of sexual sadism expressed during a sexual homicide crime. It has ten items, each scored from zero to two. Ray scored a nine, indicating the likelihood of sadism as a principal driver of the killings and rapes. For instance, he dominated the victims through the use of asphyxia, and he left bite marks.

***

It was time to discuss the complex evaluation results with Bill, Ray's attorney. Clearly, Ray was psychologically disturbed, but psychiatric conditions don't directly translate into legal defense or mitigation possibilities. Much typically depends on the defendant's mental state at the time. In Ray's case, his claim of complete innocence precluded his mental condition as a defense in response to the charges since he denied committing them.

Maybe psychological evidence could be offered at sentencing that could save Ray from capital sentencing.

I met with Bill on a Friday morning. He had a new office in the hip part of downtown, surrounded by artists' lofts and wine bars. Casually dressed, he was more relaxed than I'd ever seen him. At the jail or courthouse, his mind was always churning and cascading about. Not today. His easygoing manner made the discussion of Ray's difficult case that much easier.

We had already discussed Ray's disturbed early history, especially his father's disavowal of paternity. We had reviewed my observations about Ray's mother, her coldness and her deluded denial. We had previously discussed Ray's hypersexuality as possibly related to his early introduction to sexuality by his older sister's friend, as well as other issues in Ray's unusual early history. We had not yet considered fully the consequences of this history on his psychological development and how it related to his status as an accused serial sexual murderer. Nor had we discussed much of the psychological testing results.

I outlined Ray's profoundly arrested psychological development, including the deadness of his inner life captured so evocatively by Tanya's depiction of him as living with an "emotional void," a fragile identity, and with little sense of who he is. His father's rejection was total; he denied Ray's paternity. Worse, he cruelly flaunted the rejection by fawning over his daughters in Ray's presence. Ray's mother was both overprotective yet emotionally distant and cold. She wasn't equipped to soothe his early suffering and feelings of abandonment. And currently, she couldn't face the calamities he created in his adult life. It was another form of repudiation, albeit unwitting. These privations happened to a child who, together with the emotional limitations that come with such a disordered early milieu, had intellectual lacunae with limited problem-solving ability and a weakened capacity for efficient and organized thinking, all of which contributed to his crooked development. The confluence of his misfortunes stained his ability to construct a mature sense of himself that had meaning for his life experience.

In an attempt to be more concrete, I gave a little spiel about normal development to Bill, hoping it would help him to appreciate the implications of Ray's disordered early life. A crucial by-product of having been raised in a basically compassionate environment is a capacity to recognize and tolerate emotions, including complex ones, in oneself and others. It's bequeathed by reasonably empathic caretakers with the facility and willingness to serve as surrogates and who vicariously perceive, interpret, and regulate the feelings and fears of the child's budding mind. Eventually, the child becomes capable of independent and mature functioning, which includes the capacity to understand one's own mind and the mind of others. This is basic to the construction of an emotional self with a rich and cohesively formed inner life; in other words, it's the foundation of a sturdy identity and emotional self-awareness.

Tanya, I told Bill, looked into Ray's face and saw his void, the consequence of deprivations in nurturance and validation. But the result of such lacunae is not simply emptiness. A void that is fundamental to one's psyche produces pressure, like that of a punctured window in a high-flying jet whose hurricane-like decompression is followed by a deadly explosiveness.

Ray's distorted psychological development engendered the modus operandi for his rapes and sexual homicides that is referred to in the professional literature as catathymic in nature.[7] This particular cohort of sexual murders showed a pattern of fury and sexual violence motivated by latent sexual torments and inadequacies for which "[t]his violent act has some symbolic significance over and above its obvious meaning."[8] A buildup of tension and motivational drive inevitably leads to a sudden blitz of explosive violence.[9] It's an outburst designed to release the pressure of a long-held and festering grievance. One of Ray's surviving victims, for example, described how he "out of nowhere ran towards me . . . tackled me to the ground" with such force that "my shoe flew off and down the hallway." Although it's a displacement and symbolic of the original injury, it does the trick, if only for a while.

Bill wondered if Ray had a psychopathic personality. I did not believe so. On the Hare Psychopathy Checklist, he showed some features of the condition (e.g., failure to accept responsibility), but he wasn't coldly detached or glib like so many psychopaths. Ray's cruelty was circumscribed and sexually sadistic in nature. It served to neutralize his inner turmoil, to evacuate, at least for a while, his mounting inner chaos.

Catathymic sexual murderers like Ray tend not to be psychopathic.[10] They aren't cool and calculating; they're hot and furious. Less interested in killing, the catathymic offender's aim is to make the victim suffer, satisfying a fantasy of revenge for past hurts and narcissistic injuries.[11] Frequently, the killer's memory of the event is poor, likely a result of the disorienting nature of such frenzied emotions and behavior. This may have contributed to Ray's adamant denial of guilt; subjectively, the events become less and less real over time.

Though he had killed two women, I didn't think the homicides were intentional, I told Bill. Nor did I think the asphyxiation was integral to his sexual arousal. If it were, strangulation would likely have surfaced in his sexual life with Tanya—possibly by asking her to asphyxiate him—or at least in the porn he viewed. That didn't seem to be the case. Most of his rape victims were strangled to unconsciousness. The homicides were likely the unintended consequences of his frenzied wrath.

I told Bill that Ray had a borderline personality, which is characterized by splitting as a defense (all good and all bad emotions kept apart), and a malformed identity that lacked a mature emotional center. The pain of nonrecognition and intolerable rejections was too much for Ray, the little boy, to absorb. For Ray the man, the cadence and vagaries of emotional life were spinning and chaotic experiences. To manage, he learned to keep it simple: bifurcate emotions and keep the dark where it belongs, invisible and away from any available goodness. This becomes a way of experiencing himself and others in a black-and-white, emotionally un-complicated fashion. Handling intense or ambivalent feelings created a psychic swirl that was dangerous and threatened a fragile self.

Ray's borderline condition was severe, which profoundly compro-mised his ability to navigate the world of adult intimacy and sexuality. His splitting defense was explicitly manifest in the contrast between his relationship with Tanya and his victims. Toward Tanya, he was loving and respectful, but in a cartoonish way, as if she was a specimen of virgin purity. His savage and sadistic hatred was saved for his victims. With an emotional self in such an underdeveloped, dissected state, his dark dai-monic side was never cushioned by his more benign personal elements. Inevitably, it longed for release, for decompression.

As part of his borderline personality, Ray had gender identification conflicts, evidenced by his dressing like a girl as a child and his elevated score on the transvestism scale. It made sense that a part of him wished to be female; he witnessed his sisters being given so much of what he hopelessly longed for but was denied as a boy: attention and recognition from his father. This also points to the source of his sadism; a fiery envy of women turned to blood-boiling rage at them with a derisive urge for control. Or, to use Erich Fromm's description of sadism, [12] Ray inverted impotence into omnipotence.

Splitting and the use of primitive denial were survival mechanisms for Ray, psychically speaking. Self-examination can be a dangerous proposition if it stirs emotions too hot to handle. Anxiety is a "signal emotion" for all of us, a ringing of the bell that prepares for threats from either external situations or inner passions. But not all anxiety is the same; for someone with a fragile identity like Ray, it could be fragmenting to his psychological experience to the point that he might have moments when it was difficult to tell the difference between what is real and what isn't.

Summarizing all of his complex psychological information for Bill, I reiterated that Ray suffered from a combination of borderline and sadistic personality disorders with a misogynistic orientation. He was incapable of forming and enjoying the fruits of a mature heterosexual relationship. With his core defense of splitting, he sectioned off his fears from his hatred. Projection was an ancillary coping device. His sexual fantasies of being dominated by women were projections of his own impulses to demean and control them. Unlike a psychopath, Ray wasn't devaluating and controlling toward anyone in his way; it was women he was after, in order to exorcise his demons. He knew the women he raped were suffering; his was an atavistically perverse form of empathy, along with the joy of schadenfreude from their pain.

If we wanted to pinpoint one source of Ray's destructive psychopathology, I told Bill, my vote would go to his father's mindless insensitivity and abject rejection of Ray, while showering attention to his daughters and throwing it in Ray's face.

Bill wanted some time to consider the medical-legal implications of what he had just heard from me.

***

About two or three weeks after our meeting, Bill called. He had spoken with the prosecutor on the case, who made the following offer: if Ray pleaded guilty to all counts, he would take the death penalty off the table and recommend to the judge that Ray be sentenced to life imprisonment without parole. Ray, however, continued to claim innocence even after Bill detailed the overwhelming evidence against him. Bill briefed Ray on my findings and told Ray he was facing very limited legal options. Bill was frustrated, describing the district attorney's offer as a "gift from the heavens." He asked if I could go with him to the jail and together "we have a come-to-Jesus talk" with his client. I suspected Bill hoped I would counterbalance his blunt style with my therapeutic one. A good cop, bad cop approach, I guess.

I had not seen Ray for a while. He was now under increased pressure to face his limited legal options, which was a challenge to his denial mechanism. The pressure was taking its toll. He was more sullen, withdrawn, and distrustful.

Bill began the meeting by reviewing the plea offer. Immediately, Ray responded, "But I'm innocent." I didn't say much, quickly realizing that Bill wanted me there to have a calming effect on Bill, not to directly influence Ray. Bill reiterated the case against Ray, who occasionally glanced at me. Bill was a bit softer than usual, even sympathetic. He told Ray that if he took the case to trial, a guilty verdict was almost certain. Ray would be left with the death penalty hanging over his head. If he pleaded guilty, Bill reminded Ray, he'd have an opportunity to see his children grow up, and this whole legal mess would be easier on his family.

Still, Ray said that he wanted time to think about it.

As we left the jail, Bill gave me more details about how the plea arrangement came about. The prosecutor on the case was a very experienced litigator. Apparently, he also happened to be compassionate. He offered Ray the deal to spare the victims' families and Ray's young children from being exposed to years of appeals and newspaper reports on the status of Ray's case, which is typical with serial rape-murder death-penalty cases. It takes years to litigate because of the multiple appeals by capital defendants, while the families of all involved are put through hell. Most important, the prosecutor came to believe that Ray likely did not intend to murder the two victims but that it happened during the course of the rapes. The evidence suggested that the murders were not premeditated; rather, they were a by-product of his sexual drive to mix violence with sex.

Several weeks after our meeting with Ray at the jail, I received a call from Bill. Ray refused to accept the plea. "I guess we're going to trial," Bill said in exasperation.

***

The trial didn't get underway until approximately three years after my last meeting with Bill and Ray. The district attorney's office continued investigating Ray's link to other unsolved rapes and sexual homicides in southern California.

At the trial's opening, the prosecutor told the jury that Ray perpetrated a string of rapes and assaults and committed two murders in the process. He was arrested after having left his genetic material at one of the crime scenes. Ray's DNA also linked him to the other offenses. And there were the eyewitnesses who identified him. The prosecutor described the evidence as "airtight . . . incontrovertible."

The trial lasted less than two weeks. There was some minor controversy about the quality of the DNA evidence, but it was a Hail Mary pass of desperation. I read in the local newspaper that Ray was found guilty of rape and special circumstances double murder.

***

I expected that I might get a call from Bill to discuss the pros and cons of my testifying at the penalty phase of Ray's trial, but it never came. I read in the newspaper that Ray was sentenced to death. The article mentioned the name of the defense attorney who made the closing statement, imploring the jury to impose a life term without the possibility of parole, contending that Ray "was a soft-spoken and polite man who grew up in poverty." The lawyer was not Bill.

I called his office, but Bill's partner answered with a message that he was no longer in practice and to call her if records were needed on a case previously handled by him. Puzzled, I called Andrew, a friend and colleague of Bill and someone I had worked with, to get the scoop.

A grim-sounding Andrew told me that Bill had killed himself. Less than a year earlier, he said he was taking some time off to go back East and visit family. Instead, Bill was found dead in the Northwest where he sometimes vacationed and spent downtime fishing. He blew his brains out in a hotel room, alone. Shaken and shocked, I was mute for a moment. Andrew spoke, "Yeah, I know. We were all dumbfounded. Bill had a problem with alcohol and he was moody, but still. . . ."

I keep reviewing in my mind the times we struggled together on cases, especially Ray's. I pictured Bill's muted smile, brightened by an easy chuckle. We worked well together, and I prized his intelligence and intensity. Did it make me oblivious to his struggles? Not that I would have had any standing to help. He was a colleague, not a friend. I didn't even know about his alcohol problem. I didn't feel guilty; it was more of a shame and disappointment in myself for being so unaware of what must have been a festering pain. Why didn't I have a scintilla of recognition?

Ray's case was so bleak and tragic. So much pathos and unnecessary pain. Now, the darkness burrowed deeper.

10

MAN-CHILD OR TROUBLED TEEN?

Juveniles Tried as Adults

One cannot in the nature of things expect a little tree that has been turned into a club to put forth leaves.—Martin Buber

After quickly reading the first hundred pages of a voluminous stack of documents sent by Phillip's attorney, the facts of the case were plain and appalling. A twenty-two-year-old drug dealer was shot in the stomach and died in a dank dusky apartment hallway. A drug deal had gone tragically bad. Eyewitnesses heard two shots and saw two males running from a building into a waiting black Toyota, which then fled. The apparent shooter jumped in the front passenger seat as the vehicle sped away. The other man, who witnesses said was standing outside the building when the shots were fired, jumped into the backseat. Phillip was later identified as the male outside the building, an apparent lookout.

Two days later, Phillip and three companions, including the two other suspects, were picked up by the police as they drove around in that same black Toyota Tundra. They were first arrested for possession, since methamphetamines were found in the vehicle.

Phillip was interviewed by two detectives, first about the drugs in the car before quickly pivoting to the homicide. He denied knowing anything about a killing. One detective confronted him, reminding Phillip that "it's all over the media." He held tight to his ignorance, saying he didn't watch TV and that he just listened to music. After about an hour and a half of stoic denial, the interview ended, and Phillip was transferred to juvenile hall.

Phillip was just fifteen years old at the time of his arrest. He was charged with felony murder.

A few days later at juvenile hall, a staff member overheard Phillip telling a gang member, "My homie smoked a drug dealer."

At his first court hearing, the prosecutor requested that Phillip be transferred to adult court for trial. Phillip was charged with murder that occurred during the commission of a felony—attempted robbery of the drug dealer. Thus, if tried as an adult, he could face life in prison without the possibility of parole.

Phillip's attorney, Sara Feldman, retained me to conduct a juvenile transfer 707 evaluation. Californians had recently passed Proposition 57, which requires a juvenile court judge to decide whether a juvenile is fit to be transferred to adult court for adjudication. The specific criteria to be considered are set forth by California's Welfare and Institution Code 707.[1] A psychological expert may submit a report and opine on the minor's fitness to be tried as adult.

***

I continued wading through the sixteen hundred pages of documents related to the homicide, including the police and court reports, educational records, medical records, and hours of videos related to the case. The basic calamitous facts remained the same but more sordid. Killing the drug dealer appeared to have been *planned*.

Phillip was the only juvenile suspect at the time of the murder. The two others were adults. At twenty-seven years of age, Tony, the driver of the Tundra, was the oldest. The shooter, Jose, was nineteen years old and a local gang member.

I first watched the videotape interviews of Tony. He had a record of prior drug busts and two domestic violence arrests. He had driven to the drug deal but said he didn't know Jose had a weapon. Jose was to buy drugs, and Phillip was to be a lookout.

The Tundra that Tony drove belonged to his employer. A dash cam had been installed several months earlier. Tony apparently forgot that it was set to record whenever the truck's engine was engaged. The plan to rob and kill the drug dealer was recorded. Tony could be heard telling

Jose not to forget his "piece." At another point, he made reference to taking "your baby with you," apparently meaning Jose's revolver. They discussed shooting the drug dealer multiple times, ensuring that he "bleeds out."

They spoke of the planned attack for about ten minutes before picking up Phillip. As the three of them drove, they talked about "scoring meth," with Tony telling Jose to "stay calm . . . don't look concerned." Some of the conversation was difficult to hear over the sounds from the street and the radio, but there was no talk among the three of killing the drug dealer.

Tony's interview was brief. Soon after the detectives reminded him of the dash cam, he asked for a lawyer.

I watched Phillip's interview with the detectives after reading a brief summary about it in a police report. He steadfastly claimed innocence in any plan to murder; he only wanted to score methamphetamines. Watching the video was my first encounter with him. Phillip is about five feet, seven inches tall. At that time, soon after his arrest, he looked even younger than his fifteen years, thin and drawn. I thought to myself, *here's a meth addict who needs a good meal.*

But mostly it was his attitude that caught my attention, even trumping his impoverished appearance. Phillip was cavalier and indifferent to the seriousness of his plight. He dismissed the Miranda warnings with a "Yeah, yeah" to each of the questions. His replies were pithy and with an easy irritability ("I told you I didn't know. . . . Fuck this!"). He refused any gesture of support from the detectives. Maybe because he looked so thin and malnourished, they actually seemed sympathetic, offering to get him a McDonald's hamburger. He declined. He refused water. He refused to make eye contact. Was this fifteen-year-old already so hardened, or was his attitude a drug-induced masquerade?

***

Phillip's mother called me not long after she was given my number by his attorney. "I could meet at any time." Ms. Sanchez clearly had a story she wanted to tell. We spoke for about two and a half hours. She wanted me to know the circumstances surrounding the homicide. For the first hour, I listened without saying much; I took notes as she told her story.

As Phillip entered his teen years, he began spending more time away from home and on the streets. He was never a great student. Though never placed in a learning disability program, he received resource specialist assistance during his elementary school years. During junior high, he began sluffing off his homework assignments and failed a few subjects. He was never aggressive or violent, but he began to talk back to his mother and rebelled more than he had during his early years. Ms. Sanchez first thought this was typical adolescent behavior. She became concerned over time. He had the same friends since his elementary school years, but several of them had become gang members, judging by the way they dressed. Phillip told her he wasn't a gang member, and he didn't dress like one.

Her worries became acute after she received a call from the police, telling her to pick Phillip up at the police station. He was detained while walking home with two teenage gang members whom the police suspected of committing a burglary earlier that week. They told his mother that Phillip was now identified as a gang member.

At that point, Ms. Sanchez decided to take action. Phillip just turned fourteen, and she was worried about what might happen if he spent his teen years in the neighborhood. She decided to send him to Mexico to live with his father, Hector. Though she hadn't talked to Phillip's father for a number of years and he had a bad temper, especially when he drank, she wanted to protect her son from "the gangs and other bad influences around here." Phillip was more than agreeable.

All went well at first. Phillip seemed happy during their occasional conversations. But he became increasingly listless and remote. He eventually told Ms. Sanchez that a woman had moved in the house along with her two children. She didn't like him. "She wants my daddy's attention," Phillip told her. And she wanted his father to pay more attention to her children.

A month or so after this woman moved in, Hector asked Phillip to find a job. He was financially stressed by the extra mouths to feed. Their relationship became increasingly strained as a result of Phillip's inability to find work. Hector limited Phillip's access to food. He ate dinner alone, in his room.

Ms. Sanchez arranged for Phillip to move in with her own father, who lived not too far away in Mexico, though she was reluctant to do so. "My father is a selfish old man. But I had no choice."

Phillip's situation went from bad to worse. His grandfather forced him to do ranch work and wouldn't feed Phillip if he made mistakes or didn't complete enough work. Showing emotion for the first time, Ms. Sanchez became tearful, saying she had sent her father money to help support Phillip.

She arranged for Phillip to return home from Mexico. When she first saw him, she was shocked. "Phillip was very changed." Thin and fragile looking, he was preoccupied and very sad. At times, she heard him crying in his room. Being in Mexico "really, really affected him." He became rebellious, more so than before moving to Mexico. She noticed that he wasn't eating well, and he continued to lose weight. She was worried, saying, "He was so drawn looking. I didn't know what to do. He would come home very late and sleep during the day."

In retrospect, Ms. Sanchez realized that Phillip was using drugs. She felt the incident that led to Phillip's arrest had something to do with his drug use and his "very bad time in Mexico."

Mrs. Sanchez told me about Phillip's developmental and family history. His birth and delivery were normal. She and her husband separated when Phillip was about seven years old. She was vague and somewhat evasive when we discussed the marital relationship. "He drank." I asked if there was any domestic violence. "There was some pushing and shoving at times." Their marital problems didn't seem to affect Phillip. "He was a happy kid." It was after his father left that he became moody. She was called by the school on several occasions because of his behavior. She knew Phillip missed his father, but they were better off without him, she said.

Not long after the separation from Phillip's father, Ms. Sanchez developed a relationship with Manuel, who moved in with her and Phillip. They separated during the time Phillip was in Mexico.

Because he missed his father, Phillip developed a close relationship and Manuel. "They were a lot alike . . . touchy-feely. Unlike me."

I asked Ms. Sanchez if Manuel's absence was a shock to Phillip when he returned home from Mexico. "I don't think so." He didn't have a response, she said.

In a no-nonsense, serious manner, Ms. Sanchez emphasized facts and events she wanted me to consider. Speaking in a monotone with a fixed, deadpan expression, she came across as a level-headed historian, clearly concerned for the fate of her child. Yet I wondered if her constricted emotions and detached style aborted a fuller appreciation of Phillip's psychological predicaments.

***

Before I began my interviews with Phillip, I read his pretrial probation department report. Almost invariably, these reports present an exacting portrait of the minor. It's understandable: typically, the probation officer has a one-off interview with a guarded adolescent who was instructed by his attorney to avoid any discussion of the crime. The details of the offense were summarized in the report as being "atrocious." The probation officer hadn't yet completed an interview with Phillip's mother and didn't have access to any experts' reports. In addition to the police and school records, she relied on Phillip's self-reported personal history and his interview behavior to complete her probation evaluation.

I expected the worst. I was surprised. The summary of the crime was indeed ghastly and tragic: a young man was intentionally shot to death with two bullets in his stomach, after which Phillip and two other perpetrators fled the scene. Toward the end, the report outlined protective and risk factors, which are conditions or attributes that bode well or ill regarding the likelihood of future criminal behavior. Phillip's only protective factors were his clean criminal history and his part-time job before he got arrested. Risk factors were many, including chronic junior high school problems such as poor attendance, gang associations, drug use, inadequate home supervision, and so forth. But the probation officer also made the point that Phillip was free of behavior problems during his elementary school years, and he was regularly described by teachers as "a pleasure to have in class." She softened the impact of his gang affiliation by adding that Phillip denied it and that these gang members had been his friends since childhood. The picture she provided of Phillip was not that of a cold-hearted criminal. That was unusual.

In her concluding remarks, the officer recommended detention in juvenile hall—a given considering the charges against Phillip. Most significant to me was her conclusion that, "The minor's degree of criminal sophistication is unknown." Sophistication is one of the criteria to be considered when a judge decides if a minor should be adjudicated in juvenile or adult court. Probation reports almost always emphasize the minor's criminally sophisticated behavior. Many times, the conclusions are a non sequitur to the narrative, which may include deficits like an intellectual disability that belies sophistication. This report was notably different. The probation officer, I suspected, saw something redeeming about Phillip.

***

When Phillip walked into the consulting room, he was handcuffed and escorted by two juvenile hall staff members. I thought they had the wrong teen. He looked nothing like the one in the police video. It had been almost a year since Phillip had been first arrested. Incarceration had altered him for the better. He looked taller. He sported a pair of glasses and a light mustache. Expecting a sullen adolescent, I was taken aback by his bright smile as he greeted me. I asked the staff to remove his handcuffs, which they did. A staff member sat outside the consulting room (with the door closed) throughout my long interviews with him, a requirement because of the nature of his alleged offense.

I've evaluated many minors over the years. This one was different in demeanor and appearance. Phillip's clothes were crisp and fresh looking, as though his gray shirt and burgundy pants had been carefully ironed. With his black hair neatly combed and parted, he looked less like an alleged murderer and more akin to a wannabe preppy.

Phillip listened as I explained to him the reasons for my presence and that we would be meeting several times over the next couple of months. I told him I had already met with his mother. "I know," he said, sadness washing over his bright expression.

I began by asking about his life before the arrest. Phillip lived with his mother and worked at a laundromat owned by a friend's father. His mother was clearly in the forefront of his mind. "My mother, she always tries [sic] to make me happy when I was growing up." He described her as strong, "no matter what I put her through." Chastising himself further, he went on, saying, "She works day and night cleaning houses." He was "another problem" atop her financial worries.

After a year in juvenile hall, he was clearly thinking about the impact that his conduct had on her. I wondered how Phillip felt about the victim.

We continued to talk about his mother and his earlier life. Phillip blamed his mother when his father left for Mexico. He was about seven or eight years old, he said. He misbehaved at school and was "mean" to other children, "just because . . . I don't know . . . I was mad." He loved the occasional phone conversations with his father. He had "scary" memories of arguments between his parents. He saw his father push and shove his mother. He punched her on one occasion. Still, he wanted his father around.

Curiously, Phillip never mentioned Manuel, his mother's boyfriend. I asked why he hadn't mentioned him. "I don't talk about it." A few moments later, "He was like a father figure." He cryptically added, "I hide myself."

In addition to asking about his "mean" behavior at school, I queried Phillip about symptoms during his early years such as stealing, bullying others, animal torture, fire setting, enuresis or encopresis, and so on. He denied them all, except bullying. Most interesting was his curiosity about my questions. He wanted to know the reason behind them. "Why'd you ask those things?" Minors are typically dismissive or annoyed by questions. He seemed genuinely curious about the meaning behind them. It revealed an introspective bent, though in a nascent stage.

I asked about his bullying of others. He was "mad all the time" and getting into fights. "At school, I was like a demon." Before his teen years, "I was a follower. I wanted to be liked, make people think I was big." During those early years, "I just didn't like my life. I didn't give a fuck about school. Now I do." Still, for some reason, his elementary school teachers frequently described him as a pleasure to have as a student. He couldn't say why.

His high school years were interrupted by his stay in Mexico, where Phillip didn't attend school at all. Upon return, he enrolled in a continuation high school and attended until his arrest. By then he was "kicking it with gang members" to get drugs. He never "jumped in"; that is, he wasn't a gang member proper. He admitted, "I was mad [about] what happened to me" in Mexico.

At juvenile hall, his grades were good, as was his behavior. "I'm happy about my grades," Phillip said. When he grew up, he said he'd like to work in a body shop customizing cars.

During our second session, I continued soliciting his perspective on his early life. With a halting hesitation, Phillip disclosed, "When I was a kid, an older man touched me . . . made me smoke cigarettes." It happened multiple times, more than five. He never informed his mother, as he felt too ashamed and guilty.

Though registered with the police as a gang member, Phillip had no record of charges or arrests, gang related or not. He admitted to spending time and "hanging" with gang members. It was how he became friendly with Jose, his codefendant and classmate during the elementary school years. But he denied having "jumped in" to the gang; he was not a formal member and didn't participate in their criminal activities and gang violence. His major reason for hanging around with gang members was their easy access to drugs, he told me. He had begun using marijuana during his junior high school years. At the time of his arrest, it was a daily habit. And he smoked methamphetamine "mostly every day," followed by snorting air dust, the refrigerant-based cleaner used to remove dust from computers. He use it "a lot. It helped knock me out."

Phillip never liked alcohol, but for reasons unknown to him, "I drank a lot of beer and liquor" in Mexico. I pressed him to consider why. He admitted, "'cause I was sad . . . kicked out of my dad's house . . . I'd drink."

***

Phillip was elated when his mother told him he was going to Mexico to visit his father. "I remember the exact day and time I landed, 7:23 a.m. I didn't see my daddy for years."

"It was great in Mexico" during the early months. Then, his father's girlfriend moved in with her kids. His father spent "more time with her kids . . . carrying them on his shoulders."

It made Phillip sad. His paternal grandfather told Phillip, "Let your father be happy."

"His girlfriend never liked me," Phillip said. They argued all the time. "When things went wrong, she screamed at me . . . no food." Either he'd go to bed without supper or was told to eat alone in another room. He soon decided, "Screw it. I have to find my way. That's when I started using methamphetamines. It made me happy. It made me not hungry."

Eventually his father "kicked me out." Phillip went to live with his maternal grandfather on a ranch. "It got worse. I had to work to eat. I got things wrong, I didn't know how to work."

Phillip spent about a year in Mexico. He admitted to using drugs before going to Mexico, mostly marijuana. Upon his return to California, he kept smoking marijuana, but he also used methamphetamines, having gotten hooked on them in Mexico.

Now back home, "I was using it. I was sad because of what I went through. I don't feel nothing." He found that alcohol also did the trick.

I asked Phillip about his current thoughts regarding his father and their relationship. He was very circumspect, "He's alright." He added that his mother and Manuel were "a perfect match" and that Manuel "was more of a dad to him than my real dad."

When he returned from the trauma of Mexico, Phillip had not only lost his bond with his father but also his relationship with Manuel. He was now psychologically bereft of a reunion fantasy with a loving father that he had so coveted for years.

**

An hour or so into our second meeting, we began to explore the events surrounding the killing of Miguel, the drug dealer. We did so over the course of multiple sessions, with increasing levels of depth. It was like we were peeling an onion; the more we peeled away, the harder it was for Phillip to tolerate. At first, he tried to avoid the topic with a few summary remarks. "I admit I was there," Phillip said. "I never ever touched any-body. I just left." Confronting Phillip, I said, "We have to go into what happened. In detail." He looked worried and scared. Little by little, we got there.

The night before the homicide, Phillip had not slept; he smoked weed and meth until the morning hours. He napped briefly. He couldn't recall when, but sometime in the afternoon, he left the house, hoping to "score more meth." He made some calls and soon made contact with Jose, one of his "homies from the neighborhood and school." Jose was a gangbanger but "cool." And he had quick access to drugs, which they frequently used together. He told Phillip he and another homie were on their way to buy meth from a local dealer. Jose told Phillip, "I'll pick you up."

Jose arrived with a "dude" named Tony. Phillip didn't know him. After picking up Phillip, they stopped to buy some cigarettes and smoked meth and weed together in the car. Jose told Phillip that he and Tony were on their way to meet Miguel, a drug dealer, and rob him. I asked how he reacted. "Fuck, I just wanted more meth," Phillip responded. I asked if he heard Jose and Tony discuss how they intended to rob Miguel. He had no clear recollection, saying he was high on methamphetamines. "They were talking . . . all I know, I wanted drugs. I wasn't thinking straight." I asked if he saw Jose with a gun. He didn't, although he had seen Jose with a gun in the past.

Jose, Phillip said, told him to wait outside the hallway of the building to make sure no one entered. I asked if he suspected Jose had a weapon, given that he was going to rob a drug dealer. Again, Phillip said he wasn't thinking, other than of scoring meth. He admitted to having "a bad feeling" after getting out of the vehicle and walking toward the building. He was becoming more and more anxious when he heard shots fired. He was not sure how many. Although witnesses have described Phillip as running back into the car with the other assailant, Phillip said that wasn't accurate. After hearing the shots, "I thought, 'Fuck it' and ran." Not long after, Tony and Jose picked him up. Jose was very agitated, but they didn't talk about what happened. Jose commented, "It was fucked up."

Phillip admitted he didn't ask any questions. He smoked some meth with Tony and Jose and went home that night. "I didn't think about what happened."

A few days later, Phillip was again looking to score meth. He figured he'd call Jose and get some from him. Not long after being picked up by Jose, Tony, "and another dude," the police stopped and arrested them.

This is when Phillip heard Jose and Tony talking about the shooting, shortly before they were stopped by the police. Phillip knew then that Miguel was dead.

I told Phillip I reviewed the dash cam footage, and it was clear Tony and Jose planned to shoot and kill the drug dealer. Phillip again said he had no recollection of that conversation. He had told the police he had been in the car for only a few minutes prior to the homicide. Now he realized that they were together longer. Still, he never heard plans to shoot the drug dealer, and he didn't see Jose with a gun.

Phillip emphasized how different he is when he is on drugs. "When I'm sober and people tell me what I said, I go 'oh shit, I said that?'"

***

Almost always, I include psychological testing as a part of my forensic psychological evaluation. In this particular case, given the questions about Phillip's maturity and capacity for psychological sophistication, testing was especially germane.

Phillip completed a number of neuropsychological tests, including intelligence and achievement testing. I wasn't interested in his intelligence per se, but I wanted to get a handle on his overall level of neurocognitive development and its influence on his behavior, including judgment, impulse control, and decision making. Of particular importance to his maturity was his level of executive functioning capacity, which is the ability to plan, think through situations, and problem solve effectively.

The Wechsler IQ test[2] places an examinee's performance within several categories of ability. Phillip obtained a score that placed him within the borderline category. With an IQ of 73, he was in the fourth percentile, which means that 96 percent of his peer group scored at or above him. His vocabulary and verbal reasoning were weak. He had difficulty, for instance, understanding the similarity between two words (e.g., table and couch). He was close to normal on nonverbal tasks such as making a design with blocks within a limited time period. This resonated with Phillip's desire to work in an auto repair shop, where visuospatial abilities are at a premium.

Phillip's achievement scores in reading words and math were low, consistent with his IQ scores. Surprisingly, Phillip's reading comprehension was better, just below average. This suggested that when given a context (a story as opposed to two words whose similarity he was asked to judge) he could think in a more verbally abstract fashion.

The Connors Continuous Performance Test[3] is a computer-based instrument that measures sustained attention, response inhibition, and concentration. Phillip was average on multiple measures of concentration, attention, and impulse control.

I further examined Phillip's capacity for executive functioning with the Iowa Gambling Test (IGT).[4] It's designed to simulate real-life decision making. His overall score on the IGT placed him within the nonimpaired range of decision making. Yet he was above average in a measure of insensitivity to loss, and he showed an inclination to expect defeat.

Overall, Phillip's cognitive testing revealed that he functioned within the borderline range of intellectual ability. He was weak in language comprehension, with nonverbal reasoning a relative strength. He had adequate impulse control and decision-making ability but was handicapped by his tendency to expect loss and failure.

I completed testing of Phillip's emotional functioning as well. From my review of his juvenile hall records, I knew he had been diagnosed there with post-traumatic stress syndrome. I administered an adolescent version of the PTSD Symptom Scale.[5] Phillip was within the severe range due to symptoms such as recurring bad dreams and memories.

I completed the adolescent psychopathy checklist,[6] similar to the one I described in chapter 6. The youth version provides factors that measure interpersonal-emotional features of the adolescent, as well as antisocial-behavioral ones. Compared to the scores of institutionalized adolescents, Phillip's total score placed him in the second percentile, meaning that ninety-eight out of one hundred incarcerated minors scored higher. He was below the twentieth percentile on all subscales of psychopathic functioning, including antisocial behavior, interpersonal destructiveness, and cruelty. The results indicated that Phillip was not a budding psychopath nor was he an adolescent prone toward misconduct.

As several of the crucial questions I needed to address concerned Phillip's level of maturity and sophistication, I completed the Risk-Sophistication Treatment Inventory (RSTI).[7] It's a semi-structured interview and rating scale used to estimate sophistication/maturity, dangerousness, and treatment amenability. The scores within each domain are then compared to a juvenile offense reference group and placed within three categories: low, medium, or high.

Phillip's total maturity/psychological sophistication score placed him within the middle range. Compared to other offenders, he was higher in self-control and introspection. Phillip's risk for dangerousness was low, and his treatment amenability was high. Save the arrest charge, he was free of a history of violence or psychopathic behavior. He related well with others, and he thought about his future.

Finally, Phillip completed a comprehensive inventory of his budding personality, the Millon Adolescent Clinical Inventory.[8] In addition to scales that address the validity of responses, it includes scales that identify various patterns of personality, symptoms, and psychiatric syndromes.

Because Phillip's validity scales indicated that his responses were influenced by a significant tendency to debase himself, the clinical scales were adjusted to account for this. His profile revealed a considerable amount of depression, anxiety, and pessimism, as well as a strong tendency toward guilt and self-reproach. Not surprisingly, he functioned with a chronic sense of insecurity and inferiority. He struggled with painful memories activated by minor stressors, and he was resentful of others because of his unmet dependency needs.

Overall, the testing results identified Phillip as an adolescent with a variety of symptoms, including depression, anxiety, a self-defeating tendency, substance abuse, and post-traumatic stress. He was not a predator, budding psychopath, or prone to violence. He had intellectual limitations buttressed by academic disruption.

Phillip's substance abuse began before his stay in Mexico but was exacerbated there. So were any preexisting stress and anxiety. His depression had a longer duration, present at least by the age of seven. His mother recognized behavior changes after his father left for Mexico. Phillip began acting out more at school. At home, Ms. Sanchez told me he punched the walls and cried more. He was not his previously compliant self. Children at that age don't recognize their moods in the way that adults might; rather, they act them out. Phillip's behavioral symptoms are sometimes characterized as depressogenic in nature, the result of an underlying mood disruption. He clearly felt the loss of his father's presence.

Phillip was also burdened with intellectual limitations. And he was exposed to a period of sexual abuse and a measure of neglect, albeit unwitting. His mother worked long hours, leaving Phillip to fend for himself much of the time. Manuel's presence helped, but he was at work a lot too. I reviewed a Child Protective Services report that was part of the records subpoenaed by his attorney. It wasn't clear who reported possible neglect (likely a school official). When I questioned Phillip about it, he became defensive and protective of his mother. "It was stupid." The allegation of neglect was found to be unsubstantiated by the investigating social worker.

The issue at home was more subtle than neglect. Though Phillip felt close to his mother, there was an emotional mismatch; he's the demonstrative type and needs affection, whereas she's impassive, matter of fact, and reserved, even distant. With the loss of his father, Phillip was left feeling needier yet prematurely forced to function independently beyond his means, emotionally and intellectually. This may have disrupted his ability to get close to Manuel, lest he risk loss and abandonment again.

Being temperamentally different from her son, Ms. Sanchez misunderstood his yearnings. She described Phillip as a child who "doesn't mature. He likes to cuddle. That's not like me." Although her observations were accurate, she didn't grasp the reasons behind his seemingly childlike behavior, his craving for emotion security and affection.

Ms. Sanchez was, nonetheless, attuned to Phillip's year-long trauma in Mexico not long before his arrest and charge of murder. He had already begun to use drugs to manage his depression before Mexico. It ramped up as an antidote and continued after his return to California.

***

Over the course of the evaluation sessions, Phillip's mood alternated from bright to hopeless. Sometimes upbeat and pleasant, at other times downcast and fatigued. He had regular nightmares. "I don't know. I get nightmares. I wake up quick. I sweat and sweat. I get cold and then I sweat." The nightmares had occurred for years, but the content had changed since his arrest. Before his arrest, "I got nightmares about people getting killed . . . stuff like that. I try to open my eyes. I can't." Since his arrest, the nightmares were about "the court . . . standing in front of the judge."

He was sometimes guilt ridden. "I get nightmares the night before [court]. I'm getting paid back for what I'd done." Here, I thought, was an opportunity to explore his guilty feelings about the killing. I directly asked if he felt remorse about it. Phillip responded defensively, reiterating, "I wasn't there. I didn't know." He pivoted to his mother's grief caused by his misdeeds.

Phillip didn't think it was fair that he was being charged with murder. He was clearly angry and fearful. Any guilt he may have felt about the homicide was buried under his anger and fear. And it was abated by a juvenile perspective about what it meant to be implicated in the death of another.

***

My appreciation of Phillip's psychological life deepened as we spent more time together. Early on, I wondered how he would react to me, aware of his repeated disappointment and hurt by men who were supposed to be good to him. I was an unknown, and we needed to discuss topics that were personal and painful. At our first encounter, he commented, "My lawyer said you're coming to help." I had to correct him. After explaining the evaluation process, I told him that the results might or might not help. He seemed surprised and a little disappointed. We went on.

After spending hours together, Phillip and I built a warm bond, one able to employ humor to navigate tough times and topics. While he at first resisted my attempts to explore the circumstances of the homicide with shrugged-off responses like, "I wasn't there" or "I don't know," I began reacting in a playfully sardonic fashion to questions he asked of me, meant as sideways confrontations. At the end of a session, he asked when I'd be back. In a quizzical tone, I said, "Gee, I don't know." He gave me a knowing smirk. At our next session, I asked him an innocuous question, "Did you have breakfast?" He was ready with a broad grin, "I don't know." Humor helped.

I clearly had positive feelings for Phillip, sort of a paternal transference, but I didn't want my evaluation to be colored by these feelings. I took notice that my overall impressions of Phillip's psychological state resonated with those of professionals at juvenile hall. A psychologist there diagnosed Phillip with stimulant dependency, major depressive disorder, and post-traumatic stress disorder. He had good relations with the juvenile hall staff, evidenced by their banter as they escorted him to our sessions. I could sense it in their clinical notes that I reviewed as well. And I thought about that mellow probation report that I read, even before meeting Phillip. I took heart that it wasn't just me and my transference.

It was Phillip's interpersonal and emotional strengths that contributed to his likability and our good working relationship. He had a natural warmth and a capacity for empathy, along with a reflective honesty. He couldn't yet tolerate the righteous remorse suitable for having been a participant in the death of another; that may have been too much to ask at this point, given his age. Plus, he was fighting for his future.

***

Phillip suffered from a number of psychological disorders. At juvenile hall, he had been diagnosed with a major depression. I didn't think he had the severity of symptoms to warrant that condition, which the latest Diagnostic Statistical Manual of the American Psychiatric Association[9] describes as a depressed mood and irritability nearly every day for weeks at a time. This kind of depression manifests in ways such as a sapped level of energy that makes everyday functioning almost impossible. Phillip's depressed condition was low grade and long term in nature and may have existed most of his life. Besides a low mood, he had felt hopeless and had a damaged self-esteem for many years. Recall that his mother noticed his depression after his father left for Mexico when Phillip was seven. He began to have crying spells and misbehaved at school, symptoms of an underlying depression. During and after Mexico, he used drugs as an antidote. He told a juvenile hall staff member that he always "hated my life."

The symptoms of post-traumatic stress include nightmares, a sense of numbness, intermittent mood states, and negative thoughts resulting from a life-threatening or near-lethal event. At home, Phillip's life was threatened on two occasions, with guns pointed at his head. He had been exposed to abject neglect in Mexico, where food was withheld and he felt alienated for a sustained period of time. He also had a history of being sexually abused. All of which affected his emotional state in a chronic way. I felt he warranted the post-traumatic stress diagnosis.

Phillip's intellectual ability was significantly below normal. More important, I thought, was his multiple substance abuse disorder. Until his arrest, he had continued to abuse methamphetamines and marijuana.

***

After many hours with Phillip, it was time to address the issues most important to the court and to Phillip's future. There were five factors the judge would need to consider when deciding whether Phillip was fit to be judged as a minor or tried in adult court.

They included:

1. What degree of sophistication did Phillip exhibit?
2. What was Phillip's previous delinquent history?
3. How successful were previous attempts by the court to rehabilitate him?
4. Could Phillip be rehabilitated before the expiration of the juvenile court's jurisdiction?
5. What were the circumstances and gravity of Phillip's alleged offense?

In Phillip's case, the first and last of these issues were the most pivotal. The middle three, it seemed to me, clearly skewed in favor of Phillip being viewed as best managed from within the juvenile court's purview. He had no previous history of criminal charges or convictions. As such, there were no earlier attempts by the court to rehabilitate him, a point mentioned in his probation report as well. Since his arrest, Phillip had become increasingly cooperative and responsive. At first, he seemed like an angry and defiant minor; for instance, telling another teen, "My homie smoked someone." Over time, it became clear to the staff that his bravado masked emotional difficulties including depression and trauma. The staff, clinical progress notes, and Phillip's psychological evaluation reports clearly showed a trajectory of increased emotional stability and engagement with staff, along with accruing benefits from his counseling sessions. One entry from a counseling session quoted him as saying, "Talking helps me think."

The question of Phillip's degree of sophistication was complicated and had to be teased out from an array of psychological test findings and interview information. California's Welfare and Institution 707 code doesn't provide a definition of what is meant by "sophistication." I tackled the issue by parsing out two areas of development, cognitive and emotional. Their gradual maturation and blending leads to psychological maturity, good judgment, and self-control.

First, I summarized the results of Phillip's psychological testing results. His overall cognitive maturity intelligence was borderline intellectual, in the fourth percentile compared to his peers. His verbal ability was lower, in the second percentile. He was sixteen at the time of testing. In terms of age equivalency, Phillip's verbal ability and capacity to verbally abstract and use language was equal to that of an average nine-year-old. [10]

Phillip's RSTI score exposed a potential for psychological reflection and maturity but also immature problem solving and judgment. Additional testing revealed an excessive willingness to tolerate loss and an inability to appreciate the consequences of his risk taking.

Generally, cognitive development lags behind emotional development and doesn't reach maturity until young adulthood, around the age of twenty-five. [11] It's around that time that neurons in the frontal part of the brain—the area most responsible for planning, complex problem solving, and self-control—have completed their gradual pruning process. [12] Emotional development, on the other hand, occurs abruptly at the advent of adolescence because of hormonal influences.[13] This disparity results in adolescents having adultlike emotional, sexual, and social desires yet underdeveloped capacities to regulate them.

Normally developing adolescents are less competent in decision making and judgment than are adults. The average adolescent is at least 20 percent less mature and sophisticated than the average adult.[14] What's more, Phillip's emotional and cognitive abilities were immaturely developed compared to the average adolescent. His lag in development was exacerbated by a series of traumas during his early youth: exposure to domestic violence, parental divorce, loss of a father figure for years, emotion neglect caused by limited adult supervision, and sexual abuse. During the year before the crime, he was especially traumatized by the physical and emotional abandonment of his father and his raw mistreatment by other adults in charge.

Phillip sought solace and relief by abusing street drugs. At the time of the murder, he was not only under the influence of methamphetamines, he was suffering chronic depression flanked by long- and short-term traumas, all atop an arrested neuropsychological development.

The police record strongly supported his claim that he had known only of a plan to rob the victim, not to kill him.

Based on his clear lack of psychological development and sophistication, I concluded that Phillip was a proper subject to be dealt with under juvenile court law.

The final consideration was that of the circumstances and gravity of Phillip's offense. The allegation of murder couldn't have been more grievous. Phillip admitted that he was going with his fellow assailants to purchase drugs. He knew that the intent was to rob the drug dealer, but he adamantly denied any knowledge of a plan to murder him. Astonishingly, there was a video recording of the conversation that occurred between the two adult assailants as they planned the murder that occurred as they drove to pick up Phillip, before he entered the vehicle, supporting his claim.

My evaluation clearly indicated that Phillip was free of any psychopathic features. He was in the second percentile when compared to other juvenile inmates, meaning that 98 percent of them had greater tendencies toward psychopathy. He was without a history of violence. The testing results clearly showed him to be free of a delinquent disposition or a budding antisocial personality. He wasn't impulsive or egocentric. Phillip's misconduct is best explained by a combination of drug addiction, trauma, and depression occurring in a developmentally delayed adolescent.

I saw no evidence that Phillip was involved in the plot to murder the victim. He was a juvenile with developmental and emotional difficulties and a substance abuse disorder. At the time of the homicide, he was under the influence of two adults and drugs. Although the gravity of the circumstances of his arrest was great, he appeared nonetheless to be fit to be dealt with in the juvenile court system.

***

Ms. Feldman, Phillip's lawyer, told me that Phillip had a "good judge" in family court who would preside over the transfer hearing. By "good," she meant the judge had a reputation for being interested in and responsive to the details of the juvenile's history and development before making her rulings. All triers of fact must consider the five factors laid out in the California ruling, which should prompt a close look at the juvenile's personal history, but some are more fastidious and detailed than others. Other judges bring a strict law-and-order perspective to the bench, placing a premium on the crime itself and the juvenile's recent history, making them less apt to consider personal history and psychological makeup. Everybody, including judges, bring a personal perspective and temperament to the courtroom. Nobody is a blank slate.

***

About two weeks before I was scheduled to testify, Phillip's lawyer called, saying that the district attorney's office had dropped the juvenile transfer request. The case would proceed in juvenile court. Though not privy to the reasons behind the district attorney's change of heart, Ms. Feldman and I concluded that it was due to a number of reasons. The prosecution had two adult defendants who were being charged with felony murder in adult court. And the evidence against them was compelling—the dash cam, for one. Phillip admitted to participating in the planned robbery, but he adamantly denied knowledge of a plan to kill. And that claim seemed clear and convincing from the dash cam video. Phillip's probation report was at least obliquely supportive, this from a member of a professional group that almost invariably takes a hard line in their reports. My report addressed the five criteria that were to be considered before a juvenile transfer decision could be made. It provided findings that were specific to Phillip's life and the circumstance of the crime, the sum of which supported his fitness to be adjudged as a juvenile. In addition, when summarizing the transfer criteria, I included important U.S. Supreme Court decisions involving juvenile criminal justice and the evolving nature of the law's perspective on adolescent development.

In *Roper v. Simons* (2005),[15] the U.S. Supreme Court ruled that the death sentence for juveniles was cruel and unusual punishment and unconstitutional. Seven years later, in *Graham v. Florida*,[16] the court ruled that life without the possibility of parole for a nonhomicidal offense was unconstitutional. In 2012, in *Miller v. Alabama*,[17] the court went even further, ruling that all mandatory life sentences without the possibility of parole were unconstitutional.

The reasoning behind these rulings was based on contemporary neuroscientific and developmental science, some of which I've already cited. For instance, studies of adolescence consistently show that teenagers are less competent than adults in their decision making and judgment.[18] Normal adolescents are deficient in their capacity for self-management and independent functioning[19] and easily influenced by peers.[20] Of particular relevance to Phillip's case is that PTSD has been found to increase impetuous risk taking in teens.[21]

These findings regarding specific psychosocial limitations in adolescence are consistent with many studies that have documented the structural immaturity of the adolescent brain, in particular the frontal cortex, the seat of thoughtful decision making, self-regulation, and emotional control.[22]

Justice Breyer, in *Miller v. Alabama*, made the point that a juvenile offender who did not kill or intend to kill has twice the diminished moral culpability than an adult who actually killed or intended to kill. Phillip, I noted in my report, had a thrice-diminished moral culpability for the murder: he didn't intend to kill, he was a juvenile at the time, and he was a minor who was psychiatrically compromised with intellectual limitations at the time of the murder.

In *Roper v. Simmons*, the court explicitly asserted that the differences between adults and juveniles make their behavior "less likely to be evidence of an irretrievably depraved character than are the actions of adults."[23] Barring adolescents with psychopathic traits who are at risk for future malice,[24] I agree.

Looking at all the facts of Phillip's case, it's clear he was a teenager without a depraved or wicked heart. That was likely the district attorney's opinion as well.

Part III

Culpability

11

MY BRAIN MADE ME DO IT

A plant cannot say anything about itself to the botanist.—Hans Kelsen, jurist and legal philosopher

Peter was accompanied by four deputies from his cell to the interview room where I waited. That's an unusual number. Looking more like a posse than escort trailing the defendant, the group's size reflected concerns about Peter's potential danger. I had been appointed by the court to conduct an insanity evaluation in this case. Peter walked slowly, burdened by heavy leg cuffs and handcuffs chained around his waist. He carried what looked like a research file of legal papers and a book, both clutched tightly to his chest, as if he was caressing them. The deputies secured him to a metal stool by attaching his leg irons to the pole beneath. He complained of the pain caused by the tightness of the irons. Without a word, the deputies left.

Already serving prison time, Peter was charged with attempted murder of a fellow prisoner. As he was being transported from prison to a court appearance on a child custody matter, he "shanked" a fellow prisoner, a rival gang member. While waiting to be transported on a bus, Peter and several inmates, including the soon-to-be victim, were chained together. In a vicious and bloody assault, Peter allegedly stabbed his rival nine times in the face and neck with a makeshift blade. The man survived after being rushed to surgery. Peter claimed he was insane at the time.

Within a few seconds of my introductory comments but before I could explain to him the limits of confidentiality, Peter showed me the book he carried with him, Erving Goffman's *Asylums*. It was one of the most powerful books I had read as an undergraduate. A sociologist, Goffman wrote about the subtle yet psychologically corrosive effects he observed in mentally ill patients that were caused by long-term stays in state psychiatric hospitals. It detailed the problems among patients who were hospitalized for years on end. After handing me the book, Peter began to argue, quite persuasively, about the dehumanizing effects of long-term incarceration. In order to survive in an institution like prison, "my worse tendencies worsened," he said. Legally representing himself, Peter wanted to argue that because of his background and his genes he was unable to control his behavior. He described himself as being in a "blind rage" when the stabbing occurred.

He was on a roll, so I just listened. Peter's father had died in prison, serving a life sentence for murder. His mother was an alcoholic and drug abuser and his brothers emotionally abused him. All three of his brothers had served multiple prison terms for gang-related crimes and violent offenses. Peter said he had been diagnosed with a "brain disease"—attention deficit hyperactivity disorder (ADHD).

Opening his folder of research documents, Peter read the insanity defense statute, enumerating its various prongs. One is that the defendant must have a mental defect at the time of the offense. Peter had a number of them, including ADHD, substance abuse, and an antisocial personality, contributing to his violent tendencies. He also had a list of neuroscience articles that "proved" that his condition was genetic and made worse by his upbringing.

At this point I stopped Peter and explained the limits of our confidentiality. Since I was appointed by the court, I would be reporting everything he told me to the court. "I have nothing to hide," he said. From the little he told me, I mentioned there were problems with his perspective on a defense. The insanity defense requires the presence of a psychotic-like disorder, such that a person cannot tell the difference between right or wrong; substance abuse and antisocial personality disorders are excluded from the statute. Peter was undeterred. Clearly, he was accustomed to shaping the discourse, no matter what. He was in propria persona ("pro per," representing himself) because "I fired my court-appointed attorney." He and the attorney had disagreed over the appropriateness of the insanity plea. Also, Peter wanted to testify at his trial, a strategy his lawyer couldn't abide. Peter was adamant about testifying and pleading insanity. He believed that he was insane at the time, and he was sure a jury would agree.

I was intrigued by Peter's self-assured charisma and his subtle sophistication. He brought Goffman's book with him, probably surmising that a PhD type of guy who was about to examine him would be familiar with it and sympathetic to his plight of psychosocial impoverishment.

I already knew a great deal about Peter's criminal background from the many police reports that documented his years of criminal conduct. I knew about his family of origin's long criminal history. I knew he was married with two boys and that on the day of the stabbing, he was on his way back to prison after having been transported from family court on a child custody matter. I asked him about his living arrangement and family life before he was incarcerated. He wasn't interested in talking to me about his family life other than to inform me that he was not a good husband or father because of his chronic drug use and aggressive tendencies. At home, he went into "blind rages" when frustrated with the kids.

As is my way, I began by gathering information about the more innocuous aspects of Peter's life that weren't threatening to talk about, allowing us time to settle in with each other. Peter wasn't interested in establishing a rapport; he got comfortable by taking charge and driving home his point of view, especially his family's violent history during his early life and his current violent tendencies and proclivity for blind rages. I figured this was a way of telling me that his most current assault was simply an extension of his background. So I let it happen: we jumped into his attempt to murder an inmate.

Consistent with statements that he had already made to the deputies who interviewed him after the stabbing, Peter insisted that he was distraught and agitated around that time. Three days before the stabbing, his brother had overdosed and died. Peter had been at court because his wife had filed for divorce and was contesting the previously agreed-upon visitation rights with his two boys. "All I remember [about the stabbing] is a lot of yelling and screaming." A "melee" had occurred among ten inmates as they waited to get on a bus to go back to prison. Peter said, "I saw someone with a shank. . . . I blanked out." His next memory was of being at the jail infirmary. A nurse was washing pepper spray off his face. He denied knowing the victim was a rival gang member who was "in the hat." I asked him what that meant. It's apparently prison lingo for someone with a contract on his head.

Peter did not deny stabbing the prisoner, although he claimed that he had no memory of it. He accepted the official account, given "my natural tendency" to become violent when threatened. Having read multiple police reports and court documents about his long-term involvement in gang activity, I confronted Peter, saying his claim of ignorance about the victim's status as a rival gang member was not credible. "I had no idea," he responded. I mentioned to him that jurors don't usually accept dissociation claims at insanity trials. Undeterred even for a moment, Peter said his situation was different and believable. He felt threatened by the melee, the developing violence, and his "brain makeup" took over.

Peter claimed a tendency toward violence that was the outcome of his genetic nature and deprived nurture. And he steadfastly claimed that his attempted murder charge was a direct outcome of his biopsychology and genealogy. My thought: not bad for someone with a brain disease.

***

Peter was impressive and imposing. In his mid-thirties, he was about six feet, two inches tall and well-built with an erect posture. His grooming was impeccable and his musculature taut, likely the result of regular workouts in the prison yard. He had tattoos on his arms and neck and one of a fading swastika on his shaved head.

With his physicality and his violent history, it was no wonder that Peter was escorted to the interview room in chains accompanied by four guards when I interviewed him. I told the deputies that I eventually would need them to remove his restraints so he could complete psychological testing. The supervising deputy was reluctant, but during the remaining sessions, he took the handcuffs off, although he kept Peter's leg irons attached to a metal bar below the stool on which he sat.

I have interviewed many men (and women) with extremely violent histories induced by various causes, including malignant psychopathy, intermittent explosive disorders, paranoid delusions, and so forth. Deputies have discouraged me from "contact visits," strongly advising me to conduct the interviews by phone behind a glass partition. Once, a deputy made quite a forceful attempt to dissuade me from contact with an inmate, saying, "In a moment's time, he could grab a pen from your pocket and stab you in the eye." Of course, anything can happen. My experience at the jail and also with volatile patients in private hospitals is that if I am respectful, listen carefully, remain observant and attentive to signs of emerging agitation or mental deterioration, I'm okay.

Peter had a very violent history and could be physically intimidating. But, curiously, he didn't make me nervous. I didn't feel the need to be especially vigilant as I might with, say, an actively delusional patient whom I need to avoid setting off. Why wasn't I apprehensive with Peter? Before coming to any formal decisions about him, I had an intuitive sense of how Peter used violence. His was the predatory type; violence was an instrument of control and dominance. He tended to employ it mostly proactively, with a goal in mind, and less as an impulsive reaction. Becoming openly aggressive or violent with me was not in his interests.

I certainly felt Peter was taking my measure as much as I was his. He forcefully attempted to influence me in a number of ways—for instance, by introducing the *Asylums* book as an opening gambit and by aggressively shaping our exchanges to drive home his point of view.

Peter was not on any medications and he denied any feelings of depression, anxiety, or stress of any kind, for that matter. His thinking was well-organized and free of any symptoms of disordered thinking. He was articulate with a vocabulary better than I would have expected; by all accounts, he did not attend elementary school or high school classes regularly (according to his records, he completed his GED in prison). He used words like "alienation" when we briefly discussed the book. He proclaimed, "I'm an institutional criminal" as though he was victimized by his prison life.

Contacting family or friends to obtain outsider views on Peter's behavior and development was impossible. All collateral contacts were unavailable. His estranged wife had refused to speak with his lawyer or anyone else. By the time I started conducting my evaluation, she had moved and her location was unknown. His parents were dead, his siblings were either dead or in prison, and his friends were gang associates who would never speak to me or were themselves incarcerated or deceased. I had only the official records and Peter's account of his life to go by, which was clearly skewed and self-serving.

***

The official criminal record of Peter's crimes was extensive, beginning in his early teen years. He was raised by his mother and siblings until her death when he was still in his teens. His first arrest was for selling drugs for a street gang notorious for its violence and drug running. Not long after he was released—and with the blessings of his probation officer and mother—he went to live in Arizona with her brother and sister-in-law. Peter and his uncle began using drugs together, with Peter eventually getting busted for having drugs at school. Soon after, he was sent to juvenile hall in Arizona for grand theft auto.

It was downhill from there, with multiple arrests during his juvenile years. In his mid-teens, Peter was sent to the California Youth Authority (CYA, now known as the Division of Juvenile Justice), a place reserved for hardened and incorrigible teens, where he stayed until the age of twenty-three. He could have been released earlier, but because of his gang involvement in multiple violent altercations leading to extended periods of solitary confinements, he was kept longer (he could have been held until the age of twenty-five).

As an adult, Peter's criminal lifestyle continued with multiple arrests for drug possession and sales, grand theft auto, witness intimidation, aggravated assault, domestic violence, forgery, and attempted murder of a rival gang member. At the time of the stabbing, he was serving a twenty-five-year-to-life sentence.

Though his early family history was sketchy on details, it was manifestly deeply chaotic and dysfunctional. Peter had little memory of his father, a violent alcoholic who left the family when Peter was quite young. The reminiscences he had were of his father beating his mother. His father eventually died in prison. His mother died of complications resulting from chronic alcoholism when Peter was in CYA custody. Peter expressed affection for her, describing her as "a good woman who wanted to help." His aunt, with whom he briefly lived before being sent to Arizona, was an alcoholic and "mean." He got along with his uncle in Arizona, the one he used drugs with.

Peter was open about his early conduct difficulties, saying, "I had a temper." He frequently fought and bullied other students at school. He was a "cool kid" and into heavy metal music during his junior high school years. By then he was already actively involved in street gang life. He seemed proud of his easy rise to a leadership position among the younger members of the gang. He not only helped sell drugs for the gang, but he used them as well, with his drug of choice being meth. He also drank daily.

With such disinterest and erratic school attendance, Peter's grades were in the tank. He was diagnosed with ADHD by a school psychologist during his elementary school years. His mother didn't want him on medication. Instead, "she had me sip alcohol to mellow me out."

Peter claimed to have been sexually abused on one occasion by an older neighbor woman. She fondled his penis and had him "lick her out." He sustained several head injuries, usually the result of physical altercations. His most serious one involved an altercation during which he was hit in the head with a pipe. He thinks he blacked out for a period of time, its length unknown. He didn't go to a hospital, so there's no record of his injury.

As he talked about his youth, Peter seemed most proud of the fact that during the time he was running the streets, before having been sent to Arizona, he was on his way to becoming a local leader of the younger wannabe gang thugs. Following in the footsteps of one of his older brothers who was a gang leader, Peter was willing to intimidate others and exercise violence when necessary. So he was on his way up the street gang food chain.

Peter met the mother of his children in his late twenties. She was about five years his junior, and they used drugs together during their early years. Though not formally married, he considered her his wife. They lived together with their two boys. She stopped using drugs during her first pregnancy and, based on his description, she matured and expected him to as well. They argued about his drug use and sales and his dicey lifestyle. He admitted to "losing my temper with her" and getting arrested twice for domestic violence. She had not been taking his boys to visit him in prison. After his last family court appearance, when he accrued the latest attempted murder charge, she had moved, possibly out of state.

***

During our second visit, I attempted to explore Peter's state of mind during the day of the assault, before his alleged blackout. He claimed to have little memory of the day. He returned to the moment of the attack with a description that was consistent—too consistent—with what he had already told me and the police. He used the same words (e.g., "melee") with me to characterize his recall of the event that he used with the investigators. His story sounded contrived and scripted. At the same time, he couldn't recall how he came to possess the shank used in the assault. He denied recall of actually slitting the victim's face and neck.

I told him that stabbing someone around the facial area seemed like an attack that was personal and emotional in nature, not just a self-protective one. Peter had no response, no recall of his motivations.

Further efforts to circle around to the issue of his mind-set around the time of the stabbing were to no avail. I reviewed the transcript of the victim's statement to the police. "He grabbed me and I fell to the ground. The next thing I knew he was on me." Unaffected, Peter repeated himself. He sounded like a politician "on message."

***

Having endured multiple psychiatric evaluations during his many incarcerations, Peter claimed to have been diagnosed with bipolar disorder on several occasions and was on medication for about a year during one prison stint. I had my doubts. The prison records I reviewed included several psychiatric evaluations, usually diagnosing him as antisocial, with one suggesting the possibility of a bipolar condition. I hadn't observed any signs of mania like, say, an overly pressured way of speaking. Sometimes, complicated personality disorders might initially be seen as possible bipolar illness. Symptoms such as unstable mood, impulsiveness, aggression, pleasure-seeking behaviors, poor judgment, and drug use are all symptoms of many conditions, including a bipolar condition. An early diagnosis of ADHD is also common in those later diagnosed with bipolar disorder. Many of the associated symptoms of the illness were better accounted for by his personality disorder. He lacked the core symptoms of a bipolar disorder, such as complaints about racing thoughts and documented episodes of unusually pressured verbalizations. Nonetheless, I had to eliminate the possibility of bipolar disorder, with its tendency to impair judgment and weaken impulse control, as a factor that influenced his assaultive conduct.

I also needed to keep in mind the head injury with loss of consciousness for an unknown time period that Peter had reported. There was no mention of a head injury in his prison records, but I did not have a complete set of all his prison documents. Given that Peter was implicating a neuropsychiatric condition in his defense, I decided to do a complete neuropsychological testing on Peter as part of the evaluation.

Given his criminal history, I completed the Hare Psychopathy Check-list (PCL), which I described earlier as an instrument that appraises an individual's degree of psychopathic traits. Peter's score of thirty-one placed him around the eighty-second percentile of prison inmates. More meaningful was his emotional callousness/lack of empathy score, which was very high, in the ninety-eighth percentile. Essentially, his moral compass had stopped working. He felt little remorse for his conduct, was self-centered, and employed violence as an instrument to control others.

Peter had no signs of a bipolar illness, but since it had been mentioned as a possibility in his "jacket" (prison record), I had him complete the self-reported Mood Disorder Questionnaire (MDQ), which lists the various behaviors associated with the illness. His score suggested he suffered with bipolar disorder. For example, he indicated that he had racing thoughts. When I asked him to tell me what it was like to experience one's thoughts fleeing by so rapidly, he couldn't give a credible response. He endorsed pressured speech as a symptom, but I didn't observe it nor was it recorded in any documents I reviewed. He seemed very likely to be dissembling.

Peter completed the Connors questionnaire for symptoms of attention deficit hyperactivity disorder, which I described in an earlier chapter. His validity and clinical scales suggested he indeed suffered with ADHD. I wanted neuropsychological testing results to confirm it.

On the Aggression Questionnaire (described in a previous chapter), Peter scored high on physical and verbal aggression, both above the ninety-fifth percentile. No surprise here; he had no qualms about using aggression to achieve dominance.

On the Minnesota Multiphasic Personality Inventory-2-RF (MMPI-2-RF), Peter's validity scores detailed his exaggeration of memory or intellectual functioning. At the same time, he presented himself in a favorable way, denying minor faults and as being more virtuous than the average person. Clinically, his highest elevation was on a scale measuring antisocial behavior and the likelihood of exercising poor impulse control. The results presented a picture of an individual who is easily bored and impulsive, abuses drugs, and is sensation seeking. Peter was unusually low on measures of negative emotionality; nothing disturbed his positive feeling or his self-esteem.

The neuropsychological testing results were helpful. On achievement and IQ tests, he scored within the average range. For example, Peter obtained a Wechsler IQ of 106. He wasn't as smart as he fashioned himself, likely conflating cognitive abilities with his "street smarts," of which he had plenty. But he wasn't dumb. And his verbal capacities like reasoning and vocabulary were higher than his nonverbal ones like reconstructing puzzles. His relative facility with language, I thought, had likely been an asset in his criminal lifestyle. Since adults who find themselves on the wrong side of the law frequently have limited verbal skills, he no doubt used this asset to his advantage. It likely helped his move up the gang leadership ladder.

To complete a comprehensive neuropsychological evaluation, I employed the Neuropsychological Assessment Battery[1] (NAB) as well as additional specialized neuropsychological instruments. Relatively new and at the cutting edge of research, the NAB assesses neuropsychological functioning in five domains: attention, language, memory, spatial abilities, and executive function, all of which include a number of individual tests within each domain module. The NAB then yields a number of scores, including a total NAB score and five individual module scores.

Peter's overall score on the full NAB was in the average range. As is common, he showed weaknesses in specific tests within various modules. For example, his attention module score was within the average range, but he faulted on everyday living skills, which entailed a driving scene task. He was slightly below average on a few scores within the language module, but none of his module scores were within the impaired range.

Most significant was that Peter's best module score on the NAB was in testing executive functioning. It is a high-level cognitive ability that requires planning, problem solving, and the sequencing of goal-directed behavior even under novel circumstances. He was within the above-average range on all of the specific tasks within this module. For instance, he was above average on a word generation test that required him to devise as many three-letter words as possible from a list of eight letters.

I conducted additional testing of his executive functioning, including the Wisconsin Card Sorting Test, the Iowa Gambling Test, and the Connors Continuous Performance Test, all of which I previously described. Except for mild impairment in his ability to maintain vigilance and sustained attention, he was without evidence of neuropsychological impairment in his abilities to plan and regulate his behavior.

What were the "take-home" neuropsychological findings? Peter functioned basically within the average range of intellectual ability and academic achievement, even with his disrupted academic career. He had some specific deficits. His nonverbal reasoning ability was lower than his verbal abilities, and he had difficulty with sustained attention and vigilance, which interfered with his ability to integrate and organize complex information that is part of everyday life. His executive functioning, which is important with regard to self-regulation, was at least average, even considering his tendency to impulsivity and his attentional problems.

I diagnosed Peter with a mild neurocognitive disorder stemming from his deficits in visuospatial ability along with an inability to sustain attention and his underdevelopment in selected areas of language. The causes of his neurocognitive limitations were likely the result of his extensive drug use and history of violence, which included at least one instance of head injury. I also diagnosed him with ADHD based on his documented history of attentional difficulties and the neuropsychological testing results.

He had a polysubstance abuse disorder, his drugs of choice included methamphetamines and alcohol. Just prior to our first interview, Peter had been placed in solitary confinement ("the hole") after being caught using and helping to distribute methamphetamines at the jail.

***

I reviewed the testing results with Peter's co-counsel, a private attorney appointed by the judge to help Peter represent himself. I also told him that Peter was psychopathic, though I formally diagnosed Peter with antisocial personality disorder. The Diagnostic Statistical Manual of Mental Disorders, fifth edition (DSM-5), the official diagnostic manual recognized and utilized by the court, doesn't include psychopathic personality. The antisocial diagnosis is focused mostly on behavior that violates the law and recognized social norms. Peter's most pernicious characteristics, I said, were his cold callousness and lack of empathy. The DSM-5 reports that a 70 percent sample of men in forensic settings have an antisocial personality.[2] Only a portion of those, the severest of the severe, are psychopaths. Peter was one of them.

Although he had a number of significant psychiatric diagnoses, I said I could not conclude that Peter was insane. To even consider it as a possibility, I would have to accept his claim that he did not recall how he obtained possession of the weapon he used to stab the victim. It was not credible, especially for a psychopath with no co-occurring conditions to support his claim, such as having been actively psychotic or dissociative at the time. I especially would have expected Peter to have some recall given his history of repeated past violence; attacking someone or being part of a melee was not aberrant and incongruent with his past behavior. I would not expect him to have been overwhelmed by the experience.

I told the attorney that Peter's memory lapse was, to put it mildly, implausible. At any rate, antisocial personality and substance abuse disorders are excluded from the insanity defense. Peter did not have any symptoms of a major mental disorder or defect at the time of the stabbing that compromised his ability to know what he did was wrong morally or legally. And Peter had adequate executive function—that is, the capacity for self-regulation. Thus, he had the neuropsychological potential to control himself. This, I thought, even constrained the mitigating factors to consider in the final adjudication of his case.

As far as insanity evaluations go, Peter's case was not one of the more difficult ones to arrive at an opinion.

* * *

Several months after I completed the evaluation, I was subpoenaed by the district attorney's office to provide testimony during Peter's trial. Not long after, I received a call from Tom Coleton, the assistant district attorney who was trying the case. A complication had arisen, and the trial was postponed. Peter decided that he wanted an attorney to represent him, and his attorney would need time to "come up to speed" on the case. Okay, I thought, a little time to relax. My preparation time before testimony is always one of my more anxious periods, even with cases for which I am confident in my opinions. Trials are inherently unpredictable, and I worry about screwing up in some unforeseen way, so I overprepare, which helps with the apprehension—somewhat.

A month or so later, I received a call from Peter's public defender, Mathew Swain, who informed me that Peter had withdrawn his insanity plea (likely at his attorney's urging). Mr. Swain was in the process of negotiating with the district attorney regarding a possible plea. He had read my report and decided to request funding from the court for a neurological evaluation of Peter. When completed, he would forward the evaluation to me to comment on the additional findings. I told him that I would read the neurologist's report and call him afterward. In all likelihood, Mr. Swain was looking for issues of mitigation to lessen the seriousness of a conviction.

Peter's neurological examination was normal, as were his MRI and electroencephalogram results. Although the results were within the normal range, the neurologist said there still was still evidence that was "consistent with an individual with traumatic brain injury." When I spoke to Mr. Swain, I told him that regardless of the possibility of a traumatic brain injury, I found that Peter's functional neurocognitive deficits mild and his executive ability above average. The new findings did not alter my opinion.

***

Peter's lawyer eventually secured a plea deal: aggravated assault with a deadly weapon. He was sentenced to additional years of prison time.

Almost certainly a trial jury would have found Peter sane and guilty of attempted murder. If he had taken the witness stand in his own defense, as he was inclined to do, his extensive criminal record of violence would have been revealed during the cross-examination. His claim of criminal lawlessness as predetermined by his origins, which he put down to his genes, would not likely have resonated with the jury. A crushing cross-examination by the assistant district attorney, together with two expert witnesses—me and another appointed by the court—opining that he had understood right and wrong when he stabbed the victim, would have almost certainly carried the day.

I did not speak with Mr. Swain after the plea bargain was made. I don't know if evidence of Peter's mild neurocognitive deficits had anything to do with the district attorney's office agreeing to lessen the charge from attempted murder to aggravated assault. I doubt it. Peter was already serving a long prison sentence, unlikely of ever being placed on parole. This conviction further dimmed that possibility.

***

When, if ever, is a neuropsychological deficit a credible legal defense? Are there times when a defendant may realistically argue that his brain caused his criminal conduct or at least significantly influenced it?

Consider the case of Andy. Like Peter, he wasn't a very sympathetic character. A glance at his mug shot and photos of the crime scene would provoke alarm. At forty-nine years of age, he was older than the typical arrestee. He stood about six feet, two inches tall and appeared drawn, with long, stringy hair, tattoos on both arms, hollow eyes, and a flat expression.

Andy was charged with attempted carjacking. He was alleged to have threatened the owner while trying to snatch the car keys in an effort to steal the car. Andy denied any intention to steal the car to the arresting officer. The problem started when he requested a cigarette from the vehicle's owner. After being rebuffed and disrespected ("get the fuck away from me"), a clash ensued: Andy threw a punch at the guy and grabbed for the car keys. A brief scuffle ended with Andy walking away, only to be arrested as he sat in a nearby park. He told the arresting officers that he grabbed the car keys in anger, to "throw them away" in response to having been "put down" by the alleged victim.

On the day of his arrest, Andy was homeless and living on the streets. He received Supplemental Security Income (SSI) and had resided in a house with an older man before being "kicked out" after an altercation. Andy claimed this man "came on to me" sexually. The day before the arrest, he was "very drunk" on malt liquor. A habitual methamphetamine user, he had not used it for a couple of days. His description of the arrest paralleled very closely that of the police reports. The only question was that of his state of mind at the time: had Andy's intent been to carjack?

When I first consulted with Andy's attorney, Lisa Stephens, she told me his history included years of drug abuse and a long criminal record. In prison, he had been diagnosed with bipolar disorder, polysubstance abuse, and, at various times, different personality disorders, including antisocial personality. His mother told the attorney that he had had behavior problems since childhood and had been diagnosed with "minimal brain disorder," an outdated catchall term used to diagnose conditions like ADHD, learning disabilities, or various cognitive issues. She also told Ms. Stephens that Andy had been hospitalized for head injuries, but she was vague about the circumstances that caused the injuries.

Ms. Stephens described Andy as "kind of weird . . . off emotionally." Like many defendants, he claimed innocence. However, his behavior after the altercation was peculiar for someone who had intended to steal a car but failed. He did not try to hide; he left the scene and rested in a nearby park. Ms. Stephens also described his demeanor as "quirky." Andy expressed frustration at his arrest but at the same time behaved in a jovial, childish fashion. She asked for a "workup" to clarify the diagnostic picture and to evaluate his intellectual level. I said that neuropsychological testing would be useful. She agreed.

During our first encounter, I explained the assessment process to Andy. Having already been in jail for a while, he was cleaned up and upbeat. His jumpsuit was a little stained and his hair still long but not as greasy. He had gained some weight. He was taking Risperdal and Depakote, both psychiatric medications usually given in combination to those with a bipolar illness.

When I mentioned to him that our sessions would include cognitive testing, Andy launched into his medical history of head injuries. For instance, "I was knocked out once after I got hit in the head with a metal bar" during a street fight. He lost consciousness, woke up in the emergency room, and was released the following day. Subsequently, he suffered from "bad hearing and headaches." He had been in many fights over the years, which included head injuries and, at times, near loss of consciousness. He proudly showed his right hand with its collapsed knuckle, the result of his many tussles over the years. Then he cheerfully admitted that when frustrated, he slammed his head into walls or hit himself in the head. He proceeded to demonstrate by smashing his forehead repeatedly with the palm of his right hand. I immediately implored him to stop, which he did with a hearty howl.

Andy had an extensive drug history beginning at the age of nine when he was given marijuana by an older brother. He dabbled in a lot of street drugs over the years, but his drugs of choice for many years had been methamphetamines and malt liquor. "I drink until I get arrested. . . . [I]t's always my downfall," he announced with an awkward sneer. He had been arrested many times and served two prison terms. He had been arrested for assaults, petty theft, grand theft auto on one occasion, a DUI, and multiple parole violations. His two prison terms were for assaultive behavior. Once he was charged with attempted assault with a utility knife after an argument in a store. He was on meth at the time. He also had been charged with assaulting a police officer. Again, he was on meth and drunk. On another occasion, he slapped a woman in the face at a shopping mall after the woman slapped her child across the head. Andy said, "I called her a fuckin' whore for hitting her kid like that."

His correctional records documented his drug abuse and psychiatric history. Andy had been hospitalized once privately, but most of his psychiatric treatment occurred in prison hospital units. He had been diagnosed with bipolar disorder on multiple occasions and with various other personality disorders, including, as I mentioned, antisocial personality. The records also documented his head-banging when angry or frustrated.

Andy described a long history of self-destructive behavior. At one point during his time in prison, he stabbed himself in the stomach, requiring surgery. His one private psychiatric hospitalization was for suicidal ideation. Another homeless person flagged down a passing police car after Andy told this man that he was about to jump off a bridge.

An evaluation completed by the probation department described Andy as volatile and with a history of learning disabilities. He reportedly was sodomized by his father at the age of five and had a shotgun placed to his head.

When I eventually spoke with Andy's mother, Ms. Thomas confirmed the history given in the probation report. She described his father as mentally ill and delusional. She divorced him after Andy's sexual abuse was exposed. Her second husband had two older boys. The oldest "was mean, even sadistic" toward Andy.

Andy's birth and delivery were "traumatic." He did not breathe, she said, for an estimated five minutes while hospital staff "worked on him." He did not like to be held during infant years and frequently rocked himself to sleep. Still, "I had a good bond with him." As a young child, he easily became frustrated and destroyed his toys. All his life, Andy had been hyperactive with severe attentional and learning problems. He never had been capable of gainful employment or a love relationship.

***

During my interviews with Andy, his recollection was similar to the information given by his mother and in his official record, including neuropsychological test results. His Wechsler IQ score of 83 placed him within the mildly impaired range of ability, in the thirteenth percentile, with limited verbal and nonverbal abilities.

I administered a version of the Neuropsychological Assessment Battery (NAB) described earlier, a form that is shorter yet yields results that are on par with the longer version. I figured it was best, given his frustration tolerance.

As might be expected, Andy's scores were uniformly within the mild to moderately impaired range across all domains, including language, memory, spatial ability, attention, and executive ability. I especially took note of his executive functioning deficiency, given Andy's history of head injuries and impulsive aggression. Additional testing helped to clarify the nature of his impairment in this domain. On the Connors test (CPT) of his attention and concentration, his overall score placed him within the range consistent with an ADHD diagnosis. His impulsiveness score was especially high, as was a measure of cognitive inflexibility, also confirmed by his performance on the Wisconsin Card Sorting Test.

In addition, I had Andy take the Stroop test,[3] which targets response inhibition. A color word-naming task, it required Andy to read the word "red" printed in blue or to read the word "blue" written in red. It is a test of the ability to suppress a natural response. Andy was overwhelmed by its demands, performing at the first percentile.

The summary results of Andy's testing revealed him to have limited intellectual ability with central deficits in attention, mental flexibility, cognitive control, and self-regulation. These executive impairments caused him to become overwhelmed when confronted with complex information and intense emotions, taxing his ability for self-control and mature decision making.

***

I did not think of Andy as a psychopath. He had been diagnosed with an antisocial personality during his periods of incarceration, but I didn't believe that was accurate. He did not have a history of serious conduct problems as a teenager, and his adult criminal history was not the result of a criminal propensity in his personality. It stemmed from his drug abuse and his other mental disorders, including his attention deficit disorder, his learning disability, and his neurocognitive deficits. I initially felt no need to administer the Hare PCL but later decided to do so. If the case went to trial and I had to testify, I wanted to be able to provide quantifiable evidence to support my opinion. I had almost no doubt that the Hare PCL results would be consistent with my clinical impression.

I completed structured clinical interviews to evaluate Andy for symptoms of various mental and personality disorders and conditions, especially bipolar disorder and antisocial personality, which he had been diagnosed with in the past. He had the symptoms and history of a bipolar condition. Regarding his personality, he did not score high on callousness on the PCL, but his score was elevated on antisocial behavior, the result of his long criminal record. Most striking were his borderline personality features. He was self-destructive and impulsive, and his identity was shaky. "I'm not sure of myself. Who am I supposed to be?" he said, a sign of an unstable self-identity, a key feature of borderline personality. At times, for example, he was grandiose and thought of himself as someone who could be a Navy SEAL. And sometimes, "I feel like I'm 50 percent human and 50 percent alien." With Andy, though, these features were in part due to his developmental conditions (ADHD and learning problems), his neurocognitive deficits, and his bipolar condition. So I diagnosed him with features of a borderline personality.

Andy's MMPI-2-RF had a larger than average number of infrequent responses, that is, a number of such infrequent responses that is statistically higher than the number given in the general population. This was likely a result of his limited verbal comprehension. Still, the overall testing results were valid, consistent with an individual who sees himself as useless and who has a tendency toward self-destructiveness. The results also suggested that he was impulsive and had difficulty organizing his thoughts. Furthermore, the findings were consistent with an individual who is prone to becoming emotionally overwhelmed and having grave difficulty regulating his behavior.

I diagnosed Andy with bipolar II disorder with episodes of a low-grade manic symptoms (hypomania) and periods of depression. I didn't think he had experienced full-blown mania or florid psychotic symptoms.

***

Most significant with regard to the carjacking charge was my diagnosis of Andy's neurocognitive disorder, which was likely the result of a traumatic brain injury due to his multiple head injuries over the years. His learning disability and ADHD also synergistically contributed to his cognitive disability. The neuropsychological test results revealed major deficits in his executive functioning, especially in his planning and foresight, along with his capacity to inhibit and forestall naturally occurring reactions. For instance, he was severely impaired in his ability to suppress the tendency to read the word that was in a different color.

These findings, together with his behavior, revealed that Andy's impairment was in the orbitofrontal region of his brain, which is just above the eye sockets, and the ventromedial portion of the brain, deeply behind it. These areas have immense influence on social judgment and decision making, as well as one's ability to suppress prepotent reactions,[4] one of Andy's most consequential deficits. He described how he surprised himself with his impulsive aggression and how he'd find himself weeping immediately afterward. Usually, he would be embroiled in an argument, react abruptly, and calm down quickly, shocked at his behavior. I observed Andy's disorder in vivo, when he began slamming his forehead with his hands to demonstrate how he became self-destructive when frustrated; once he began, he had difficulty discontinuing his behavior until I intervened. This was consistent with his description of how he easily became overwhelmed with frustration, leading to physical altercations that he immediately realized were inappropriate ("it's . . . crazy"). And it supported his assertion that he reacted in an impulsive fashion when he grabbed for the victim's car keys in an angry impulsive fashion, not with a plan to carjack. His calm behavior afterward (sitting in a nearby park) also was consistent with orbitofrontal dysfunction behavior. His ADHD didn't help his frustration tolerance either.

I submitted my report to Andy's attorney and discussed with the attorney the complex nature of my findings. His pretrial hearings led to a private meeting among the prosecutor, Andy's attorney, and the judge, at which an agreement was reached: Andy pled felony assault with probation, and the carjacking allegation was dropped. As part of his probation, Andy had to participate in psychiatric and drug treatment, take his medication, and live in a stable environment, at a board and care residence that would be financed by his SSI.

***

There were meaningful similarities between the history and neuropsychology of Peter and Andy. Both had long histories of crime and substance abuse. In many ways, both had similar dysfunctional brains (neurocognitive disorders and attention deficit hyperactivity disorder).

But there were major differences. Most important, Peter's violence did not arise from a brain condition. He had above-average executive abilities, for example. His violence stemmed from his psychopathic self and was proactive and instrumental, predatory and rapacious. Andy's violence was a direct result of his neurocognitive disorder, an orbitofrontal syndrome. His violence was reactive and impulsive, unplanned and without a desired goal. It dissipated quickly and was immediately followed by self-contempt over his behavior.

***

Nonetheless, Peter's claim that "my brain made me do it" was not unusual. Over the last several decades, neuroscientific findings have been used increasingly by the defense in criminal proceedings. About 6 percent of murder cases in the United States have introduced neuroscientific findings of one sort or another.[5] I have been retained to conduct neuropsychological investigations with defendants accused of crimes ranging from murder and attempted murder to cases involving sexual misconduct, arson, assault, and legal questions regarding various forms of legal competencies (e.g., understanding of Miranda rights), and more. The neuropsychological evidence is typically employed by the defense but increasingly has been used by prosecutors to make claims that the neuroscientific data support a longer prison term because of the defendant's biologically based violent tendencies.[6]

Peter's argument was that his genetic background and his family milieu—his biological nature combined with a damaging environment during his early life—were corrupting forces that impeded his abilities to stay within the bounds of moral norms and the law and that he therefore should be excused for his legal violations. There is indeed evidence for a temperamental and genetic disposition for antisocial and violent behavior,[7] especially if one is exposed to a dysfunctional environment during development.[8]

What's more, Peter had substantial support from a portion of the neuroscientific community. As I mentioned in chapter 6, some neuroscientists advocate an alternative view of legal responsibility that resonates with Peter's. In its most sweeping form, these scientists argue that all behavior, including criminal acts, are biologically determined by one's genes and brain activity and beyond conscious control.[9]

Unlike the plant referenced by the philosopher Keller in the epigraph of this chapter, these scientists believe that, although we might be capable of reflecting upon ourselves and our impulses and sharing our personal experience with others, our sense of psychological mastery and personal agency are illusions.

Sound similar to Peter's perspective? I think so. But there are other considerations.

The "hard" biological deterministic view asserts that the mind is just a psychological expression of the brain's biochemistry; the brain has complete hegemony over psychological experience. But not all neuroscientists subscribe to this absolutist view of the mind-brain relationship. [10] Many scientists and clinicians view the mind as emerging from the brain, but its makeup is influenced by many sources, such as early caretaking experiences, [11] social learning, [12] and cultural context. [13]

Genetic research conjures a flexible, less deterministic viewpoint, particularly when complex psychological issues—as opposed to, for instance, physical attributes—are under consideration. Genes may have a 95 percent influence on eye color, but they exert only a 40 percent influence on personality. [14] That's a lot, but it is not 100 percent, which would be determinative.

There is no evidence for a criminal gene, [15] only evidence that biology has an influence on behavior. But so does environment, especially early life experiences of maltreatment and neglect. [16] So does educational level, nutrition, and attachment experiences; [17] I could go on. The point is that all behavior is caused by *something*, whether biological, psychological, or social in nature. As legal scholar Stephen Morse points out repeatedly in his writings, [18] criminal law doesn't focus directly on the causes of behavior; it is concerned with legal violations and the accompanying thoughts, intentions, and motivation that animated the misconduct.

***

Peter's argument was the hard deterministic one: his disordered brain was responsible for his criminal conduct. He was right in the sense that his biology, as well as his nurturing deficits, were very destructive influences on him. But they were not causal influences. Not everybody with "bad" biosocial backgrounds becomes violent criminals. More important, Peter had the cognitive equipment and reasoning ability to think before he acted. He had the *capacity* for self-control; it was his personality, formed by a complex mixture of causes and influences, that drove him to violence. It was the totality of his unique makeup that formed the basis of his violent crimes. In other words, it was *him*.

Andy's history of early abuse and his learning disabilities no doubt were adverse formative influences on his adult behavior. But it was his *lack of capacity* for self-control, resulting from a brain disorder, that distinguished him from Peter.

***

Having the good fortune to be born with an easy temperament and to be raised by a nurturing family doesn't protect one from malicious thoughts or vile impulses; those inner experiences are, at varying measures of intensity, ubiquitous and part of our human nature. Wicked desire is not limited to those with broken brains. All of us must grapple with clashes between impulse and desire, with the need for restraint between the two being the price of civility.

I'm reminded of an observation attributed to the renowned developmental psychologist Jerome Kagan that most corrupt people he knew had perfectly functioning brains.

12

DAIMONIC INJUSTICE

"Hier is kein warum!" (Here there is no why!)—Shouted by an Auschwitz Nazi guard to Primo Levi after he asked why a fellow prisoner was being beaten

With a visiting order in hand allowing entrance to the jail, I was off to begin my evaluation of Thomas, a twenty-seven-year-old man accused of criminal assault. His attorney, Anthony Muñoz, had filled me in on the details of the case. Thomas had gotten into an argument with the victim over a parking spot at a mall, which escalated into a physical altercation. When he met with his client after his arrest, Mr. Muñoz said that Thomas went on and on about how he found the spot first. "He doesn't get that he can't lose his temper and start punching someone, even if that's true." At the same time, Mr. Muñoz continued, Thomas didn't seem like the kind of guy who would become so violent. He had no criminal history and no history of violence or drug abuse. He had never been under psychiatric care for strange behavior. "On the surface, he seems like your average Joe. But I don't think he is," the lawyer said. "He's a little weird . . . maybe Asperger's or something like that."

Thomas's parents told Mr. Muñoz that as a child Thomas became strangely obsessed with various topics. For instance, in elementary school he had been fixated on a particular comic book character. As an adult, he was hyperreligious. His parents were believers, but they complained that Thomas had a rigidity to his morality that was peculiar. "They always felt something was off-kilter with their son," Mr. Muñoz said. He wondered if

Thomas's "black-and-white world" and rigid thinking had something to do with his violent outburst in the parking lot that day.

The prosecutor handling the case was reluctant to sign off on any kind of plea arrangement. He had listened to the taped police interview with Thomas that had been made immediately after the incident. Thomas sounded like an angry guy during the interview, the prosecutor told Mr. Muñoz. On the other hand, since Thomas was without prior episodes of violence, the prosecutor was willing to consider a plea if he got a favorable psychological report, which included an estimate of Thomas's violence risk and a psychiatric diagnosis. He wanted some understanding of what had prompted the defendant's aggression. If a plea deal were in the cards, treatment recommendations would need to be part of it.

Thomas was housed at a jail in which I had never previously worked, and it was a distance away. As usual when I'm in for a long drive, I hooked up my smartphone to my car and prepared to listen to an audiobook, usually revolving around my second intellectual love after psychology, twentieth-century history. That day I listened to Ken Burns's book, *The War*. It's an intimate history of World War II as told by voices of men and women who experienced it and lived to tell about it. My wife thought it was strange that I listen to stories of tragedy and death as I head off to jail. She asked, "Why don't you take a break and listen to music?" She had a point. Then again, as the historian Eric Hobsbawn wrote in the *Age of Extremes*, an oeuvre to the wars of the twentieth century, these were conflicts that vividly exposed the potential of human beings to perpetrate acts that stretch from abject depravity to ones of stunning nobility and courage (think Nazi SS versus the British Royal Air Force and the Battle of London).

Such extremes in human conduct are revealed not only during times of titanic conflagrations, but in everyday life, as well, particularly among those who spend time within the criminal justice system, either by force or choice. It's a venue where the full range of our proclivities for good and ill are manifest, a direct result of having been exposed to a constant drip of raw emotionality and heaviness of heart.

So listening to Burns's work was both preparation and a form of succor that I found therapeutic.

***

Since this was my first time at this lockup, I had to be approved by the watch commander, even with my court order. Contraband gets smuggled into these facilities via ingenious methods, sometimes by those who are the least suspicious types. Recently, there had been a breach of security, which had necessitated closer scrutiny during visitations. The intake deputy told me that a lawyer had smuggled in a mobile phone to his client, who was a "shot caller" of his unit. He's the designated authority in his area, not officially, but by the sanction of the other inmates. The shot caller earned the position for one reason or another; maybe he had served a prison term that gave him standing in jailhouse lore. Armed with a phone, the shot caller could make unmonitored contact with outside associates (all jail phone calls are monitored) to find out the reasons for a new inmate's arrest and his pedigree. The shot caller then could decide if any action needed to be taken. Is the newly arrived inmate accused of child molestation? Is he a rival gang member or one with a reputation for being a snitch, a capital offense in the jailhouse world? If necessary, the shot caller gives an attack order.

I was finally vetted and directed to a private booth, where I waited to interview Thomas. I set up my laptop and reviewed my notes and the police reports. I was ready to go, but still no Thomas. I took out a newspaper and read it while waiting. After about an hour and a half, I heard the roar of a motor cranking up; the cell gates that separated the inmate section of the jail from the interview room, which contained a number of private booths, slowly opened. A lanky young man walked, quick paced, down a narrow corridor to the interview room. Tall and thin, he moved with a slight wobble to his gait, his longish straight black hair flapping from side to side. As he got nearer, I could see his dark eyes were cast down and his face tight with tension. A buzzer sounded, the door unlocked, and he entered the booth. I got a closer look at his eyes. He wasn't just tense and wound up; he was terrified. Before I was able to introduce myself, Thomas blurted out, "Call my lawyer. He's gotta get me out . . . in protective custody."

That morning, Thomas had been given an assignment by one of the deputies to mop the floors in his cellblock. That's a task with a little extra freedom, usually given to those the deputies trust will not cause trouble, the ones who do what they're told. Though Thomas was arrested on an assault charge, he clearly wasn't classified by the staff as a violent risk. That was a good sign, so what was he so anguished about? The problem occurred when Thomas was amid his assignment. An inmate approached and told him to mop somewhere else. Being his fastidious self, Thomas refused, saying he was told to mop in that area. The inmate became belligerent, ordering Thomas to leave. Another inmate, he told Thomas, had been targeted by their shot caller and was about to be attacked; in a few minutes, he was going to be thrown off the top tier, above where Thomas had been mopping. "Now fuckin' move," he told Thomas.

"What was I supposed to do?" Thomas asked me. "What if someone died?" I listened without interruption, waiting to find out what he did do. Thomas clearly felt he was faced with a real moral dilemma, possibly a life-and-death one. To him, the choice was clear.

Thomas left his assigned area, went straight to a deputy, and told him what was about to occur. He was schooled enough in jailhouse culture to know the cost of being labeled a snitch. Frantically, Thomas asked to be placed in protective custody. A smart request, I thought. At that point, I assumed his horrified look was the result of what had just transpired. But it was for another reason: the deputy refused Thomas's request. He told Thomas, "Next time, mind your fuckin' business." As he walked away, he instructed Thomas to go back to his tier.

At that point, I could not have simply proceeded with the forensic evaluation. Thomas needed to know I would help as much as I was able. I told him I was unfamiliar with this particular jail, but I would call his lawyer immediately after I left the facility. I tried to communicate to him that I understood his fear and the urgency of the situation. We spoke for about another half hour. I asked him some questions about his personal life but mostly listened and offered support, less as a forensic examiner and more like a psychotherapist listening to a person who felt trauma-tized.

I left the facility and immediately called Mr. Muñoz from my phone as I sat in my car in the jail parking lot. He was not in his office. I told the office manager that it was urgent I speak to him. She put me on hold as she made contact with him and patched me through. I told him Thomas's story. Mr. Muñoz was surprisingly calm and matter of fact: "I'll call over there," he said.

Later in the day, I called to follow up and spoke with the office manager, who told me that Thomas was now in protective custody. I suspected that Thomas's lawyer was familiar with the jail staff and how things were done there.

As the day turned to night, I thought about Thomas's situation and my conversation with Mr. Muñoz. I had told him that from what I knew about Thomas's history and my limited time with him, I suspected he was on the autism spectrum, in the higher functioning range. I was surprised and irritated at Mr. Muñoz's blasé reaction to the incident. I seemed more excited—even offended—about Thomas's situation than his attorney did. Though Thomas was safe, I had this ongoing clamor over the incident's exposure of a convoluted morality. Here was an inmate charged with felony assault who cared more about the welfare of a fellow inmate than the guy who was supposed to be wearing a white hat.

Several weeks after my visit with Thomas, I got a call from Mr. Muñoz. Thomas was able to "plead out" to a misdemeanor charge of disturbing the peace with probation requirements that he attend anger-management treatment and receive a psychiatric evaluation. The assistant district attorney had looked at all the evidence including Thomas's school records, his clean criminal record, and a lengthy statement and review of Thomas's history provided by his parents. He concluded that Thomas was a low risk for future misconduct, especially if he received treatment.

***

The moral juxtaposition exposed by Thomas's jailhouse adventure is not all that uncommon in many complex social systems. But the dangers are unique in criminal justice, where issues of judgment and morality take center stage. It's the place in our society where legal conflicts are supposed to be adjudicated objectively and fairly, at least theoretically. It's the forum in which we as a society arbitrate justice and penalize wrongdoing. As we have seen throughout this book, grievous forms of misconduct frequently flow from the dark end of our nature. Sometimes, with emotions fraught and tensions high, human frailty and base impulses overpower our ideals, even among those sworn to serve justice.

***

The spectrum of behavior from the malicious to the magnificent—what I've referred to as our daimonic and nebulous nature—has been a preoccupation of mine for years, predating my professional career. It's been with me for as long as I can remember. When I was about nine years old, my older brother took me to a movie matinee to celebrate the beginning of summer. It was a cowboy flick, *The Legend of Tom Dooley*. Like so many movies of the 1960s, its characters were turgid and blunt. But this one presented a disturbing perspective to my nine-year-old mind.

The essential storyline: A Confederate officer during the Civil War, Tom Dooley leads an attack on northern soldiers, not aware that the war is over. He is declared a murderer and is in danger of being arrested if he returns to the town where his sweetheart, Laura, lives. Dooley indeed returns, marries his Laura, and is arrested by the town sheriff, Charlie Grayson. Dooley is tried and sentenced to death by hanging. He escapes with the help of an army buddy, Country Boy. When Laura leaves town to reunite with Dooley, Grayson finds Laura and forces himself on her. Dooley and Country Boy show up, a fight ensues, and Laura is accidentally stabbed. Dooley and Grayson struggle with the knife. During the melee, Grayson and Country Boy shoot each other. Laura dies in Dooley's arms as lawmen arrive and arrest Dooley. The story ends with Dooley awaiting execution.

I left the movie in a state of emotional vertigo. How could such an unfair thing happen? Dooley did not intend to commit a crime; he was misinformed, believing he was at war. From earlier events in the movie, it was clear that Grayson was in love with Laura and wanted Dooley gone so he could "get the girl." But he was a lawman. He was supposed to be honorable and do the right thing. Not only was his pursuit of Dooley dastardly and self-serving, he forced himself on Laura. And Dooley, the righteous character, was unjustly executed.

That entire summer as I lay in bed at night slipping into sleep, I deliberated about Tom Dooley's fate and the wretched unfairness of it all. How could a righteous man be so misjudged and a lawman so unjust? The ambiguity of goodness and evil rattled my childhood illusion about a natural moral order of things. It disturbed my summer slumber.

***

How common are injustices perpetrated by those who have been given the responsibility to enforce the law? It's hard to know, though criminal justice scholars who study such matters feel that most police misconduct goes unnoticed.[1] Law enforcement officials don't like to investigate their own, and the public in general supports the police and sees them as a "blue wall" protecting them from danger. In addition, most people are cognizant of the dangers inherent in the job.

With the advent of body cams and cell phones, though, there has been an increasing awareness that the circumstances of an arrest sometimes may be more complicated than the official police version, which may even be a distortion of the circumstances surrounding the arrest. Over time, this could have a corrosive impact on how the police are perceived. In a survey released by the Cato Institute,[2] 70 percent of Americans continue to have a favorable attitude toward police. Yet almost half of Americans believe that "most" police officers think they are above the law, and 60 percent believe the justice system fails to treat everybody equally under the law.

I have seen deputies taunt psychotically confused individuals (e.g., "Hey, asshole . . .") for not immediately following their directives, seemingly unconcerned or oblivious to their disabilities. Over the years, inmates have shared with me stories of deputy mistreatment, some of which, in my judgment, were more credible than others. One inmate, a smart-mouthed young guy, told me he was "pretzeled up"—assaulted—by three deputies while being transported from his cell. He knew what was coming when the deputies took him to the elevator instead of the stairwell: the elevator doesn't have cameras. He spent a few days in the infirmary as a result of his injuries. I asked if he told his father, who at the time was a high-level law enforcement official in a different county. He had and was told that nothing could be done. "It's a rite of passage," his father said, for the deputies to violently discipline disrespectful inmates. Anyway, who would believe an inmate over a peace officer?

***

Sometimes, though, what you see is what you get: the white hat guys are just that; good and ethical and compassionate.

I frequently evaluate inmates in a specialized jail unit that houses the most florid of psychotic individuals. It's a surreal experience to enter this area. I feel like I'm stepping back in time to the way it must have been in the nineteenth or early twentieth centuries when institutions had to care for psychotic patients without the benefit of modern psychiatric drugs. In this unit are people with severe mental illnesses who have committed crimes that range from disturbing the peace to murder. Many have refused medications and have not yet gone through the legal hoops that would have allowed the psychiatric staff at the jail to medicate without their permission. As I enter the unit, the descent into atavism is immediately experienced by all the senses. Inmates are screaming incoherently and irrationally about one topic or another: the CIA is poisoning him, says one inmate; others issue screeds about the evilness of their lawyers; someone else demands to be recognized as Jesus Christ. On my way to the cell to interview a defendant, others screech directly at me. Once, an inmate claimed to be a billionaire cheated out of his money by Bill Gates. He pleaded for help as I passed his cell. Others are agitated and tormented, pacing the hall, nude or with their gowns opened, preoccupied and obsessed looking. A few may be masturbating while others sleep with their blankets covering their heads.

Almost always, the cells are in disarray, with half-eaten food trashed about the cell floors. Each cell has its own toilet, which could become a multipurpose device for the psychotic inmate. Sometimes it's used not only to defecate and urinate but to wash a jumpsuit or t-shirt, even when the toilet is backed up with feces and urine. An odious stench seeps through the cells into the unit hallways. A deputy told me, "You get used to it."

When a cell is judged to be dangerously unhygienic, deputies enter wearing protective gear to clean up the mess and the inmate as they try to manage his deranged behavior. Some of the inmates require emergency intravenous tranquilizers to tolerate the intrusion.

The wretched psychological regression of the inmates is in such stark contrast to the humane treatment I've regularly observed from the deputies. Immediately, I was struck by how engaged they were with the inmates, tolerant of their bizarreness and working hard to be as helpful and as kind as possible. Typically, deputies tend to be authoritative and demand that inmates and visitors such as I follow their directives. Here they remain calm and respectful while inmates menace and rage, sometimes threatening and sometimes spitting at them.

Once, as I was escorted off the unit by a lieutenant, I mentioned how impressed I was by the way the deputies handle the inmates. He agreed and said the deputies are specially chosen to work on the unit and want to be there. Breaking with standard procedure, deputies on the psychiatric unit are not regularly rotated to other parts of the jail system but are assigned to it for longer periods of service. An excellent strategy, I thought.

***

Why such a range of conduct among law enforcement officials—from the cruel to the merciful—so clearly on display? The lessons from the famous Stanford Prison Experiment[3] suggest that the immediate social context and culture are frequent culprits driving bad behavior. Social psychologist Philip Zimbardo chose twenty-five undergraduates, who, by the way, were deemed to be psychologically stable, to act as guards and prisoners in a mock prison. All participants understood they were taking part in an experiment. Nonetheless, over the course of several days the experiment had to be stopped because the guards became excessively cruel and aggressive toward the "inmates." About a third of the guards showed sadistic tendencies.

The standard interpretation of these findings is that our tendencies toward malice could be sparked by social context.[4] We are all too readily influenced and guided by the roles we inhabit and are willing adjust our behavior to the perceived expectations of those roles. To wit, it's not "the devil made me do it" or my character; it's my social milieu. On the other hand, many are capable of overruling social press. Not all of the "guards" in Zimbardo's experiment became cruel and sadistic. And think of those humane deputies I described earlier who work on the jail's psychiatric ward; they are members of the same authoritarian law enforcement culture that apparently sanctions meanness and reactive violence as a rite. Those deputies choose to place themselves in an environment that demands tolerance and patience to be effective.

What then leads to gaps in humane behavior? The perspective taken by law enforcement leadership is that misconduct is the result of some "bad apples" in the bunch, though the widespread nature of misconduct points to systemic problems.[5] Is it a result of individual differences among personalities, with a self-selection process occurring that draws aggressive and authoritarian personalities to police work? That's certainly the stereotype of many critics of contemporary policing. But the forces influencing police conduct are many and complex. Most officers possess adequate coping skills to manage the strain of police work adequately; those who do not have such coping skills are susceptible to becoming controlling and aggressive.[6] Most sworn officers fulfill their professional obligations professionally and ethically.[7]

The problem of law enforcement misconduct is difficult to grasp. Most police are no doubt fair-minded, yet studies suggest that the extent of bad behavior on the part of the police is seriously underestimated and unreported.[8] It paints officers with too broad a brush to say they're all controlling and bellicose, but officers who have been disciplined and faced misconduct charges have been found to be cynical and distrustful with tendencies toward aggression and irrationality.[9]

Of particular concern is that officers, both the good and bad ones, are in control of and shape the chronicle of their own behavior. Not only are they invested with the authority to arrest and use violence when necessary, but they write the reports of the official version of the crime; that is, in many ways they control the reality of what happened. Maybe what is most important is that they are assumed by the public and their leadership to be ethical in their conduct, to be moral warriors and placeholders for our ideals, holding the line against evil.

While recognizing that most police officials are in fact reputable, it has been widely known, at least since the early part of the twentieth century, that a code of secrecy exists among law enforcement officials.[10] A sense of loyalty to their peers protects all, including the "bad apples," which over time has a pernicious effect on all.

The process of socialization in the law enforcement subculture occurs early in officers' careers.[11] Training procedures and career progression serve to alter their perception of self as separate from ordinary citizens since they are responsible for enforcing the laws by which others must adhere. As exemplars of the law with the authority to use violence when necessary, they carry a heavy burden. Understandably, a strong bond develops among sworn officers that can undermine their oath. Beginning cadets are exposed to unwritten but powerful norms and forms of behavioral control that most find compelled to honor; the code of silence is one of the more pernicious ones. Essentially, it asserts that "we take care of our own," not only during the commission of their duties, but even when colleagues misbehave, break the law, or exercise brutality. This "blue curtain" serves to solidify an identity that separates the officers from other citizens and creates a "band of brothers" commitment to fellow officers.

Being trained and socialized within a quasi-military subculture[12] that places a premium on hierarchy and intense loyalty creates an unwillingness to address wrongdoing from those within the blue circle. Together with the demands of a difficult job, this creates a tendency among officers to take an absolutist view of how the world operates.[13] The thinking process that defines judgment tends to be binary in nature: right or wrong, bad or good, virtuous or sinful.[14] A problem arises when such a Manichaean perspective is wedded to a tightly knit subculture that places a premium on allegiance, secrecy, and the protection of its own above all else. Over time, this creates an "us against them" perspective. And to peace officers, the "them" encompasses those who aren't wearing the uniform. Many law enforcement personnel come to the profession with a military interest and background, which potentially adds another layer to the problem: in a military context, the "them" are enemy combatants; in law enforcement, the "them" are individuals the officers are sworn to protect.

With an established code of silence and an us-against-them perspective, it doesn't require much rationalization to perceive the abuse of a suspect by one's colleague as "something the asshole deserved," not as wrong and illegal. Police officers are known to care less about the procedures of justice (e.g., due process, the right to remain silent, etc.) than what they "know" to be true, what they have seen with their own eyes. In other words, they are more attentive to what they perceive as *factual* guilt rather than *legal* guilt.[15] It's tantamount to street justice, which officers view as a method of crime control, particularly when the formal punishment for an illegal or unacceptable behavior would likely be limited.[16] This may include using excessive violence, roughing up someone who behaves disrespectfully to officers, or lying under oath to secure a conviction. In fact, perjury by sworn officers is such an open secret that there's a name for it: testilying.[17] One scholar offered up a moral defense of the police exacting punishment on the streets, calling it a form of order maintenance that the public supports.[18]

When those vested with the responsibility to uphold the law instead violate it—even when they view themselves as acting in the service of justice—the unintended consequences are frequently stark. The Innocence Project, for instance, has documented multiple cases in which police misconduct led to innocent people being convicted of heinous crimes, including capital murder.[19] When a law enforcement culture bypasses centuries of hard-earned judicial wisdom, all kinds of unethical consequences follow. In my own backyard, for instance, a judge dismissed the case against the cofounder of a major high-tech company because of the federal prosecutor's blatant intimidation of a witness. The judge called the persecution's conduct in the case "shameful."[20]

Again in my backyard, a scandal hit the news and rocked a community known for its conservative and law-and-order values.[21] At the local jail, deputies devised a system that illegally used confidential informants (snitches) to develop evidence on inmates accused of crimes. In one particular case that exposed the long-running system, deputies placed an informant in a cell with an inmate accused of a heinous double murder, even after he had already confessed to the crimes. Placing an informant in the cell with the defendant to obtain incriminating evidence was illegal since accused had invoked his Miranda rights and was represented by counsel. By subpoenaing documents from the jail, criminal attorneys on the case exposed an informant system that had been in place at the jail for more than twenty years. This revelation occurred after deputies had sworn under oath that no such system existed. The signatures of two supervising deputies, who had denied under oath that such a system existed, were on documents directing informants to be illegally placed in cells with inmates.

The consequences were profound. Many cases that had already been adjudicated had to be revisited. Several cases of gang members who were convicted of murder had their convictions either overturned or renegotiated.

***

Not only did the deputies know about but deny the existence of the illegal informant system in open court, the prosecutors also denied knowing about it to the judge. This led to several of the prosecutors getting into legal hot water. Because of prosecutor malfeasance, the presiding judge recused the entire district attorney's office from several cases and appointed the state's attorney general to take over the criminal proceedings of those cases. This was not a case of a few "bad apples" or overzealous lawyers going rogue in the district attorney's office. The illegal informant system had been in place for years.

Prosecutorial misconduct is not uncommon. One study[22] found a wide range of prosecutorial malfeasance, including the presentation of false evidence and, most destructive, failure to disclose exculpatory evidence. As with police officials, unlawful prosecutorial conduct is implicitly accepted. Out of 707 confirmed cases of prosecutorial misconduct in California from 1997 to 2009, sixty-seven committed misconduct in more than one case and only six prosecutors were disciplined by the California State Bar.[23] None was disbarred.

Another study[24] found that prosecutorial misconduct included suppressing exculpatory evidence, abetting false testimony, coercing witnesses, and concealing evidence. Almost certainly there were many more unidentified cases of misconduct.

Undoubtedly, many of these prosecutors believed they were doing the right thing, that they were doing justice. I read a newspaper account that quoted a prosecutor as saying, "There're no swans in a sewer." He rationalized that, given some defendants' lifestyles and social standing, they probably had escaped justice in the past and were guilty as sin of *something*. Even if the evidence was tainted or didn't reach the standard of beyond reasonable doubt, they deserved harsh judgment, vigilante or otherwise.

***

As ministers of justice, prosecutors are tasked with bringing charges against those whom they believe to be guilty of illegal behavior and to employ fair and legal methods to convict the accused. They are sworn to conduct their investigations impartially, with a fundamental responsibility to seek justice, not solely to convict. Like the police, the majority of prosecutors successfully discharge these obligations. Also like police, the human elements that drive behavior come into play: the desire to compete and to win, an eye on advancement and glory, or the desire for admiration from one's peers. An ambitious prosecutor in a high-profile case might fail to disclose exculpatory evidence. Why, he might conclude, chance raising reasonable doubt among the jurors? In the prosecutor's mind, the evidence is overwhelming; the defendant is a bad guy who needs to be put away, so what's the harm?

Or consider a young peace officer who sees a veteran colleague plant evidence at a crime scene. He knows it's wrong, but it's taboo to betray a fellow officer, especially a seasoned one. Anyway, the suspect is a "bad seed" who probably got away with a lot of crimes, so what's the harm here? These kinds of justifications are easy to make if one concludes that a crooked means justifies a righteous end. To rationalize in this way and assuage a sense of wrongdoing is understandable and human. That's the problem; it is all too human.

At the same time, there are subcultures that exist within law enforcement that represent the more sublime aspects of our nature. Think of the unit with psychotic defendants who are cared for by unusually humane deputies or the many divisions within the offices of district attorney around the country that are solely dedicated to reopening cases of convicted inmates when evidence to the contrary is revealed. Or the prosecutor who offered Ray, the sex crime murderer I wrote about in chapter 9, a plea deal to spare his young children and the families of the victims the relentless psychological trauma of repeated media exposure of a capital case conviction as it grinds through legal appeals.

A number of years ago, I taught with an older gentleman who had a career in law enforcement and retired as a command-level administrative official. He went on to earn a PhD in organizational justice and taught at the same university as I. He frequently assisted professors in obtaining access to the jail system so students could tour. It was impressive how the deputies responded to my colleague, now deceased, with such warmth and admiration. I understood why; he was an extraordinarily ethical and compassionate man. As a high official in one of the local police agencies, a highly stratified subculture, he treated everyone with respect and common decency. He told me that he counseled those under his charge to respect the dignity of every inmate, whether guilty or innocent.

It should not be a surprise that a range of moral behavior exists within the agencies of law enforcement. After all, they're simply a microcosm of us all, with the same base instincts and exalted tendencies. Or, if you will, with the same daimonic nature.

***

The results of the famous Stanford Prison Experiment laid bare the ease with which, under the right circumstances, one group could dehumanize another. Even in explicitly contrived circumstances, it was seemingly easy for psychologically sturdy individuals to view the "other" as worthy of harshness and aggression, even sadism, as though their status marked them as socially or morally inferior, as less than others.

It has been known for years that people imbue their own group with a specialness that distinguishes them from other groups.[25] In-group members are usually seen as possessing an essence—biological, cultural, or religious—that makes them unique. A series of intriguing studies[26] investigated how two groups (different nationalities) perceived the emotional functioning of their own group members versus members of the other group. Each person rated the functioning of members from both groups using a list of multiple emotions and sentiments. Emotions such as anger or fear are shared by all primates, whereas sentiments are a different matter. Sentiments are composed of complex, nuanced combinations of emotions that are derived from prior social and interpersonal experience. Examples include sorrow and grief, envy and contempt, and compassion. Unlike emotions, sentiments are believed to be uniquely human experiences.

The results of the studies showed that people attributed more negative emotions to members of the other group and more positive ones to members of their own group. In addition, they rated their own group members as having more positive sentiments (e.g., compassion and astonishment), whereas the other group was regarded as having more negative sentiments (e.g., contempt) and fewer positive sentiments (e.g., pride). Out-group members were seen as having a diminished sentimentality, that unique dimension of inner life. Basically, the out-group was viewed as less than human—as infrahuman, as it were.

One of these studies was designed to measure the degree of emotions and sentiments attributed to the other group. Employing an elaborate design, the results revealed that each group was reluctant to attribute *any* sentiments to the other group.

It becomes especially problematic when the "other" is in a powerless position, as so starkly demonstrated by Zimbardo's prison experiment. But the tendency to dehumanize the "other" exists beyond the social power dynamic. Hannah Arendt, in her explorations of Nazism and totalitarianism,[27] concluded that evil results from a failure to think, from an inability or unwillingness to reflect on the wickedness of one's impulses. Such a state of mind is all too frequently incited by group identification, thus allowing for the dehumanization of others outside one's own group.

Interestingly, it was just that kind of mindlessness demanded of the Nazi guard that I referenced in this chapter's epigraph.[28] *Here there is no why!* The guard was saying that he would fulfill his duty as a soldier at Auschwitz without question, and he expected the same from Levi: that he accept his fate and the fate of all Jews without asking why. Arendt surmised that such a zombielike psychological posture allowed Germans, normal and moral ones, to accept the perpetration of human destructiveness. That's what she meant by her famous phrase, "the banality of evil." Everyday people, under certain social and psychological conditions, are capable of unspeakable cruelty.

But not all individuals succumb to the tyranny of mindlessness, whether the result of social pressure or selfish impulse. To investigate the extent to which context and personality influence altruistic behavior,[29] social psychologists John Darley and Daniel Batson had one group of seminary students from Princeton University listen to a lecture about the parable of the Good Samaritan while another group participated in a seminar about postgraduate employment opportunities. Both groups were then instructed to give a lecture across campus and to arrive on time. On the way to the lecture, all the students had to pass a person slumped in an alleyway, distressed and clearly in need of help. One research question was whether the students who listened to the parable about the Good Samaritan, a person who responds to another in need, would be primed to respond more altruistically than the other group, regardless of personal ambition or the mandate to get to the lecture hall on time. As you might— or might not—have expected, 90 percent of the students from both groups did not stop to help. Those students who listened to the Good Samaritan parable did not stop to help any more than the students from the employment-opportunities group. But 10 percent, a small but not insignificant amount, did stop.

The historian Christopher Browning studied the conduct of German men from Reserve Police Battalion 101,[30] who served on the Eastern Front during World War II. Of interest was the fact that these men of Battalion 101 were not Nazis, nor were they even members of the Wehrmacht, the German armed forces. They were uniformed police officers who had been given additional military training. They were stationed in Poland, a theater of death that witnessed the mass murder of Jews and partisans who resided there. These "ordinary men," as Browning referred to them, were given the option to step away from the killing field and perform other duties that were not so central to fulfilling the homicidal national policy. Only about 10 to 20 percent did so. Again, a small but not insignificant number.

In my next and final chapter, I explore the psychological ingredients that engender wickedness and the psychological conditions that reduce the likelihood of descending into cruelty and preventable madness.

13

CONCLUSION

Justice, Human Frailty, and the Daimonic

Humanity [is] situated between the animal and the divine. . . . Whatever the achievements of civilization, the animal still dwells within.—Thomas Nevin, *Ernst Jüng en and Germany: Into the Abyss 1914–1945*

You must have chaos within your soul to give birth to a dancing star.—Friedrich Nietzsche, *Thus Spoke Zarathustra*

After the calamity of September 11, 2001, British prime minister Tony Blair proclaimed that honorable nations must bind together to seek out "evil and drive it out of this world." Maybe the former British prime minister was attempting to slough toward the Churchillian with some inspiring rhetoric. Or maybe he was simply being naive and blind to a simple truth: we are animals with both a cortex and primordial drives that, if unchecked, are perilous. It's our indigenous, inextricable condition that cannot be outsourced to evildoing "others" and driven away. We can't throw out the bathwater without losing the baby.

***

Recently during voir dire, after the attorneys questioned me regarding my competency to render an expert opinion, the judge asked why, with all my particular training in psychoanalysis, I engage in expert witness work and not treatment. That was a question I could work with; it was like an elixir that helped to silence the foreboding disquietude that always accompanies me to the witness stand. I focused on what is most germane about my curriculum vitae, what I feel leavens its content yet is sub rosa: my temperamental proclivity toward the interior that is expressed by my specialization. I told the judge that I do both and that psychoanalysis and forensic work are harmonious. More than any other psychological approach to the understanding of human beings—including the parent disciplines of clinical psychology and psychiatry—psychoanalysis takes seriously the subjective and the internal world of the person with all of his or her moving parts. I was drawn to the psychoanalytic perspective because it recognizes that to understand someone is to grasp his or her inner life with all its darkness and light. It takes more than a cursory look at behavior or surface attitudes. As a forensic psychologist trained in psychoanalysis, I'm deeply attuned to an individual's emotional turmoil, his intentions and his purposefulness—the drivers of behavior. Since the commission of most crimes requires both criminal behavior and an accompanying mental state that is intentional and purposeful, my comfort and expertise in dwelling within the deeply subjective is nothing but an asset when conducting forensic examinations.

My strict Catholic education was a blessing and a curse. Early on, I internalized a sense of the moral—think of the Sermon on the Mount. I was exposed to the notion of original sin, an inbred spiritual stain on the soul. It portends a lurking malevolence that's just around the corner. Though I sometimes feel like a "fallen angel" tainted by my original sin, I have long given up a belief in the spiritual basis of evil. But it's primed me to a psychoanalytic perspective, with its unblinking willingness to take human destructiveness seriously.

Here's how the historian Norman Brown puts it: "It is a shattering experience for anyone seriously committed to the Western traditions of morality and rationality to take a steadfast, unflinching look at what Freud has to say. It is humiliating to be compelled to admit the grossly seamy side of so many grand ideals."[1] My training as an analyst and my years as a psychoanalytic patient didn't introduce me to the complexity of human experience or to our capacity to do good and ill. What it did was to steel me with the courage to face it. Criminal forensic work has been a full-bore entrée into the depths of human nature: it's where psychoanalytic understanding confronts lived experience that is often dashing toward our seamy side. We don't like knowing it's there, that seamy side. Or that it can show up anywhere. It's a part of human nature that Freud referred to as the id.[2] Translated from German, "id" means "it": Freud referenced the id as the part of us that's like a daimonic presence that doesn't feel as if "it" belongs to us. It is a human potential that animates not only the seamy but also the sublime side of our beings. As I did at the outset in chapter 1, I call upon Plato's observation that Eros is daimonic. Or consider psychoanalyst Rollo May's elegant observation that to view "creativity on one side, and anger and rage on the other side, as coming from the same source. That is, constructiveness and destructiveness have the same source in human personality. The source is simply *human potential*."[3]

The daimonic in us is revealed in every aspect of our lives: in its generative (think van Gogh) and destructive forms (Auschwitz), in humane acts of courage and in mindless cruelty. The psychological exploration of our human nature is what I have been most interested in as a psychoanalyst and as a forensic psychologist. It's this dimension of the human experience that lights up the people and stories I've written about.

***

The raw emotionality, impetuosity, and psychic madness that drives us to the dark daimonic edge are writ large in the criminal justice system. Despite such starkness, though, the light shines through. Consider several of the the instances I described in the previous chapter, such as the prosecutor in Ray's rape/murder case (chapter 9) who wished to spare the defendant's children from the years of media exposure that comes with a capital conviction by offering instead a life-in-prison deal. Or, on a more abstract level, consider the noble values of fairness and impartiality that are encoded within our system of justice.

The light is all around. I have a friend, a gifted writer of fiction, who told me that story narratives frequently come to him as he sleeps, like a spirit in the night. He keeps a pad near his bed so that he can record his thoughts when the muse arrives. It's as though he is transcribing a story that has already been written by his daemon, demanding a voice.

The more august side of our nature is evident quite early in development.[4] For instance, Paul Bloom in his book *Just Babies*[5] writes about how a one-year-old reacted to his nascent sense of fairness. The infant, whom I'll call Tommy, watched a show starring three puppets. The puppet in the middle rolled a ball to the puppet on the right, who then rolled it back to her. She then rolled the ball to the puppet on the left. That puppet took the ball and ran away with it. After the show, the nice puppet and the naughty puppet were taken from the stage and placed in front of Tommy. Treats were placed in front of the naughty and nice puppets and Tommy was invited to take one of the treats. As predicted by the researchers, he took the treat from the naughty puppet, as did most of the other infants who participated in the study, thereby exercising their intuitive moral judgments.

The point Bloom makes throughout the book, one replicated by other researchers,[6] is that humans have an innate capacity for compassion and justice toward others. By contrast, he also cites a nineteenth-century cleric who wrote that infants are also brought into the world replete with evil propensities and offers evidence of the cleric's perspicacity, affirming much of what has been documented in these pages.

The roots of our daimonic range go deep, beyond and before infancy to our essential biological makeup. We may be animals, but Homo sapiens are of a different sort. Anthropologist Richard Wrangham describes us as a domesticated and house-trained species.[7] That being so, we tend to be more tolerant and far less aggressive than our cousin chimps. For instance, primatologist Jane Goodall, who spent years observing chimpanzees in the wild, recorded their tendency to attack rival tribe groups, kill the males, eat the babies, and mate with the females.[8]

Being housetrained, we live in close association with one other, form clans, and are dependent upon one another for safety and nurturance. To say that we are tame, though, does not mean that we are not aggressive. On the whole, our aggressiveness is not wanton in nature—not usually. We do not indiscriminately attack, as a matter of practice, those different from us. In most of the civilized world, we don't kill off the males from an adjacent neighborhood and take their women for mates. Our violence toward one another is largely reactive and defensive in nature.[9] And through our justice system, we impose harsh retribution on those who premeditate violence.

At the same time, our justice system, while demanding self-restraint and the use of reason before action, recognizes our emotional fragility and vulnerability to the aggressive instinct. Simon, for example, the husband from chapter 7 who strangled his wife to death in a fit of shameful rage, was convicted of manslaughter, not murder. Our laws codify an understanding of ourselves, our nature: we are domesticated, yet as a result of emotional or psychic interruptions, we are capable of aberrant acts of madness and violence. Otherwise, we are expected to exercise moral character, restraint, and respect for the other.

***

There is an abundance of neuropsychological evidence of the normative nature of morality and nonviolence. As I have noted in previous chapters on psychopathy and the brain, dysfunctions in the prefrontal and limbic areas of the brain systems increase the likelihood of aberrant and violent conduct. More to the point, studies in which healthy subjects were faced with life-altering decisions reveal this neuropsychological foundation of morality. We naturally possess a tendency to avoid harm along with a preternatural hesitancy to employ violence.

In a series of classic experiments with philosophical underpinnings, researchers investigated the neurocognitive underpinnings of our automatic reactions to the use of violence and how we unconsciously react when faced with tough moral decisions.[10] Subjects were confronted with a set of dilemmas while MRI machines recorded the functioning activity of their brains. In all of the scenarios, a runaway trolley is headed for five people who would be killed if it proceeded on its usual course. The only way to save them is to somehow stop the trolley. The subjects were asked to imagine themselves standing next to a large stranger on a footbridge that spans the tracks between the oncoming trolley and the five people. In this scenario, the only way to save the five people is to push the husky stranger off the bridge onto the tracks below. He will die but his body will stop the trolley from reaching the others. The question is: "Ought one save the lives of five people by pushing a stranger to his death?"

When people were surveyed, most said that such an act is morally unjustified. So do the lion's share of professional philosophers. The MRI results indicated that when the subjects are making such decisions, the parts of their brains most activated are those associated with emotionally ladened moral judgments: specifically, sections of the medial prefrontal cortex (posterior cingulate) and portions of the temporal sulci. These are the areas that that help us to manage conflicting impulses and wishes as we come to a decision. These subjects were experiencing viscerally intense, ambivalent emotions as they considered how to respond.

Most interesting is the contrast in attitude and brain functioning when subjects are confronted with a slightly different moral decision. In the second experiment, while the trolley is headed toward five people, the subjects are given the opportunity to trip a switch that turns the trolley on an alternate track, killing one individual. They're not in proximity to the person who is about to die, and they don't have to push him to his death. In that scenario, most surveyed people and philosophers opined that it was acceptable to kill one person to save five. Different parts of the subjects' brains were activated by this chain of events—those that are utilized to make impersonal types of intellectual decisions (the upper lateral parts of the prefrontal cortex). The more abstract and impersonal a relationship to the other becomes, the easier it becomes to access our more violent side.

I'm reminded of a comment attributed to the dictator Joseph Stalin: the death of one is a tragedy, but the death of a million is a statistic.

***

Evolutionary psychologist David Buss highlights a troubling drive toward our dark nature. In his book, *The Murderer Next Door: Why the Mind Is Designed to Kill*, he asserts that there is a "fundamental logic to murder."[11] From his perspective and that of evolutionary science, violence and murder are products that have emerged in the mechanisms of our mind over time during which humans were confronted with a need to compete with one another for scant resources to survive. Buss argues that it was adaptive to form kin ties and to distrust strangers outside the tribe. As such, one adapts willingly to the cruel killing of those outside one's group, especially when there is a struggle for available resources such as food.

There are myriad reasons for killing—greed, envy, jealousy, fear, even mercy and self-protection. Buss's point is that our access to homicidal impulses does not stem from our reactive violence or madness but, more fundamentally, from our humanness.

As evidence for the commonplace and prosaic nature of evil impulses, Buss presented results of a survey involving more than five thousand participants from various regions of the world and cultures. It revealed that a startling 91 percent of men and 84 percent of women have had at least one vivid fantasy of killing someone.[12] Buss concluded that homicidal violence is not an aberration or due to an illness, but a potential woven into our minds—we are prewired to kill.

In my private, non-forensic practice, I have indeed had many patients over the years who have expressed violent, even homicidal, desires. Almost all were very decent individuals who by any standard would be judged to be ethical and socially in high regard. For instance, Drs. Lindsay and Edward Wallace sought couple's treatment for their "communication problems." Both were physicians with busy schedules, she as an anesthesiologist and he as a neurologist. Although they had inhouse help, they argued incessantly over time-management issues involving household chores and childcare. Edward was kind but something of a cold fish. Lindsay found his detachment maddening. During one of our sessions, she rather matter-of-factly said she had seriously considered poisoning Edward. Besides being an anesthesiologist, she had an interest in chemistry. She knew how to do it. Edward, in his typically flaccid style, simply did not react. Frankly, I was not concerned, either. Although Lindsay had the expertise to kill, she, like many patients, felt the urge and an accompanying fantasy, but that was where it ended. I was confident this was the case with Lindsay and that she wasn't about to kill her husband. It was more of an expression of her feelings of helplessness and her inability to elicit emotional reactions from Edward.

***

The mind may be wired to kill, as Buss indicated, such that a murderer could be living next door to you, prepared to exercise his dark instincts. Or it could be *you* or *me* with the murderous wishes toward our neighbor. Yet the picture is a complicated one, with more at play than our evolutionary instincts. For instance, Buss claimed that most premeditated killings are done out of ruthlessness, not the result of a mental disorder or culture. That does not seem to be the case. A recent study[13] found that premeditated murderers are almost twice as likely to have histories of psychosis and serious mood disorders as those of impulsive murderers. And those statistics on premeditated murderers do not take into account individuals who are free of a diagnosed psychosis or serious mood condition but killed due to a prolonged experience of hopelessness and loss of dignity and self-efficacy. Consider a battered woman, for instance, who kills her husband after years of brutalization. She may have premeditated the killing, or she may have reacted impulsively. But the killing wasn't a product of biologically based ruthlessness; it was more that her natural potential to access violence was activated. Having been forced to endure unremitting shame is almost a surefire prologue to violence. [14]

In the Buss survey, many men and women fantasized about killing someone, although the vast and overwhelming number of them never attempted it. They were like my patient Lindsay, and unlike many of the defendants I've written about, they were self-possessed enough and un-willing to traverse that bright line between fantasy and reality.

***

What's the difference between those who contemplate malice and those who exercise their daimonic darkness? There are a number of factors such as context and in-group identifications, as revealed by the Stanford Prison Experiment, for example. When an individual or group is "other-ized" and seen as less than fully human, all hell breaking loose becomes a real possibility. Nonetheless, beyond circumstances, psychological make-up undoubtedly is crucial, particularly in those situations that breed temp-tation to animate one's dark side. I introduced the concept of mentaliza-tion [15] in chapter 2, contrasting the troubled adolescent Rodrick with Deb-orah, my private patient who, though anguished by early loss, was raised in a supportive family. Having formed secure attachments during the critical periods of her early childhood, she developed this crucial psycho-logical capacity to self-reflect on her thoughts, needs, and desires. She experienced her mind as separate from other minds: as such, she recog-nized others as distinctly stamped by their unique personal histories and temperaments, motivations, desires, and sentiments. In other words, she experienced herself as a unique identity and viewed others as such. She possessed a seemingly simple ability to empathize and respect others for their individuality.

This type of mentalized ability is *not* tantamount to sentient self-awareness. It is a level of development that results in large measure from a history of secure attachments and bonding with responsive, reliable, and empathic caregivers. It is a deeply structured psychological process with crucial by-products, including empathic awareness and a readied endowment to manage personal urges and desires, even the dark ones.[16] Mentalized reflection creates an inner psychological space that allows for consideration before action, even when complex and intense emotions hold sway. It provides a psychological distance between the immediate pressure of an event and the emotional state that it instigated. As such, one has the ability and vantage to reappraise in real time the current emotional demands and to fashion a less reactive response.

Most important, this form of reflection results in the creation of a firm identity that includes an implicit recognition of one's personal history and its accumulated morals[17] and expectations. As such, reactions to current demands and frustrations are constrained by a "long view" of oneself and are not a result of immediate displeasure. Such a perspective allows for a kind of "time travel" to experience the self (and others) in the context of past experience[18] and an imagined future,[19] thereby loosening one from the immediate moment. When such a psychological achievement has been developed, one is more likely to act with personal integrity. Thus, a range of less destructive emotional behavioral options becomes available.

***

Deficits in the developmental achievement of mentalization are very much implicated in those who find themselves on the wrong side of the law. For instance, one study within a prison population found that 80 percent of inmates had various forms of insecure attachments and low levels of mentalization.[20] Those inmates serving time for violent offenses (murder, armed robbery) were lowest on measures of mentalization. Consider Peter from chapter 11, who claimed to have a brain deficiency that caused him to be violent. He came from a family environment that was rife with violence and neglect and certainly lacked any normal type of interpersonal attachment among family members. His compromised capacity to mentalize his emotional experience was clearly revealed in his complete lack of empathy for victims and his awareness of his complete focus on his own needs as opposed to those of others. Or consider Randall, who killed his child, most likely to cover up his rage killing of his wife. He then went on blithely with his life. His lack of reflective mentalization was revealed in his abject void of any guilt or shame.

Interestingly, many successful psychopaths, like the ones I've written about in chapter 6, have a truncated mentalizing ability that could be very destructive. They have an intellectual understanding of how an emotionally responsive person is supposed to react, while lacking the associated inner emotional experience. For example, when administered the Reading the Mind in the Eyes Test, which requires the identification of mental states from photographs of the eye region alone, psychopathic subjects performed as well as nonpsychopathic individuals.[21] However, children identified as at-risk to become adult psychopaths showed deficits in the processing of facial expressions, especially fear and sadness.[22] It appears that, over time, psychopathically prone individuals learn to present a mask of mentalization. Their well-developed social skills allow them to appear sensitive and thoughtful, but they do not experience the underlying emotions that usually prompt such prosocial behavior as empathy or compassion.

This can be dangerous. Ted Bundy, the well-known serial killer, is a tragic example. Good looking and smooth, he lured women to violent deaths by easily convincing them that he was a kind, gentle, nonthreatening law student. After gaining their trust, he abducted and brutally killed his victims, after which he would have sex with the victim's corpse. The memory psychologist Elizabeth Loftus, who interviewed Bundy, found him to be "a charming man."[23] This, about an individual who, before his execution, said in regard to his victims: "What's one less person on the face of the earth, anyway."[24] Or again consider Randall, who also was good looking and charming on the surface, but insidiously narcissistic and malevolent.

Other studies[25] have found that various types of personality disorders in the prison population, including those with borderline personality and sex offenders, involved low levels of mentalization ability, especially if the prisoners were violent.

***

Of course, not all bad behavior and wickedness can be accounted for by an underdeveloped ability to mentalize and self-reflect. Individuals with various forms of mental illness such as paranoid schizophrenia could become violent. Consider for instance Michael from chapter 3 who, while actively paranoid, killed his mother. When psychologically stable, his relationship with his mother was warm and loving. Most people with mental disorders, even those with a schizophrenic illness, don't become violent. It's only when particular types of symptoms like paranoid think-ing or beliefs become intense and override reality and self-control that violent behavior becomes a possibility.

Contemplate what can happen when one is under the influence of drugs or raised in a context in which antisocial behavior and violence is normalized. Phillip, the adolescent from chapter 10, was involved in a robbery that ended in the death of a drug dealer. He was dependent on meth, neglected and abused, and raised in street-gang culture.[26] All kinds of situations and mental conditions may lead to violent or aggressive conduct, regardless of the level of mentalization of the people involved.

Consider a situation of intense emotional experience and chronic stress. This is another context that might propel an individual with a self-reflected mentalization and psychological mindedness to go "off-line." In such conditions, one may regress to a lower mode of thinking, such as that referred to as psychological equivalence. In this mode, external circumstances and psychological reality become one. An individual's im-mediate reality is experienced as absolute and a reflection of "truth." Thinking becomes inflexible and concrete. Recall Rodrick from chapter 2 who senselessly assaulted another teenager for simply looking at him. Rodrick had such a damaged self that he misinterpreted the victim as looking down at him. Or consider what might happen in high-conflict families, when parents regress as a result of prolonged stress; their normal style of discipline may be supplanted by abusive reactions.

***

The roots of malevolence and destructive behavior are many and varied: an improvised development in mentalization allowing for the easy release of cruelty and violence; severe mental illness; a neuropsychological con-dition that results in poor self-control; mind-altering substance abuse; and disturbances in personality, especially psychopathy. In addition, the nar-row identification with one group could engender the disidentification with and "otherizing" of those outside the chosen group. If outsiders are perceived as less than fully human, all kinds of hellish behavior become possible.[27]

The degrees of human cruelty vary in their intensity as well. This is exemplified in many of the cases I have presented here. At one end of the spectrum was my private-practice patient who repeatedly undermined his

son with devaluing comments; there was Phillip, the drug-addicted adolescent who unwittingly participated in a drug deal that ended in a homicide; and then there was a stone-cold psychopath like Randall who resided at the malignant tip of the daimonic spectrum.

Adding to the evidence of our potential for cruelty is the montage of
brutality laid bare by even a cursory look at our recent history. Consider
the examples of organized human calamity such as the various "isms":
Nazism, Stalinism, and Maoism. Or consider the Holocaust, Hiroshima,
the Vietnam War, events in Rwanda, the siege of Sarajevo, terrorist attacks—I could go on. Freud even proposed a death drive[28] that lies beneath all our rakishness and propels the impulses toward wantonness.

***

At the same time, there is compelling evidence that we are neuropsycho-
logically endowed with a moral impulse as demonstrated, for instance, by
the train track example I discussed earlier. In addition, multiple sources
of social science research[29] confirm a natural proclivity toward goodness.
And we need not rely simply on scientific evidence: our goodness is
evidenced in our philosophical and religious traditions[30] as well.

As writer Thomas Nevin observed in the epigraph that began this final
chapter, humanity is situated between the animal *and* the divine, with a
benevolent, even sublime, side. Thinkers as far-flung as Rollo May and
Plato have observed the range of our potentialities, from feats of great
generativity to the perpetration of vile destruction and depravity.

Psychologist Steven Pinker makes the bold assessment early in his
book *The Better Angels of Our Nature* that, in spite of the calamities of
recent history, "Believe it or not—and I know that most people do not—
violence had declined over long stretches of time, and today we may be
living in the most peaceable era in the species' existence."[31] He goes on
to document how, over centuries, the social acceptability of violence and
indiscriminate cruelty has steadily diminished. There are multiple pro-
cesses that led to this, which are beyond the scope of this work to describe in detail. In brief and over the course of several chapters, Pinker
highlighted the "better angels" of our nature that have helped: empathy,
self-control, our moral intuitions, and our cognitive/reasoning ability.
Similar to Wrangham's description of humans becoming domesticated
over a geological time frame, Pinker emphasized a profound cultural

evolution he calls the "pacification process." The epoch of modernity has delegitimized violence as an acceptable reaction to social or interpersonal conflicts, with the state given control over the decision to employ violence. Expressed via our legal systems, the state imposes justice and metes out the just deserts for misconduct. This monopoly on the use of violence has had a mollifying impact. Even in the face of the catastrophes of the twentieth century, which include two world wars, there has been up to a fifty-fold decline in violence since the Middle Ages.[32]

Social institutions reflect the characteristics of their citizenry. The process of pacification over time has increasingly allowed our civic institutions to enshrine and realize the "better angels" side of the people, where our moral human qualities are embodied and tilt toward our elevated nature. It is how we have ameliorated so much capricious violence and the arbitrary application of justice over centuries of time.

***

> A man, after he has brushed off the dust and chips of life, will have left only the hard, clean questions: Was it good or was it evil? Have I done well—or ill?—John Steinbeck, *East of Eden*

Throughout this book, I have documented times in which the most malevolent of crimes have exposed our darkest side. Cruelty has been perpetrated even by those tasked with representing our enlightened selves. In contrast, we have also observed instances of deep compassion and humanity in the face of the most primordial of human behavior.

And there are signs that the judicial system as a whole is slowly tilting toward the humane. In the 1990s, forensic psychiatrist James Gilligan became director of the Random, Massachusetts, prison system. At the beginning of his tenure, the prison system was a den of violence. Inmates were killing one another, attacking attorneys, and killing and assaulting guards. Over the course of his tenure, the violence in the system was reduced by more than 90 percent.[33] Gilligan provided an anecdote that helps to explain the approach he eventually employed to stem the violence. He asked a violent inmate who was in solitary confinement with a total loss of privileges what drove him to such lengths that he would give up everything. This usually inarticulate inmate "stood tall," looked Gilligan in the eye, and responded: "Pride. Dignity. Self-respect. . . . If you ain't got pride you got nothing."[34] One inmate after another—those who had assaulted or had killed—told the warden they reacted because "He dissed me" or because they were disrespected in one form or another. Clearly, shame and humiliation were driving forces behind much of the reactive violence.

Gilligan went on to reorganize the system in response to the inmate's misconduct. Prison staff were given mental health training and various options were made accessible to inmates, including crisis intervention, greater access to protective custody, and psychiatric hospitalization and treatment. In addition, discipline of inmates was more modulated and designed to be less humiliating. This type of thoughtful, humane, and disciplined approach is what reduced prison violence so dramatically.

In more recent years, the restorative justice perspective has been integrated into the legal system in conjunction with the traditional retributive one.[35] Used with nonviolent offenders, the goal is to lessen the psychological damage resulting from the crime by having a dialogue between offender and victim, together with a mediator or counselor. Though not appropriate in many cases (such as many extreme violence offenses), such an approach offers the possibility for the victim's trauma and pain to be recognized in a potentially powerful and therapeutic way and for the offender to grow as a result of his or her willingness to repair harm caused to another.

Since the early 1990s, a mode of practice called therapeutic jurisprudence has been developed, which focuses on the impact of the legal system and its practitioners on the well-being of those affected by judicial decision making.[36] What's unique about this approach is its emphasis on the value of human dignity of all in the system and its adoption of insights from kindred fields such as the social sciences—especially psychology and criminology—to reach its goals. This innovative method was first developed after the courts realized the ineffectiveness of simply punishing repeat drug offenders. Drug courts were established to adjudicate offenders and provide treatment to those afflicted with drug and alcohol disorders, along with incentives (e.g., reduced sentences) to successfully complete the program requirements. Over the years, specialized courts with similar approaches were developed in the areas of domestic violence and homelessness and for veterans.[37]

Courts that specialize in adjudicating mental disordered offenders have been especially active, given the increased of the number of defendants who suffer from mentally illness.[38] Michael Perlin, a therapeutic jurisprudence practitioner, professor, and prolific writer, has emphasized the need for lawyers and others who work within the justice system to confront their implicit and unconscious prejudices toward defendants with mental illnesses (referred to as "sanism"), which may have a deleterious impact on the legal services provided to the mentally disturbed.[39]

In general, there has been an increasing acceptance of social science and neuroscientific research by the courts and its influence on legal decision making is evidenced by recent Supreme Court decisions.[40] Whole new subspecialty disciplines like neurolaw and neuroethics have sprung up within the last two decades that are sure to have a salutary influence on our legal system.[41] Increasingly, we can expect new case law to be influenced by contemporary scientific findings.

Indeed, researchers are calling for a broader appreciation of the roots of criminal behavior and a more nuanced understanding of criminal responsibility.[42] This is in part a reaction to the legal reforms introduced in the 1980s that placed stringent limits on mental state defenses. These changes in the law were in response to the attempted assassination of President Reagan by John Hinkley and the social outcry over his subsequent insanity determination.[43] Mostly, though, contemporary views on criminal responsibility are based on decades of research, some of which I have already cited. It has become increasingly clear that an individual's personal and biological history, along with social context, are constituent elements that shape the mental state required for specific crimes (e.g., arson defined as the *specific and willful intent* to torch a building). Issues such as past physical or emotional abuse, neglect, poverty and malnourishment, learning disabilities and mental illness, etc. are features of a person's life that mold the mindset of an individual at the time of an offense. Such mitigating factors are usually considered when a psychological expert is called to consult. Still, as I've noted at times throughout this book, there are controversies and disagreements regarding the degree of control and responsibility a defendant might have for his misconduct, even when social context and person background are considered. Nonetheless, those advocating for a science-based and humanizing adjustment to our justice system argue that a biopsychosocial model of jurisprudence should counterbalance our essentially punitive perspective of criminal conduct, especially when addressing issues of sentencing and correctional placement.

Finally, a notable number of prosecutors throughout the country have committed to review cases in which new evidence has raised reasonable doubt about an inmate's conviction.[44] The Innocence Project[45] and its findings that so many inmates have been wrongly convicted has helped fashion social and political support for criminal justice reform.

***

I have highlighted the profound advantages of a psychologically matured self-examining capacity. It allows for the integration of long-held personal values and future considerations, thus cultivating integrity to one's behavior and self-control, along with the possibility of reining in malevolent impulses. Indeed, one author has described mentalization as not simply a skill or capacity, but a virtue.[46] As noted, though, even well-developed mentalization is vulnerable to regression for a number of reasons ranging from individual fatigue, a symptom of acute mental illness, self-deception, and the ubiquitous pull to irrational thinking to which we are all vulnerable in some measure or another. Sadly, history has demonstrated that most of us are prey to the subjugation and tyranny of group pressure.[47]

Psychological awareness is not uniformly distributed, and there's an unhealthy dose of social and financial reinforcement for dark personality traits, which include narcissism, psychopathy, and Machiavellianism.[48] I've already written about how successful psychopaths function in many professions. At times, they're perceived as strong leaders, though psychopathy is also associated with negative job performance.[49] Narcissists are self-centered, lack self-reflection, empathy, and authentic concern for others. Still, they tend to experience success in their careers, likely due to their grandiosity and their single-minded motivation to get ahead.[50] Those with Machiavellian traits don't dither when placing expedience over moral principle. Because of a willingness to manipulate others and, like narcissists, a laser focus on winning and success, they tend to be in positions of organizational leadership.[51]

Unfortunately, individual moral thinking and behavior are malleable and subject to the vagaries of personality and temperament. And moral considerations bend to social context and moment-to-moment psychological instabilities.[52]

***

As an insurance policy against human nature's primitive pull and the fragility of individual conduct, cultural institutions like the justice system serve as a hedge against inevitable individual failure. Our institutions embody the best of our collected ideals, including the promotion of civility and the rule of law. The justice system's commitment to the fair and reasoned administration of law to everybody, with no exemptions for political or social status, provides a cultural layer that serves to correct any tilt toward dark injustice. At least that's the case theoretically, as long as our system prevails over individual corruption.

Supreme Court Justice Oliver Wendell Holmes pointed out that the history of law is the history of experience, not of logic. Our legal system continues to improve and will evolve as it reflects upon itself and self-corrects. Like all of us as individuals, our system of jurisprudence is imperfect but, with luck, will continue its enlightened ascent.

APPENDIX
Psychological Test Descriptions

The *Aggression Questionnaire* consists of thirty-four items in which participants rank certain statements along a five-point continuum from "extremely uncharacteristic of me" to "extremely characteristic of me." The scores are normalized on a scale of one to five, with five being the highest level of aggression. The questionnaire yields scores on four dimensions of aggression: anger, physical aggression, verbal aggression, and hostility. A fifth scale provides a measure of overall aggression. Separate norms are included for males and females.

The *b Test* is a letter recognition task designed to detect individuals who are feigning cognitive dysfunction or those who exert less than adequate effort. A fifteen-page stimulus booklet contains an array of lowercase b's interspersed among d's, q's, and letters rotated at an angle. Individuals taking the test may not be aware that the task requires very little intellectual ability and that individuals with documented cognitive impairments are able to score within the normal range. Individuals feigning cognitive deficits are identified by a performance that is less than normal based on their age and gender.

The *Clarke Sex History Questionnaire for Males Revised (SHQ-R)* is a comprehensive instrument used for sex offender assessments. It examines a wide range of conventional and deviant sexual behaviors from common sexual disorders and dysfunctions to sexual abuse and assault. It includes multiple scales that evaluate sexual functioning and disorders in a number of areas including childhood and adolescent sexual experiences, sexual dysfunction (e.g., hypersexuality, impotence), gender sexual outlets, fantasy and pornography, assessment for the presence of the paraphilias (e.g., pedophilia), identity and fantasy assessment, and courtship disorders (e.g., voyeurism). The scales discriminate clinically relevant groups from control subjects and therefore meet a clinical need in the assessment of anomalous sexual behavior. It also has a validity scale to help ensure the accuracy of the responses.

The *Conners Continuous Performance Test, Third Edition* (CPT-III), is a computerized test of sustained attention, response inhibition, and vigilance. The examinee is presented with sequential series of letters at various rates and must press a key on the computer when the letter is not *X* and inhibit a response to the letter *X*. This task requires the examinee to maintain a continuous response set. It lasts about fourteen minutes. The CPT-III is part of a clinical assessment of attention and vigilance but is not used as the sole basis for a diagnosis.

The *Conners Adult ADHD Rating Scale* (CAARS) is a sixty-sixty-item questionnaire that assesses for core symptoms of ADHD in adults, which include problems in attention, hyperactivity, and impulsiveness. The instrument includes within it eight subscales, all of which have been empirically derived to assess a broad range of problem behaviors associated with ADHD. The eight scales are: inattention/memory problems, hyperactivity/restlessness, impulsiveness/emotional lability, self-concept problems, DSM-IV inattention symptoms, DSM-IV hyperactivity/impulsiveness symptoms, DSM-IV ADHD symptoms total, and an ADHD index. All the scores and results are based on an enlarged normative data base and yield reliable and valid assessments of ADHD-related symptoms.

The *Hare Psychopathy Checklist, Second Edition* (PCL-R), is a twenty-item rating scale designed to measure traits of psychopathic personality disorder. The items cover the nature of an individual's interpersonal relationships and his or her emotional investment in others and probe for the presence of a socially deviant lifestyle and history of criminal behavior. The information is assessed from within four facets and two overall domains that define psychopathy: selfish callousness/unfeeling victimization of other people and antisocial lifestyle.

The *Hare Psychopathy Checklist for Adolescents* (PCL:YV) is a structured interview used to assess disturbances in four factors of adolescence functioning: interpersonal, affective, behavior, and antisocial. The first two factors assess for the presence of selfish callousness and remorselessness and the second two factors assess social deviancy and conduct. The instrument includes norms for institutionalized offenders and offenders who are on probation.

The *Hypersexual Behavior Inventory (HBI)* is a nineteen-item scale that assesses hypersexuality via three factors. The coping factor (seven items) assesses sex and sexual behaviors as a response to emotional distress such as sadness, restlessness, or daily life worries. The control factor (eight items) assesses the degree of self-control in sexuality-related behaviors. The consequences factor (four items) assesses the diverse consequences of sexual thoughts, urges, and behaviors, such as sexual activities that interfere with educational or occupational duties.

The *Iowa Gambling Test, Second Edition* (IGT-2), is a psychological test that simulates real-life decision making. The examinee is presented with four visual decks of cards on a computer screen and told that the decks hold cards that will reward or penalize them using the game money. The goal is to win as much money as possible. The decks are different from each other in the balance of reward versus penalty. The examinee is told that some decks are "bad" decks and some are "good" decks, as some reward the player more than others. Each time the examinee selects a card, he receives feedback as to whether he won or lost money. The "bad decks" yield immediate large gains of money, but at unpredictable points the gains are followed by a very high penalty so that in the long run these decks are disadvantageous. The feedback given to the examinee creates a conflict between immediate reward and a delayed probabilistic punishment, simulating real-life decision making. The IGT-2 has been found to identify individuals whose decision-making difficulties are related to neuropsychological dysfunction in the prefrontal cortex. The examinee's raw score is the number of times he has made selections from the card decks. Raw scores are translated into T-scores, with a T-score at or below thirty-nine considered impaired.

The *Mood Disorder Questionnaire* (MDQ) was developed to address a critical need for timely and accurate diagnosis of bipolar disorder. The questionnaire takes about five minutes to complete and can provide important insights into diagnosis and treatment. The MDQ screens for bipolar spectrum disorder.

266 DECODING MADNESS

The *Minnesota Multiphasic Personality Inventory-2-Restructured Form (MMPI-2-RF)* is a revised 338-item version of the MMPI-2. It is psychometrically up to date and linked to current models of psychopathology and personality. It contains eight validity scales, three higher order scales, nine restructured scales, and a number of scales measuring somatic/cognitive factors, internalizing behavior, externalizing, interpersonal, and interest variables, as well as five personality psychopathology scales. A score of 1.5 standard deviations above the norm (T-score = 65, ninety-second percentile) is considered clinically significant.

The *Miller Forensic Assessment of Symptoms Test (M-FAST)* is a twenty-five-item structured interview designed to provide information regarding the probability that an individual is malingering psychotic symptoms and psychopathology. The twenty-five questions investigate whether the individual's symptoms are of typical severity even for a truly psychotic individual. The M-FAST allows for the investigation of whether the patient is endorsing an unusual combination of symptoms or unusual psychiatric symptoms in general. An individual's score is compared with known group samples of scores. A score of six or greater suggests symptom magnification and the possibility of malingering.

The *Neuropsychological Assessment Battery (NAB)* is composed of five module index tests and scores. The five modules are as follows: attention, language, memory, spatial, and executive functions. Each module index score is scaled to have mean of one hundred and a deviation of fifteen. The attention index score is an overall measure of the examinee's multifaceted attentional functioning. The language index score is multifactorial and measures the examinee's overall language functioning. The memory index score is an omnibus measure of the examinee's memory functioning across all the specific areas of learning and memory tapped by the nine memory module tests. The spatial index score is a measure of the examinee's over-functioning in the areas of spatial processing tapped by the NAB spatial module. It is based on visual discrimination, design construction, figure drawing copy, and map reading. Executive function refers to behaviors and skills that allow one to successfully carry out instrumental and social activities such as planning, engaging with others effectively, problem solving, and successfully interacting with the environment to get one's needs met. The total NAB index score is based on the sum of the five full module index scores. It serves as an overall measure of performance on the NAB and as omnibus measure of neuropsychological functioning. Similar to the module index scores and the total NAB index scores, scores of less than eighty-five are categorized in the impaired range.

The *Personality Assessment Inventory (PAI)* is a 344-item instrument consisting of twenty-two non-overlapping full scales covering the constructs most relevant to broad assessment of mental disorders. It includes four validity scales plus a number of specialized validity scales, eleven clinical scales, five treatment scales, and two interpersonal scales. In addition, the ten full scales also contain a number of conceptually derived subscales to facilitate the full range of complete clinical constructs and issues. All PAI scales and subscales are expressed in T-scores referenced against a community sample, with a T-score of fifty being average. A T-score of sixty represents a person in the eight-fourth percentile in terms of experiencing symptoms and problems of a particular type, whereas a T-score of seventy represents a score in the ninety-sixth percentile on most of the scales. Once a problem that merits clinical attention has been identified, a contextual shift is made to a clinical focus. Scores are then standardized against a representative clinical sample.

The *Porteus Deception Scales (PDS)* is a self-report questionnaire designed to measure two major forms of socially desirable responding, self-deception and impression management. The instrument has extensive validity and reliability confirmation. A T-score between sixty and sixty-five is considered slightly above average, and a T-score greater than sixty-five is considered above average.

The *Psychiatric Diagnostic Screening Questionnaire (PDSQ)* is a 111-question self-report instrument designed to screen for various diagnostic conditions. It assesses for the following conditions: major depression, post-traumatic stress disorder, eating disorder, obsessive-compulsive disorder, panic disorder, psychosis, agoraphobia, social phobia and alcohol abuse, drug abuse, generalized anxiety, somatization disorder, and hypochondriasis. The total score can be used as a global measure of psychopathology, and a follow-up interview is done to assess the various syndromes noted above.

The *Risk Sophistication Treatment Inventory* (RSTI) is a semi-structured interview and rating scale used to assess the functioning of juvenile offenders. It could be used for the assessment of dangerousness, sophistication, maturity, and treatment amenability. Note that I use it for the assessment of sophistication and maturity. Normative data based on juvenile offender participants are used, and T-scores and percentiles are developed for each of the three domains.

The *Sexual Homicide Crime Scene Rating Scale for Sexual Sadism* is an instrument that dimensionally measures the degree of offender sexual sadism in suspected sexual homicide cases. Scoring is based on crime scene and related investigative information. Norms for the scale indicate that it correctly classified offenders with and without sexual sadism.

The *Structured Inventory of Malingered Symptoms* (SIMS) is a seventy-two-item self-administered questionnaire given in a variety of clinical and forensic settings. It assesses for symptom exaggeration and malingering in the areas of neurological symptomatology, intelligence, psychosis, affective disorders, and amnestic disorders. The patient responds to each of the seventy-two items by answering true or false and obtains a score. A score of fourteen or greater suggests symptom exaggeration and/or malingering.

The *Repeated Battery for the Assessment of Neuropsychological Status* (RBANS) is a brief individually administered neurocognitive test measuring attention, language, visual, spatial/constructional abilities and immediate and delayed memory. The RBANS index scores are metrically scaled and normed by age group with a mean of one hundred and a standard deviation of fifteen. Sixty-eight percent of all examinees obtain a score between 85 and 115.

The *Stroop Color and Word Test* (Stroop) is a timed procedure that tests an individual's ability to rapidly read words aloud under conditions of interference. The patient's performance is compared across three trials: word reading, color naming, and color word naming, with the latter task requiring the patient to name the ink color as quickly as possible. That is, the examinee is required to name the ink color of a written word, not the written word itself, suppressing the natural tendency to read the word. For example, when presented with the word *blue* written in red ink, the examinee should identify the color red (rather than the word *blue*). The Stroop is a measure of cognitive control, shift-setting ability, and response inhibition.

The *Test of Memory Malingering* (TOMM) is a fifty-item visual memory recognition test for adults that includes two learning trials and a retention trial. During the two learning trials, the examinee is shown fifty line drawings of common objects. The examinee is then shown fifty recognition panels, one at a time, with each panel containing one of the previously presented target pictures and a new picture. The examinee is requested to select the previously shown picture. Scores lower than chance on any trial is indicative of the possibility of exerting limited effort or malingering. Any score lower than forty-five on trial two or the retention trial indicates the possibility of malingering. Extensive data has been collected from cognitively intact normal subjects and clinical samples with cognitive impairment, aphasia, traumatic brain injury, dementia, and no impairment at all.

The *Wechsler Adult Intelligence Scale, Fourth Edition* (WAIS-IV), is a verbally administered test of a person's intellectual ability and cognitive strengths and weaknesses. It has a number of separate subtests measuring both verbal and specific nonverbal abilities, such as constructing blocks and arranging pictures to tell a story. It yields a full-scale IQ and four indexes that provide additional information about an individual's cognitive ability and style. The four are: verbal comprehension index (VCI), perceptual reasoning index (PRI), working memory index (WMI), and processing speed index (PSI). The VCI assesses verbal reasoning ability and language ability, and the PRI is a measure of nonverbal reasoning and visual-spatial ability. The WMI provides information regarding an individual's ability to attend to verbally presented information, to process information in memory, and then to formulate a response. The PSI reflects psychomotor processing speed. The average (mean) IQ score is one hundred, with a standard deviation of fifteen. The average scaled score (SS) for each WAIS-IV is ten. An IQ score of 100 and a SS of ten on individual subtests define the average performance for an age group. Based on testing scores, one is placed in one of seven categories, from "very superior" to average to extremely low.

The *Wisconsin Card Sorting Test (WCST)*, administered via a computer, uses 128 cards that are equally divided into three categories: forms (i.e., shapes), numbers, and colors. The forms that are used include circles, triangles, stars, and crosses. The colors used are red, green, yellow, and blue. The number of items on the cards range from one to four. The first four cards (the stimulus cards) are presented to the subject in specific orders and patterns. At the beginning of the test, the subject is told to place one of his cards (i.e., the response card) in front of one of the four stimulus cards. This process continues until all of the cards are used. The subject is never told the purpose of the test or the methods used during the test. Once the test begins, the subject is told if a card placement is correct or incorrect only. The procedure selects the cards in a set format of ten or so cards in either color, form, or number configurations. It is a test of problem-solving ability and executive functioning.

The *Wide Range Achievement Test 4* (WRAT4) is a standardized achievement test, individually administered and nationally normed. It yields a measure of the individual's achievement levels in various academic tasks, including reading, spelling, and math.

NOTES

1. THE DAIMONIC PARADOX

1. Christopher Bollas, *The Shadow of the Object: Psychoanalysis of the Unthought Known* (New York: Columbia University Press, 1987).

2. Sigmund Freud, *Introductory Lectures on Psychoanalysis* (New York: W. W. Norton, 1977).

3. Carl Gustav Jung, *The Basic Writings of C. G. Jung* (New York: Random House, 1959).

4. I explore the complexities and tragedy that beset Simon and his wife in chapter 7.

5. More on Thomas in chapter 12.

6. Rollo May, *Love and Will* (New York: Dell, 1969), 163.

7. Erich Fromm, *The Anatomy of Human Destructiveness* (New York: Macmillan, 1992).

8. Coline Covington, *Everyday Evils: A Psychoanalytic View of Evil and Morality* (London: Taylor & Francis, 2017).

9. Steven Pinker, *The Better Angels of Our Nature: Why Violence Has Declined* (New York: Penguin Group, 2012).

2. THE PAST IMPERFECT

1. Sigmund Freud, "Beyond the Pleasure Principle," in *The Standard Edition of the Complete Psychological Works of Sigmund Freud, Volume XVIII* (London: Hogarth Press), 28.

2. Saha, Sukanta, David Chant, Joy Welham, and John McGrath. "A Systematic Review of the Prevalence of Schizophrenia," *PLoS Med* 2, no. 5 (2005): e141.

3. Peter Fonagy, "The Mentalization-focused Approach to Social Development," in *The Handbook of Mentalization-based Treatment*, ed. J. G. Allen and P. Fonagy (Chichester: John Wiley & Sons, 2006), 53–99.

4. More on the limits and strengths of mentalization in chapter 13.

3. TIES THAT BLIND

1. Roberto Catanesi, Gabriele Rocca, Chiara Candelli, and Felice Carabellese, "Matricide by Mentally Disordered Sons: Gaining a Criminological Understanding beyond Mental Illness—A Descriptive Study." *International Journal of Offender Therapy and Comparative Criminology* 59, no. 14 (2015): 1550–63. A. Ogunwale and Olukayode Abayomi, "Matricide and Schizophrenia in the 21st Century: A Review and Illustrative Cases," *African Journal of Psychiatry* 15, no. 1 (2012): 55–57.

2. Minnesota Multiphasic Personality Inventory-2-Restructured Form (University of Minnesota Press/Pearson, 2008).

3. Minnesota Multiphasic Personality Inventory-2-Restructured Form; Catanesi, Rocca, Candelli, and Carabellese (2015).

4. Lisa A. Callahan, Henry J. Steadman, Margaret A. McGreevy, and Pamela Clark Robbins, "The Volume and Characteristics of Insanity Defense Pleas: An Eight-State Study," *Journal of the American Academy of Psychiatry and the Law Online* 19, no. 4 (1991): 331–38. Gerald Cooke and Cynthia R. Sikorski, "Factors Affecting Length of Hospitalization in Persons Adjudicated Not Guilty by Reason of Insanity," *Bulletin of the American Academy of Psychiatry & the Law* 2, no. 4 (1974): 251–61.

5. Henry J. Steadman, Lydia Keitner, Jeraldine Braff, and Thomas M. Arvanites, "Factors Associated with a Successful Insanity Plea," *The American Journal of Psychiatry* 140, no. 4 (1983): 401–5. See also Michael L. Perlin, "The Insanity Defense: Nine Myths That Will Not Go Away," in *The Insanity Defense: Multidisciplinary Views on Its History, Trends, and Controversies*, ed. Mark D. White (Santa Barbara, CA: Praeger, 2016), 3–22.

4. LADY KILLER

1. See the appendix for psychological test descriptions.

2. Nancy McWilliams, *Psychoanalytic Diagnosis: Understanding Personality Structure in the Clinical Process* (New York: Guilford Press, 2011), 101–3.

3. American Psychiatric Association, *Diagnostic and Statistical Manual of Mental Disorders*, 5th ed. (Arlington, VA: American Psychiatric Association, 2013), 645–84. See also McWilliams, *Psychoanalytic Diagnosis*, 61–65.

4. McWilliams, *Psychoanalytic Diagnosis*, 112–14. For a comprehensive but highly technical understanding to the complexity of this defensive function in personality organization, see Vittorio Lingiardi and Nancy McWilliams, eds., *Psychodynamic Diagnostic Manual: PDM-2* (New York: Guilford Publications, 2017).

5. David Spiegel and Etzel Cardeña, "Disintegrated Experience: The Dissociative Disorders Revisited," *Journal of Abnormal Psychology* 100, no. 3 (1991): 366. J. F. Kihlstrom, D. J. Tataryn, D, and I. P. Hoyt, "Dissociative Disorders," in *Comprehensive Handbook of Psychopathology*, ed. P. J. Sutker and H. E. Adams, 2nd ed. (New York: Plenum, 1993), 203–34.

6. B. A.van der Kolk, O. van der Hart, and C. R. Marmar, "Dissociation and Information Processing in Posttraumatic Stress Disorder," in *Traumatic Stress: The Effects of Overwhelming Experience on Mind, Body, and Society*, ed. B. A. van der Kolk, A. C. McFarlane, and L Weisaeth (New York: Guilford Press, 1996), 303–27.

7. *R. v. Parks* (1992) 2 S.C.R. 871.

8. McWilliams, *Psychoanalytic Diagnosis*, 107–12.

9. Samuel Adjorlolo, Heng Choon Oliver Chan, and Matt DeLisi, "Mentally Disordered Offenders and the Law: Research Update on the Insanity Defense, 2004–2019," *International Journal of Law and Psychiatry* 67 (2019).

10. Guy Hall, Marion Whittle, and Courtney Field, "Themes in Judges' Sentencing Remarks for Male and Female Domestic Murderers," *Psychiatry, Psychology and Law* 23, no. 3 (2016): 395–412.

11. Kristie A. Thomas, Melissa E. Dichter, and Jason Matejkowski, "Intimate versus Nonintimate Partner Murder: A Comparison of Offender and Situational Characteristics," *Homicide Studies* 15, no. 3 (2011): 291–311.

12. Gordon Morris Bakken and Brenda Farrington, *Women Who Kill Men: California Courts, Gender, and the Press* (Lincoln: University of Nebraska Press, 2009).

13. More on the issue of women and violence in chapter 6.

14. Hall, Whittle, and Field, "Themes in Judges' Sentencing Remarks for Male and Female Domestic Murderers," 395–412.

15. Hall, Whittle, and Field, "Themes in Judges' Sentencing Remarks for Male and Female Domestic Murderers," 399–405.

16. Patricia Easteal, Lorana Bartels, Noni Nelson, and Kate Holland, "How Are Women Who Kill Portrayed in Newspaper Media? Connections with Social

Values and the Legal System," *Women's Studies International Forum* 51 (2015): 31–41.

17. Joanne Belknap, Dora-Lee Larson, Margaret L. Abrams, Christine Garcia, and Kelly Anderson-Block, "Types of Intimate Partner Homicides Committed by Women: Self-Defense, Proxy/Retaliation, and Sexual Proprietariness," *Homicide Studies* 16, no. 4 (2012): 359–79.

5. THE CASE OF THE BODY SNATCHERS

1. Patients suffering from schizophrenia are at greater risk for suicide when their most acute symptoms have lessened. Possibly, with improved reality testing comes a sense of despair. With Andrew, that turned out not to be the case.

2. Carolina A. Klein and Soniya Hirachan, "The Masks of Identities: Who's Who? Delusional Misidentification Syndromes," *Journal of the American Academy of Psychiatry and the Law Online* 42, no. 3 (2014): 369–78.

3. Emily A. Currell, Nomi Werbeloff, Joseph F. Hayes, and Vaughan Bell, "Cognitive Neuropsychiatric Analysis of an Additional Large Capgras Delusion Case Series," *Cognitive Neuropsychiatry* 24, no. 2 (2019): 123–34.

4. Wayne R. LaFave, *Principles of Criminal Law* (St. Paul, MN: Thomson/ West, 2003), 397–410. H. J. Steadman, M. A. McGreevy, J. P. Morrissey, L. A. Callahan, P. C. Robbins, and C. Cirincione, *Before and after Hinckley: Evaluating Insanity Defense Reform* (New York: Guilford Press, 1993).

5. Gregory B. Leong, "Revisiting the Deific-Decree Doctrine in Washington State," *Journal of the American Academy of Psychiatry and the Law Online* 36, no. 1 (2008): 95–104.

6. *U.S. v. Guiteau*, 10 F. 161 (D. D.C. 1882).

7. A. Vita, L. De Peri, C. Silenzi, and M. Dieci, "Brain Morphology in First-Episode Schizophrenia: A Meta-analysis of Quantitative Magnetic Resonance Imaging Studies," *Schizophrenia Research* 82, no. 1 (2006): 75–88. P. Fusar-Poli, R. Smieskova, M. J. Kempton, B. C. Ho, N. C. Andreasen, and S. Borgwardt, "Progressive Brain Changes in Schizophrenia Related to Antipsychotic Treatment? A Meta-analysis of Longitudinal MRI Studies," *Neuroscience & Biobehavioral Reviews* 37, no. 8 (2013): 1680–91. Michael D. Nelson, Andrew J. Saykin, Laura A. Flashman, and Henry J. Riordan, "Hippocampal Volume Reduction in Schizophrenia as Assessed by Magnetic Resonance Imaging: A Meta-analytic Study," *Archives of General Psychiatry* 55, no. 5 (1998): 433–40.

8. Aslı Enzel Koc and Cicek Hocaoglu, "What Is Capgras Syndrome? Diagnosis and Treatment Approach," in *Little Known Syndromes in Psychiatry* (London: IntechOpen, 2020). Alain Barrelle and J-P. Luauté, "Capgras Syndrome and Other Delusional Misidentification Syndromes," in *Neurologic-Psychiatric Syn-*

dromes in Focus: Part 2: From Psychiatry to Neurology, vol. 42 (Basel: Karger Publishers, 2018), 35–43.

9. See the appendix for a more complete description of psychological tests.

10. R. Rogers, R. T. Salekin, K. W. Sewell, A. Goldstein, and K. Leonard, "A Comparison of Forensic and Nonforensic Malingerers: A Prototypical Analysis of Explanatory Models," *Law and Human Behavior* 22 (1998): 353–67.

11. Barbara E. McDermott and Gregory Sokolov, "Malingering in a Correctional Setting: The Use of the Structured Interview of Reported Symptoms in a Jail Sample," *Behavioral Sciences & the Law* 27, no. 5 (2009): 753–65.

12. Holly A. Miller, *M-FAST: Miller Forensic Assessment of Symptoms Test* (Odessa, FL: PAR, 2001).

13. R. Rogers, *Clinical Assessment of Malingering and Deceit*, 3rd ed. (New York: Guilford Press, 2008).

14. L. Morey, *Professional Manual for the Personality Assessment Inventory* (Odessa, FL: Psychological Assessment Resources, 1991).

15. Stephen J. Morse, "Excusing and the New Excuse Defenses: A Legal and Conceptual Review," *Crime and Justice* 23 (1998): 329–406. If accepted by the trial of fact, a partially excusing condition lessens the severity of culpability but, unlike an insanity finding, the accused is found criminally responsible for a lesser offense.

16. "Code, Model Penal, and Proposed Official Draft" (Philadelphia: American Law Institute, 1985).

17. Randy Borum and Solomon M. Fulero, "Empirical Research on the Insanity Defense and Attempted Reforms: Evidence toward Informed Policy," *Law and Human Behavior* 23, no. 1 (1999): 117–35.

6. HEART OF DARKNESS

1. D. L. Paulhus, *Paulhus Deception Scales: The Balanced Inventory of Desirable Responding User's Manual* (Toronto: Multi-Health Systems, 1999).

2. Irving B. Weiner, *Principles of Rorschach Interpretation* (London: Routledge, 2003).

3. Robert D. Hare, *Hare Psychopathy Checklist Revised* (Toronto: Multi-Health Systems, 1990).

4. Robert James R. Blair and Karina S. Blair, "Empathy, Morality, and Social Convention: Evidence from the Study of Psychopathy and Other Psychiatric Disorders." *The Social Neuroscience of Empathy* (2009): 139–52.

5. Adam R. Fox, Trevor H. Kvaran, and Reid Griffith Fontaine, "Psychopathy and Culpability: How Responsible Is the Psychopath for Criminal Wrongdoing?" *Law & Social Inquiry* 38, no. 1 (2013): 1–26.

6. Diana Ribeiro da Silva, Daniel Rijo, and Randall T. Salekin, "Child and Adolescent Psychopathy: Assessment Issues and Treatment Needs," *Aggression and Violent Behavior* 18, no. 1 (2013): 71–78. S. Berthoz, J. Armony, R. J. R. Blair, and R. Dolan, "Neural Correlates of Violation of Social Norms and Embarrassment," *Brain* 125 (2002): 1696–1708.

7. Arielle R. Baskin-Sommers, John J. Curtin, and Joseph P. Newman, "Specifying the Attentional Selection That Moderates the Fearlessness of Psychopathic Offenders," *Psychological Science* 22, no. 2 (2011): 226–34.

8. James R. Blair, "Neurocognitive Models of Aggression, the Antisocial Personality Disorders, and Psychopathy," *Journal of Neurology, Neurosurgery & Psychiatry* 71, no. 6 (2001): 727–31.

9. Stephen Morse, "Neuroscience in Forensic Contexts: Ethical Concerns," *Ethics Challenges in Forensic Psychiatry and Psychology Practice* (2018): 132–58.

10. Stephen J. Morse, "Psychopathy and Criminal Responsibility," *Neuroethics* 1, no. 3 (2008): 205–12.

11. Of course, one could be a psychopath *and* psychotic. In that case, a mental state defense may be possible.

12. S. Zeki, O. R. Goodenough, Joshua Greene, and Jonathan Cohen, "For the Law, Neuroscience Changes Nothing and Everything," *Philosophical Transactions of the Royal Society of London Series B: Biological Sciences* 359, no. 1451 (2004): 1775–85.

13. Eyal Aharoni, Walter Sinnott-Armstrong, and Kent A. Kiehl, "Can Psychopathic Offenders Discern Moral Wrongs? A New Look at the Moral/Conventional Distinction," *Journal of Abnormal Psychology* 121, no. 2 (2012): 484. As is usual in science and the professions, not all agree. See note 12.

14. M. Cima, F. Tonnaer, and M. D. Hauser, "Psychopaths Know Right from Wrong but Don't Care," *Social Cognitive and Affective Neuroscience* (2010): 59–67.

15. A. L. Glenn, R. Iyer, J. Graham, S. Koleva, and J. Haidt, "Are All Types of Morality Compromised in Psychopathy?" *Journal of Personality Disorders* 23 (2009): 384–98.

16. Julia Marshall, Ashley L. Watts, and Scott O. Lilienfeld, "Do Psychopathic Individuals Possess a Misaligned Moral Compass? A Meta-analytic Examination of Psychopathy's Relations with Moral Judgment," *Personality Disorders: Theory, Research, and Treatment* 9, no. 40 (2018).

17. R. D. Hare, "Psychopathy, Affect and Behavior," in *Psychopathy: Theory, Research and Implications for Society*, ed. D. J. Cooke, A. E. Forth, and R. D. Hare (Dordrecht: Kluwer Academic Publishers, 1998), 105–39. K. Kiehl and J. Buckholtz, "Inside the Mind of the Psychopath," *Scientific American Mind* (September/October 2010): 22–29.

18. Paul Babiak, Craig S. Neumann, and Robert D. Hare, "Corporate Psychopathy: Talking the Walk," *Behavioral Sciences & the Law* 28, no. 2 (2010): 174–93.

19. M. Stroud, *The Sociopath Next Door* (New York: Crown Publishing Group, 2005).

20. P. Babiak and R. Hare, *Snakes in Suits : When Psychopaths Go to Work* (New York: Harper, 2006).

21. Babiak, Neumann, and Hare, "Corporate Psychopathy," 174–93.

22. Shanna R. Van Slyke, Michael L. Benson, and Francis T. Cullen, eds., *The Oxford Handbook of White-Collar Crime* (New York: Oxford University Press, 2016).

23. Sharon S. Ishikawa, Adrian Raine, Todd Lencz, Susan Bihrle, and Lori Lacasse, "Autonomic Stress Reactivity and Executive Functions in Successful and Unsuccessful Criminal Psychopaths from the Community," *Journal of Abnormal Psychology* 110, no. 3 (2001): 423–32.

24. Cima, Tonnaer, and Hauser, "Psychopaths Know Right from Wrong but Don't Care," 59–67.

25. Robert M. Sapolsky, *Behave: The Biology of Humans at Our Best and Worst* (New York: Penguin, 2017).

26. Patrick D. McGorry and Barnaby Nelson, "Clinical High Risk for Psychosis—Not Seeing the Trees for the Wood," *JAMA Psychiatry* (2020).

27. S. Rachman, "Final Report: Psychological Analyses of Courageous Performances in Military Personnel," *U.S. Army Research Institute for the Behavioral Sciences* (1990).

28. S. Karson and J. O'Tool, *A Guide to the Use of the 16 PF* (Champaign, IL: Institute for the Personality and Ability Testing, 1976).

7. TILL DEATH DO US PART

1. K. S. Douglas, C. D. Webster, S. D. Hart, D. Eaves, and J. R. P. Ogloff, eds., *HCR-20, 3rd edition: Violence risk management companion guide.* Vancouver, BC: Mental Health Law and Policy Institute, 2013.

2. Richard Singer and John la Fond, *Criminal Law*, 4th ed. (New York: Wolters Kluwer Law and Business/Aspen Publishers, 2007), 179–84.

3. *People v. Beltran*, 301 P.3d 1120, 56 Cal. 4th 935, 157 Cal. Rptr. 3d 503 (2013).

4. Christopher Randolph, *Repeatable Battery for the Assessment of Neuropsychological Status (RBANS)* (San Antonio, TX: Psychological Corporation, 2012).

5. J. Briere, *Trauma Stress Inventory Professional Manual* (Odessa, FL: Psychological Assessment Resources, 2011).

6. Randy Borum and Solomon M. Fulero, "Empirical Research on the Insanity Defense and Attempted Reforms: Evidence toward Informed Policy," *Law and Human Behavior* 23, no. 1 (1999): 117–35.

7. Cynthia Lee, *Murder and the Reasonable Man: Passion and Fear in the Criminal Courtroom*, vol. 37 (New York: New York University Press, 2007).

8. Steven J. Sherman and Joseph L. Hoffmann, "The Psychology and Law of Voluntary Manslaughter: What Can Psychology Research Teach Us about the 'Heat of Passion' Defense?" *Journal of Behavioral Decision Making* 20, no. 5 (2007): 499–519.

9. Valeria Abreu Minero, Hannah Dickson, Edward Barker, Sandra Flynn, Saied Ibrahim, and Jennifer Shaw, "The Patterns of Homicide Offence Characteristics and Their Associations with Offender Psychopathology," *Journal of Investigative Psychology and Offender Profiling* 15, no. 3 (2018): 304–18. Joshua Dressler, "Provocation: Explaining and Justifying the Defense in Partial Excuse, Loss of Self-Control Terms," in *Criminal Law Conversations*, ed. Paul H. Robinson, Stephen P. Garvey, Kimberly Kessler Ferzan (Cambridge: Oxford University Press, 2009), 319–26.

10. Andrew Ashworth and Jeremy Horder, *Principles of Criminal Law* (Cambridge: Oxford University Press, 2013).

11. Joshua Dressler, "Provocation: Explaining and Justifying the Defense in Partial Excuse, Loss of Self-Control Terms," in *Criminal Law Conversations*, ed. Paul H. Robinson, Stephen P. Garvey, Kimberly Kessler Ferzan (Cambridge: Oxford University Press, 2009), 319–26.

12. Cheryl A. Terrance, Karyn M. Plumm, and Katlin J. Rhyner, "Expert Testimony in Cases Involving Battered Women Who Kill: Going beyond the Battered Woman Syndrome," *North Dakota Law Review* 88 (2012): 921.

13. Jennifer S. Lerner and Larissa Z. Tiedens, "Portrait of the Angry Decision Maker: How Appraisal Tendencies Shape Anger's Influence on Cognition," *Journal of Behavioral Decision Making* 19, no. 2 (2006): 115–37.

14. Steven J. Sherman and Joseph L. Hoffmann, "The Psychology and Law of Voluntary Manslaughter: What Can Psychology Research Teach Us about the 'Heat of Passion' Defense?" *Journal of Behavioral Decision Making* 20, no. 5 (2007): 499–519.

15. Terry A. Maroney, "Emotional Competence, Rational Understanding, and the Criminal Defendant," *American Criminal Law Review* 43 (2006): 1375.

16. L. Walker, *The Battered Woman Syndrome* (New York: Springer Publishing, 2009).

17. Melvin R. Lansky, *Fathers Who Fail: Shame and Psychopathology in the Family System* (London: Routledge, 2013).

18. *Maher v. People* (1862) 10 Mich.

19. See Richard Wrangham's *The Goodness Paradox* (New York: Pantheon Books, 2019). A biological anthropologist, he traces the evolutionary foundation of society's most fundamental paradox, to be both highly civilized yet capable of crimes such as mass murder and genocide.

8. BABY KILLER

1. Timothy Y. Mariano, Heng Choon Oliver Chan, and Wade C. Myers, "Toward a More Holistic Understanding of Filicide: A Multidisciplinary Analysis of 32 Years of U.S. Arrest Data," *Forensic Science International* 236 (2014): 46–53.

2. Michelle Oberman, "Mothers Who Kill: Crosscultural Patterns in and Perspectives on Contemporary Maternal Filicide," *International Journal of Law and Psychiatry* 26 (2003): 493–514.

3. Phillip J. Resnick, "Child Murder by Parents: A Psychiatric Review of Filicide," *American Journal of Psychiatry* 126, no. 3 (1969): 325–34. Susan Hatters Friedman and Phillip J. Resnick, "Child Murder by Mothers: Patterns and Prevention," *World Psychiatry* 6, no. 3 (2007): 137.

4. Susan Hatters Friedman, Debra R. Hrouda, Carol E. Holden, Stephen G. Noffsinger, and Phillip J. Resnick, "Child Murder Committed by Severely Mentally Ill Mothers: An Examination of Mothers Found Not Guilty by Reason of Insanity," *Journal of Forensic Science* 50, no. 6 (2005): 1466–71. Li Eriksson, Paul Mazerolle, Richard Wortley, and Holly Johnson, "Maternal and Paternal Filicide: Case Studies from the Australian Homicide Project," *Child Abuse Review* 25, no. 1 (2016): 17–30.

5. Susan Hatters Friedman, R. C. Hall, and Renée M. Sorrentino, "Commentary: Women, Violence, and Insanity," *The Journal of the American Academy of Psychiatry and the Law* 41 (2013): 523–28.

6. Timothy Y. Mariano, Heng Choon Oliver Chan, and Wade C. Myers, "Toward a More Holistic Understanding of Filicide: A Multidisciplinary Analysis of 32 Years of U.S. Arrest Data," *Forensic Science International* 236 (2014): 46–53.

7. Heather Leigh Stangle, "Murderous Madonna: Femininity, Violence, and the Myth of Postpartum Mental Disorder in Cases of Maternal Infanticide and Filicide," *William & Mary Law Review* 50 (2008): 699.

8. Luísa Saavedra and João Manuel de Oliveira, "Transgressing Motherhood: Media Reports on Infanticide," *Deviant Behavior* 38, no. 3 (2017): 345–55.

9. Julia Stroud, "A Psychosocial Analysis of Child Homicide," *Critical Social Policy* 28, no. 4 (2008): 482–505.

10. Michelle Oberman, "Mothers Who Kill: Coming to Terms with Modern American Infanticide," *American Criminal Law Review* 34 (1996): 1.

11. Catherine F. Lewis and Scott C. Bunce, "Filicidal Mothers and the Impact of Psychosis on Maternal Filicide," *Journal of the American Academy of Psychiatry and the Law Online* 31, no. 4 (2003): 459–70.

12. Patricia Pearson, *When She Was Bad: Violent Women & the Myth of Innocence* (New York: Viking, 1997).

13. Barbara Barnett, "Medea in the Media: Narrative and Myth in Newspaper Coverage of Women Who Kill Their Children," *Journalism* 7, no. 4 (2006): 411–32. Luísa Saavedra and João Manuel de Oliveira, "Transgressing Motherhood: Media Reports on Infanticide," *Deviant Behavior* 38, no. 3 (2017): 345–55.

9. A HYDRA-HEADED PASSION

1. W. Birnes and R. Keppel, *Signature Killers: Interpreting the Calling Cards of the Serial Murderer* (New York: Pocket Books, 1997).

2. See the appendix for a description of the neuropsychological tests.

3. Robert K. Heaton, Gordon J. Chelune, Jack L. Talley, Gary G. Kay, and Glenn Curtiss, *Wisconsin Card Sorting Test (WCST) Manual: Revised and Expanded* (Odessa, FL: Psychological Assessment Resources, 1993).

4. Theodore Millon, *Millon Clinical Multiaxial Inventory Manual* (Minneapolis, MN: National Computer Systems, 1983).

5. Ron Langevin and Dan Paitich, *Clarke Sex History Questionnaire for Males—Revised* (North Tonawanda, NY: Multi-Health Systems, 2002).

6. S. Jones, H. C. O. Chan, W. C. Myers, K. M. Heide, "A Proposed Sexual Homicide Category: The Psychopathic-Sexually Sadistic Offender," in *Criminal Psychology*, ed. J. B. Helfgott, vol. 2, *Typologies, Mental Disorders, and Profiles* (Westport, CT: Praeger, 2013), 403–22.

7. J. Reid Meloy, "The Nature and Dynamics of Sexual Homicide: An Integrative Review," *Aggression and Violent Behavior* 5, no. 1 (2000): 1–22.

8. Frederic Wertham, "The Catathymic Crisis: A Clinical Entity," *Archives of Neurology & Psychiatry* 37, no. 4 (1937): 974–78.

9. Louis B. Schlesinger, "Sexual Homicide: Differentiating Catathymic and Compulsive Murders," *Aggression and Violent Behavior* 12, no. 2 (2007): 242–56.

10. Jessica Yakeley and J. Reid Meloy, "Understanding Violence: Does Psychoanalytic Thinking Matter?" *Aggression and Violent Behavior* 17, no. 3 (2012): 229–39.

11. Mervin Glasser, "On Violence: A Preliminary Communication," *International Journal of Psycho-Analysis* 79 (1998): 887–902.

12. Erich Fromm, *The Anatomy of Human Destructiveness* (New York: Macmillan, 1992).

10. MAN-CHILD OR TROUBLED TEEN?

1. CA Welfare and Institution Code §707.

2. See the appendix for descriptions of the tests.

3. C. K. Conners, *Conners Continuous Performance Test 3rd Edition (CPT3)* (North Tonawanda, NY: Multi-Health Systems, 2014).

4. A. Bechara, *Iowa Gambling Test, Version 2 Professional Manual* (Lutz, FL: Psychological Assessment Resources, 2016).

5. Edna B. Foa, Anu Asnaani, Yinyin Zang, Sandra Capaldi, and Rebecca Yeh, "Psychometrics of the Child PTSD Symptom Scale for DSM-5 for Trauma-Exposed Children and Adolescents," *Journal of Clinical Child & Adolescent Psychology* 47, no. 1 (2018): 38–46.

6. A. E. Forth, D. S. Kosson, and R. D. Hare, *Hare Psychopathy Checklist: Youth Version* (North Towanda, NY: Multi-Health Systems, 2003).

7. S. Salekin, *Risk-Sophistication-Treatment Inventory* (Lutz, FL: Psychological Assessment Resources, 2004).

8. T. Millon, *Millon Adolescent Clinical Inventory Manual* (Minneapolis, MN: National Computer Systems, 1993).

9. American Psychiatric Association, *Diagnostic and Statistical Manual of Mental Disorders*, 5th ed. (Arlington, VA: American Psychiatric Association, 2013).

10. D. Wechsler, *Wechsler Adult Intelligence Scale Manual*, 4th ed. (San Antonio, TX: Pearson, 2008).

11. B. J. Casey and K. Caudle, "The Teenage Brain: Self-Control," *Current Directions in Psychological Science*, 82 (2013): 82–83. B. Vallabhajosula, *Murder in the Courtroom: The Cognitive Neuroscience of Violence* (Cambridge: Oxford University Press, 2015): 125–39.

12. Jay Giedd, Jonathan Blumenthal, Neal Jeffries, Francisco Castellanos, Hong Liu, Alex Zijdenbos, Tomas Paus, Alan Evans, and Judith Rapoport, "Brain Development during Childhood and Adolescence: A Longitudinal MRI Study," *Nature Neuroscience* 2 (1999): 861–62. L. Steinberg and E. Cauffman,

"Maturity and Judgment in Adolescence: Psychosocial Factors in Adolescent Decision-Making," *Law and Human Behavior* 20, no. 3 (1996): 253.

13. H. L. Gallagher and C. D. Frith, "Functional Imaging of 'Theory of Mind,'" *Trends in Cognitive Sciences* 7, no. 2 (2003): 77–83.

14. Frances E. Jensen and Amy Ellis Nutt, *The Teenage Brain* (Blackstone Audio, 2014).

15. *Roper v. Simmons* 543 U.S. 551, 125 S. Ct. 1183, 161 L. Ed. 2d 1 (2005).

16. *Graham v. Florida*, 560 U.S. 48, 130 S. Ct. 2011, 176 L. Ed. 2d 825 (2010).

17. *Miller v. Alabama*, 132 S. Ct. 2455, 567 U.S. 460, 183 L. Ed. 2d 407 (2012).

18. Beatriz Luna, David J. Paulsen, Aarthi Padmanabhan, and Charles Geier, "The Teenage Brain: Cognitive Control and Motivation," *Current Directions in Psychological Science* (2013): 98–99.

19. Steinberg and Cauffman, "Maturity and Judgment in Adolescence," 253.

20. D. Albert, J. Chein, and L. Steinberg, "The Teenage Brain: Peer Influences on Adolescent Decision Making," *Current Directions in Psychological Science*, 22, no. 2 (2013):114–20.

21. T. Wojciechowski, "PTSD as a Risk Factor for the Development of Violence among Juvenile Offenders: A Group-Based Trajectory Modeling Approach," *Journal of Interpersonal Violence* (2017): 1–25.

22. Nitin Gogtay, Jay N. Giedd, Leslie Lusk, Kiralee M. Hayashi, Deanna Greenstein, A. Catherine Vaituzis, Tom F. Nugent III, David H. Herman, Liv S. Clasen, Arthur W. Toga, Judith L. Rapoport, and Paul M. Thompson, "Dynamic Mapping of Human Cortical Development during Childhood through Early Adulthood," *Proceeds of the National Academy of Sciences*, no. 101 (2004): 8174–79.

23. *Roper v. Simmons*, 570.

24. R. Salekin, "Psychopathy in Children and Adolescents," in *Handbook of Psychopathy*, ed. C. Patrick (New York: Guilford Press, 2006), 389–414.

11. MY BRAIN MADE ME DO IT

1. Grant L. Iverson, Brian L. Brooks, Travis White, and Robert A. Stern, *Neuropsychological Assessment Battery: Introduction and Advanced Interpretation* (New York: Springer, 2008).

2. American Psychiatric Association, *Diagnostic and Statistical Manual of Mental Disorders*, 5th ed. (Washington, DC: American Psychiatric Publishing, 2013).

3. C. J. Golden, *A Manual for the Stroop Color and Word Test* (Chicago: Stoetling, 1978).

4. Raymond C. K. Chan, David Shum, Timothea Toulopoulou, and Eric Y. H. Chen, "Assessment of Executive Functions: Review of Instruments and Identification of Critical Issues," *Archives of Clinical Neuropsychology* 23, no. 2 (2008): 201–16.

5. Nita A. Farahany, "Neuroscience and Behavioral Genetics in US Criminal Law: An Empirical Analysis," *Journal of Law and the Biosciences* 2, no. 3 (2016): 485–509.

6. Deborah W. Denno, "How Prosecutors and Defense Attorneys Differ in Their Use of Neuroscience Evidence," *Fordham Law Review* 85 (2016): 453.

7. Paul J. Frick and Amanda Sheffield Morris, "Temperament and Developmental Pathways to Conduct Problems," *Journal of Clinical Child and Adolescent Psychology* 33, no. 1 (2004): 54–68. Joel T. Nigg, "Temperament and Developmental Psychopathology," *Journal of Child Psychology and Psychiatry* 47, nos. 3–4 (2006): 395–422.

8. Avshalom Caspi, Karen Sugden, Terrie E. Moffitt, Alan Taylor, Ian W. Craig, HonaLee Harrington, Joseph McClay, Jonathan Mill, Judy Martin, Antony Braithwaite, and Richie Poulton, "Influence of Life Stress on Depression: Moderation by a Polymorphism in the 5-HTT Gene," *Science* 301, no. 5631 (2003): 386–89.

9. Joshua Greene and Jonathan Cohen, "For the Law, Neuroscience Changes Nothing and Everything," in "Law and the Brain," special issue, *Philosophical Transactions of the Royal Society London* 359 (2004): 1775–81.

10. Liad Mudrik and Uri Maoz, "'Me & My Brain': Exposing Neuroscience's Closet Dualism," *Journal of Cognitive Neuroscience* 27, no. 2 (2014): 211–21.

11. Kristen Kelly, Arietta Slade, and John F. Grienenberger, "Maternal Reflective Functioning, Mother-Infant Affective Communication, and Infant Attachment: Exploring the Link between Mental States and Observed Caregiving Behavior in the Intergenerational Transmission of Attachment," *Attachment & Human Development* 7, no. 3 (2005): 299–311. Elliott L. Jurist, Arietta Slade, and Sharone Bergner, eds., *Mind to Mind: Infant Research, Neuroscience, and Psychoanalysis* (New York: Other Press, 2008).

12. Sytske Besemer, Shaikh I. Ahmad, Stephen P. Hinshaw, and David P. Farrington, "A Systematic Review and Meta-analysis of the Intergenerational Transmission of Criminal Behavior," *Aggression and Violent Behavior* 37 (2017): 161–78.

13. Lisa Feldman Barrett, *How Emotions Are Made: The Secret Life of the Brain* (New York: Houghton Mifflin Harcourt, 2017).

14. Robert Plomin, *Blueprint: How DNA Makes Us Who We Are* (Cambridge, MA: MIT Press, 2019), 6.

15. William Bernet, Cindy L. Vnencak-Jones, Nita Farahany, and Stephen A. Montgomery, "Bad Nature, Bad Nurture, and Testimony Regarding MAOA and SLC6A4 Genotyping at Murder Trials," *Journal of Forensic Sciences* 52, no. 6 (2007): 1362–71.

16. Caspi et al., "Influence of Life Stress on Depression," 386–89.

17. Clara Möller, Fredrik Falkenström, Mattias Holmqvist Larsson, and Rolf Holmqvist, "Mentalizing in Young Offenders," *Psychoanalytic Psychology* 31, no. 1 (2014): 84. Hyunzee Jung, Todd I. Herrenkohl, Martie L. Skinner, and Ashley N. Rousson, "Does Educational Success Mitigate the Effect of Child Maltreatment on Later Offending Patterns?" *Journal of Interpersonal Violence* (2018). Thomas G. Blomberg, William D. Bales, Karen Mann, Alex R. Piquero, and Richard A. Berk, "Incarceration, Education and Transition from Delinquency," *Journal of Criminal Justice* 39, no. 4 (2011): 355–65.

18. Stephen J. Morse, "Neurohype and the Law: A Cautionary Tale," in *Casting Light on the Dark Side of Brain Imaging* (London: Academic Press, 2019), 31–35.

12. DAIMONIC INJUSTICE

1. Amanda D. Johnson, "Police Subcultural Traits and Police Organizational Failure," *International Journal of Criminal Justice Sciences* 14, no. 2 (2019): 120–31. Philip Matthew Stinson, *Criminology Explains Police Violence* (Berkeley: University of California Press, 2020).

2. Emily E. Ekins, *Policing in America: Understanding Public Attitudes toward the Police: Results from a National Survey* (Washington, DC: Cato Institute, 2016).

3. See www.prisonexp.org. For a critique of the research results, see Stephen Reicher and S. Alexander Haslam, "Rethinking the Psychology of Tyranny: The BBC Prison Study," *British Journal of Social Psychology* 45, no. 1 (2006): 1–40.

4. Philip Zimbardo, *The Lucifer Effect: Understanding How Good People Turn Evil* (New York: Random House, 2007).

5. Philip Matthew Stinson, *Criminology Explains Police Violence* (Berkeley: University of California Press, 2020), 73–90.

6. Sean P. Griffin and Thomas J. Bernard, "Angry Aggression among Police Officers," *Police Quarterly* 6, no. 1 (2003): 3–21.

7. Anthony M. Tarescavage, David M. Corey, and Yossef S. Ben-Porath, "Minnesota Multiphasic Personality Inventory-2-Restructured Form (MMPI-2-RF) Predictors of Police Officer Problem Behavior," *Assessment* 22, no. 1 (2015): 116–32. Matthew R. Durose, Erica Leah Schmitt, and Patrick A. Langan, *Contacts between Police and the Public: Findings from the 2002 National Sur-*

vey (Washington, DC: US Department of Justice, Office of Justice Programs, Bureau of Justice Statistics, 2005).

8. Adam Dunn and Patrick J. Caceres, "Constructing a Better Estimate of Police Misconduct," *Policy Matters Journal* 7, no. 2 (2010): 10–16.

9. Martin Sellbom, Gary L. Fischler, and Yossef S. Ben-Porath, "Identifying MMPI-2 Predictors of Police Officer Integrity and Misconduct," *Criminal Justice and Behavior* 34, no. 8 (2007): 985–1004.

10. Wickersham Commission, *United States National Committee on Law Observance and Enforcement: Report on the Police* (Washington, DC: US Government Printing Office, 1931). Neal Trautman, "Police Code of Silence Facts Revealed," in *Annual Conference of the International Association of Chiefs of Police*, available at www.aele.org/loscode2000.

11. Stinson, *Criminology Explains Police Violence*, 76–80.

12. Radley Balko, *Rise of the Warrior Cop: The Militarization of America's Police Forces* (New York: PublicAffairs, 2013).

13. See Stinson, *Criminology Explains Police Violence*, 59–72.

14. Richard J. Lundman, *Police and Policing: An Introduction* (New York: Holt, Rinehart and Winston, 1980). See Stinson, *Criminology Explains Police Violence*, 59.

15. Herbert Packer, *The Limits of the Criminal Sanction* (Stanford, CA: Stanford University Press, 1968).

16. Carl B. Klockars, "Street Justice: Some Micro-Moral Reservations: Comment on Sykes," *Justice Quarterly* 3, no. 4 (1986): 513–16.

17. Christopher Slobogin, "Testilying: Police Perjury and What to Do about It," *University of Colorado Law Review* 67 (1996): 1037.

18. Gary W. Sykes, "Street Justice: A Moral Defense of Order Maintenance Policing," *Justice Quarterly* 3, no. 4 (1986): 497–512.

19. Kathleen M. Ridolfi and Maurice Possley, *Preventable Error: A Report on Prosecutorial Misconduct in California 1997–2009* (Santa Clara: Northern California Innocence Project Publications, 2010), http://digitalcommons.law.scu.edu/ncippubs/2.

20. Transcript of Record at 5195-5201, *United States v. William J. Ruehle*, SACR 08-00139-CJC.

21. https://voiceofoc.org/2015/10/prior-murder-adds-another-layer-to-wozniak-case/; https://www.ocregister.com/2016/01/18/inside-the-snitch-tank-read-the-full-story-of-murder- misconduct-and-justice-delayed/.

22. Ridolfi and Possley, *Preventable Error*.

23. Ridolfi and Possley, *Preventable Error*. See also David Alan Sklansky, "The Problems with Prosecutors," *Annual Review of Criminology* 1 (2018): 451–69.

24. Emily M. West, "Court Findings of Prosecutorial Misconduct Claims in Post-Conviction Appeals and Civil Suits among the First 255 DNA Exoneration Cases," Innocence Project Report (2010), www.innocenceproject.org/wp-content/uploads/2016/04/pmc_appeals_255_final_oct_2011.pdf.

25. N. Haslam and S. Loughnan, "Dehumanization and Infrahumanization," *Annual Review of Psychology* 65 (2014): 399–423. Muzafer Sherif and Carolyn W. Sherif, *Reference Groups Exploration into Conformity and Deviation of Adolescents* (New York: Harper and Row, 1964).

26. Jacques-Philippe Leyens, Armando Rodriguez-Perez, Ramon Rodriguez-Torres, Ruth Gaunt, Maria-Paola Paladino, Jeroen Vaes, and Stéphanie Demoulin, "Psychological Essentialism and the Differential Attribution of Uniquely Human Emotions to Ingroups and Outgroups," *European Journal of Social Psychology* 31, no. 4 (2001): 395–411.

27. Hannah Arendt, *Eichmann in Jerusalem* (New York: Penguin, 2006). Hannah Arendt, *The Origins of Totalitarianism* (New York: Harcourt, Brace Jovanovich, 1973).

28. Primo Levi, *Survival in Auschwitz* (New York: Simon and Schuster, 1996).

29. John M. Darley and C. Daniel Batson, "'From Jerusalem to Jericho': A Study of Situational and Dispositional Variables in Helping Behavior," *Journal of Personality and Social Psychology* 27, no. 1 (1973): 100–108.

30. Christopher Browning, *Ordinary Men: Reserve Police Battalion 101 and the Final Solution in Poland* (New York: HarperCollins, 1992).

13. CONCLUSION

1. Norman O. Brown, *Life against Death: The Psychoanalytical Meaning of History* (Middletown, CT: Wesleyan University Press, 1985), ix.

2. Sigmund Freud, "The Ego and the Id," in *The Standard Edition of the Complete Psychological Works of Sigmund Freud, Volume XIX (1923–1925): The Ego and the Id and Other Works* (London: Hogarth Press, 1961), 1–66.

3. Cited in S. Diamond, *Anger, Madness, and the Daimonic* (Albany: State University of New York Press, 1996). See also R. May, *Love and Will* (New York: Dell, 1969). Kirk J. Schneider, "Radical Openness to Radical Mystery: Rollo May and the Awe-based Way," in *Humanity's Dark Side: Evil, Destructive Experience, and Psychotherapy* (Washington, DC: American Psychological Association, 2013), 19–33.

4. Claire Holvoet, Céline Scola, Thomas Arciszewski, and Delphine Picard, "Infants' Preference for Prosocial Behaviors: A Literature Review," *Infant Behavior and Development* 45 (2016): 125–39.

5. Paul Bloom, *Just Babies: The Origins of Good and Evil* (New York: Broadway Books, 2013).

6. Betty M. Repacholi and Alison Gopnik, "Early Reasoning about Desires: Evidence from 14- and 18-month-olds," *Developmental Psychology* 33, no. 1 (1997): 12–21.

7. Richard Wrangham, *The Goodness Paradox: The Strange Relationship between Virtue and Violence in Human Evolution* (New York: Vintage, 2019).

8. Jane Goodall, *Patterns of Behavior* (Cambridge, MA: Harvard University Press, 1986). Jane Goodall, *Reason for Hope: A Spiritual Journey* (New York: Grand Central Publishing, 1999).

9. Fiona Brookman, "Confrontational and Revenge Homicides among Men in England and Wales," *Australian & New Zealand Journal of Criminology* 36, no. 1 (2003): 34–59. Johan M. G. van der Dennen, "Review Essay: The Murderer Next Door: Why the Mind Is Designed to Kill," *Homicide Studies* 10, no. 4 (2006): 320–35.

10. Lewis Petrinovich and Patricia O'Neill, "Influence of Wording and Framing Effects on Moral Intuitions," *Ethology and Sociobiology* 17, no. 3 (1996): 145–71. Kuninori Nakamura, "The Footbridge Dilemma Reflects More Utilitarian Thinking Than the Trolley Dilemma: Effect of Number of Victims in Moral Dilemmas," in *Proceedings of the Annual Meeting of the Cognitive Science Society* 34 (2012): 5.

11. David M. Buss, *The Murderer Next Door: Why the Mind Is Designed to Kill* (New York: Penguin, 2006), 5.

12. Buss, *The Murderer Next Door*, 8.

13. Robert E. Hanlon, Michael Brook, John Stratton, Marie Jensen, and Leah H. Rubin, "Neuropsychological and Intellectual Differences between Types of Murderers: Affective/Impulsive versus Predatory/Instrumental (Premeditated) Homicide," *Criminal Justice and Behavior* 40, no. 8 (2013): 933–48.

14. Leon Wurmser, *The Mask of Shame* (Baltimore: Johns Hopkins University Press, 1981). Melvin R. Lansky, *Fathers Who Fail: Shame and Psychopathology in the Family System* (London: Routledge, 2013).

15. For a fuller understanding of the mentalization concept, see Peter Fonagy and Mary Target, *Psychoanalytic Theories: Perspectives from Developmental Psychopathology* (New York: Brunner-Routledge, 2003), 270–82.

16. Elliot Jurist, *Minding Emotions: Cultivating Mentalization in Psychotherapy* (New York: Guilford, 2018), esp. part II, 83–160.

17. One can see how such a mentalization process is absent or terribly deformed in malignant types of personalities.

18. E. L. Jurist, "Mentalized Affectivity," *Psychoanalytic Psychology* 22, no. 3 (2005): 426–44.

19. This exquisite psychological achievement, mentalization, may be viewed as the apogee of a fundamental evolutionary process that is designed to keep us alive and well. It does so by enacting a neurobiological process called simulation. According to the neuroscientist Lisa Feldman Barrett, simulation allows the brain to function as a fortune-teller, predicting future events by drawing on past emotionally lived experience and adapting accordingly, all in the service of enhancing survival. See Lisa Feldman Barrett, *How Emotions Are Made: The Secret Life of the Brain* (New York: Houghton Mifflin Harcourt, 2017). Lisa Feldman Barrett, "Emotional Intelligence Needs a Rewrite. Think You Can Read People's Emotions? Think Again," 51 *Nautilus* (2017). The greater the mentalization ability, the greater one's emotional agility and understanding of the interpersonal milieu, thereby improving psychosocial functioning and aliveness.

20. P. Fonagy and A. Levinson, "Offending and Attachment: The Relationship between Interpersonal Awareness and Offending in a Prison Population with Psychiatric Disorder," *Canadian Journal of Psychoanalysis* 12, no. 2 (2004): 225–51.

21. Rebecca A. Richell, Derek G. V. Mitchell, C. Newman, A. Leonard, Simon Baron-Cohen, and R. James R. Blair, "Theory of Mind and Psychopathy: Can Psychopathic Individuals Read the 'Language of the Eyes'?" *Neuropsychologia* 41, no. 5 (2003): 523–26.

22. D. Stevens, Tony Charman, and R. J. R. Blair, "Recognition of Emotion in Facial Expressions and Vocal Tones in Children with Psychopathic Tendencies," *The Journal of Genetic Psychology* 162, no. 2 (2001): 201–11.

23. Lance Workman, "Interview: The Memory Warrior," *The Psychologist* 25 (2012): 526–29.

24. Elliott Leyton, *Hunting Humans: The Rise of the Modern Multiple Murderer* (New York: Carroll & Graf, 2003).

25. Peter Fonagy, "Attachment, the Development of the Self, and Its Pathology in Personality Disorders," in *Treatment of Personality Disorders* (Boston: Springer, 1999), 53–68. Glen O. Gabbard, Lisa A. Miller, and Melissa Martinez, "A Neurobiological Perspective on Mentalizing and Internal Object Relations in Traumatized Patients with Borderline Personality Disorder," *Handbook of Mentalization-Based Treatment* (Chichester: Wiley, 2006), 123–40. Tamara S. Lyn and David L. Burton, "Adult Attachment and Sexual Offender Status," *American Journal of Orthopsychiatry* 74, no. 2 (2004): 150–59.

26. Interestingly, Phillip was nonetheless capable of mentalized self-reflection. This was likely due to the quality of his attachment to his mother, regardless of her relative insensitivity, and probably to his innate temperamental push to bond.

27. I presented some interesting research findings on the consequences of "otherizing" in chapter 12.

28. Sigmund Freud, "Beyond the Pleasure Principle," in *The Standard Edition of the Complete Psychological Works of Sigmund Freud, Volume XVIII (1920–1922): Beyond the Pleasure Principle, Group Psychology and Other Works* (London: Hogarth Press, 1920), 1–64.

29. Christopher Peterson and Martin E. P. Seligman, *Character Strengths and Virtues: A Handbook and Classification* (Cambridge: Oxford University Press, 2004). M. Gazzaniga, *The Ethical Brain* (New York: Dana Press, 2005).

30. P. Foot, *Natural Goodness* (Cambridge: Oxford University Press, 2001). C. Taylor, *Sources of the Self: The Making of the Modern Identity* (Cambridge, MA: Harvard University Press, 1989).

31. Steven Pinker, *The Better Angels of Our Nature: Why Violence Has Declined* (New York: Penguin, 2012), xxi.

32. Pinker, *The Better Angels of Our Nature*, 189–294.

33. James Gilligan, *Preventing Violence* (London: Thames & Hudson, 2001). James Gilligan, *Violence: Our Deadly Epidemic and Its Causes* (New York: G. P. Putnam, 1996).

34. Gilligan, *Preventing Violence*, 29.

35. Howard Zehr, *The Little Book of Restorative Justice: Revised and Updated* (New York: Simon and Schuster, 2015).

36. David B. Wexler, Michael L. Perlin, Michel Vols, Pauline Spencer, and Nigel Stobbs, "Guest Editorial: Current Issues in Therapeutic Jurisprudence," *QUT Law Review* 16, no. 3 (2016): 1–3.

37. Kimberly A. Kaiser and Kirby Rhodes, "A Drug Court by Any Other Name? An Analysis of Problem-solving Court Programs," *Law and Human Behavior* 43, no. 3 (2019): 278–89.

38. Jeremy Travis, Bruce Western, and F. Stevens Redburn, *The Growth of Incarceration in the United States: Exploring Causes and Consequences* (Washington, DC: National Academy Press, 2014), esp. 159–64.

39. Michael L. Perlin, "'Too Stubborn to Ever Be Governed by Enforced Insanity': Some Therapeutic Jurisprudence Dilemmas in the Representation of Criminal Defendants in Incompetency and Insanity Cases," *International Journal of Law and Psychiatry* 33, no. 5–6 (2010): 475–81.

40. *Miller v. Alabama*, 132 S. Ct. 2455, 567 U.S. 460, 183 L. Ed. 2d 407 (2012). With reference to *Graham v. Florida*, 130 S. Ct. 2011, 560 U.S. 48, 176 L. Ed. 2d 825 (2010).

41. See "Sociability, Responsibility, and Criminality: From Lab to Law," *Annals of the New York Academy of Sciences* 1299, no. 1 (2013): v–97. The issue is devoted to relevant findings in the social sciences and neuroscience to criminal law.

42. Craig Haney, *Criminality in Context: The Psychological Foundations of Criminal Justice Reform* (Washington, DC: American Psychological Association, 2020).

43. Henry J. Steadman, Margaret A. McGreevy, Joseph P. Morrissey, Lisa A. Callahan, Pamela Clark Robbins, and Carmen Cirincione, *Before and after Hinckley: Evaluating Insanity Defense Reform* (New York: Guilford Press, 1993).

44. Brandon L. Garrett, "Wrongful Convictions," *Annual Review of Criminology* 3 (2020): 245–59.

45. https://californiainnocenceproject.org/?gclid=Cj0KCQiA0fr_BRDaARIsAABw4Et0Trare2rj7pjVwvo70U_AuIfI04Lw CJD8zPfic0jJj0-uHVemNLAaArt0EALw_wcB.

46. Jon G. Allen, "Psychotherapy: The Artful Use of Science," *Smith College Studies in Social Work* 78, nos. 2–3 (2008): 159–87.

47. One would hope that psychoanalysts would be psychologically minded and reflective enough as a group to be cognizant of pernicious social forces and capable of emotionally resisting its pull. During the Nazi era in Germany, many analysts did resist, and many fled the country. But some adapted to the regime and accommodated to Nazi ideology. See Ervin Staub, "The Evolution of Bystanders, German Psychoanalysts, and Lessons for Today," *Political Psychology* (1989): 39–52.

48. Daniel Spurk, Anita C. Keller, and Andreas Hirschi, "Do Bad Guys Get Ahead or Fall Behind? Relationships of the Dark Triad of Personality with Objective and Subjective Career Success," *Social Psychological and Personality Science* 7, no. 2 (2016): 113–21.

49. Seth M. Spain, Peter Harms, and James M. LeBreton, "The Dark Side of Personality at Work," *Journal of Organizational Behavior*, supplement, *The IRIOP Annual Review Issue* 35, no. S1 (2014): S41–S60.

50. Peter K. Jonason and Gregory D. Webster, "The Dirty Dozen: A Concise Measure of the Dark Triad," *Psychological Assessment* 22, no. 2 (2010): 420.

51. Jason J. Dahling, Brian G. Whitaker, and Paul E. Levy, "The Development and Validation of a New Machiavellianism Scale," *Journal of Management* 35, no. 2 (2008): 219–57.

52. Benoît Monin and Alexander H. Jordan, "The Dynamic Moral Self: A Social Psychological Perspective," in *Personality, Identity, and Character: Explorations in Moral Psychology*, ed. D. Narvaez and D. Lapsley (Boston: Cambridge University, 2009), 341–54.

ACKNOWLEDGMENTS

Writing is a solitary endeavor. I spent countless hours at my desk, reviewing my files and notes on hundreds of forensic cases as I prepared myself for the writing task ahead. And then came the writing. It was sometimes onerous, sometimes exhilarating.

It's a special privilege and responsibility to have had access to the psychological lives of those with whom I worked, especially since many were in the throes of the most tragic of circumstances. Reviewing decades of my work was at once painful and soulful.

Although ensconced and isolated in my home library as I wrote and labored over this book, I never felt alone. Always, I felt cheered on by my close colleagues and neighborhood friends.

All of you were unfailingly supportive and affirming of what I was trying to accomplish.

You all know who you are: thank you.

I especially want to thank my wife Jeanne for her selfless love and patience with me as I labored and wrote. She was willing to read and reread (and yet again reread) drafts of the various chapters without any displays of frustration or fatigue with the process. Her criticisms were offered with sensitivity and gentleness. Still, I sometimes got irritated by her observations, especially when I knew she was right. Even then, I was met with tolerance. What else can a partner ask for?

My children, Erik and Gina, and daughter-in-law, Autumn, would always light up when I talked about my book in progress. They matter-of-factly communicated their confidence in me and quietly tolerated my periods of mental preoccupation and physical isolation. With their obvious and genuine affections, less was so much more.

I want to give a special thanks to my granddaughters, Mollie and Penelope, for not giving a damn about what Papa was doing when they burst into my library seeking attention. They'd want me to help them find coloring pages of elephants or unicorns on the computer or to sit and read to them. Who can resist such beautiful little faces with their wonderstruck expressions and unbounded spirit?

Proverbs 17:6 got it right: Grandchildren are the Crown of the Aged.

INDEX

ADHD (attention deficit hyperactivity disorder): and attempted murder case, 206, 211, 215, 221, 222; and CAARS, 213, 264

adolescent crime. *See* drug dealer shooting; juveniles

The African Queen quotation, 3

Aggression Questionnaire, 213, 263. *See also* violence

alcohol abuse: leading to spousal strangulation, 124–128, 129, 130–131; and mixed personality disorder diagnosis, 57, 59, 60–62. *See also* substance abuse

American Law Institute, 88

amnesia after crimes, 51–53, 54–55, 63

Andrew (defendant). *See* stepbrother murder case

Andy (defendant). *See* carjacking case

anger: and fear, 135–136, 195; infantile rage, 25–26; management training for, 52; in mutilation and murder case, 47, 49, 51–52, 58, 59–62, 65

antipsychotic medications, 76–77

antisocial personalities, 113, 206, 215, 216

Arendt, Hannah, 241–242

assault case. *See* criminal assault case

Asylums (Goffman), 205

attachment, importance of, 24, 27, 252–254

attempted murder case: crime description, 113, 205, 211–212; defendant's claims of mental illness and insanity, 205–208, 212, 213, 215–216; earlier life of defendant, 207, 209–211; evaluations, testing, and diagnosis, 212–217; first impressions of defendant, 208–209; similarities to carjacking case, 223–226; trial preparation and plea deal, 216–217

attention deficit hyperactivity disorder (ADHD): and attempted murder case, 206, 211, 215, 221, 222; and CAARS, 213, 264

Auschwitz and lack of "why", 227, 242

"banality of evil", 242

Barrett, Lisa Feldman, 288n19

Batson, Daniel, 242

battered woman syndrome, 135, 251

The Better Angels of Our Nature (Pinker), 256

Bettleheim, Bruno, 15

biological deterministic perspective, 224–226

bipolar disorder, 222, 265

Blair, James, 111

Blair, Tony, 245

Bloom, Paul, 247–248

Bollas, Christopher, 7